Global Issues Series

General Editor: **Jim Whitman**

This exciting new series encompasses three principal themes: the interaction of human and natural systems; cooperation and conflict; and the enactment of values. The series as a whole places an emphasis on the examination of complex systems and causal relations in political decision-making; problems of knowledge; authority, control and accountability in issues of scale; and the reconciliation of conflicting values and competing claims. Throughout the series the concentration is on an integration of existing disciplines towards the clarification of political possibility as well as impending crises.

Titles include:

Roy Carr-Hill and John Lintott
CONSUMPTION, JOBS AND THE ENVIRONMENT
A Fourth Way?

Malcolm Dando
PREVENTING BIOLOGICAL WARFARE
The Failure of American Leadership

Brendan Gleeson and Nicholas Low (*editors*)
GOVERNING FOR THE ENVIRONMENT
Global Problems, Ethics and Democracy

Roger Jeffery and Bhaskar Vira (*editors*)
CONFLICT AND COOPERATION IN PARTICIPATORY NATURAL RESOURCE MANAGEMENT

Ho-Won Jeong (*editor*)
GLOBAL ENVIRONMENTAL POLICIES
Institutions and Procedures
APPROACHES TO PEACEBUILDING

W. Andy Knight
A CHANGING UNITED NATIONS
Multilateral Evolution and the Quest for Global Governance

W. Andy Knight (*editor*)
ADAPTING THE UNITED NATIONS TO A POSTMODERN ERA
Lessons Learned

Kelley Lee (*editor*)
HEALTH IMPACTS OF GLOBALIZATION
Towards Global Governance

Graham S. Pearson
THE UNSCOM SAGA
Chemical and Biological Weapons Non-Proliferation

Andrew T. Price-Smith (*editor*)
PLAGUES AND POLITICS
Infectious Disease and International Policy

Michael Pugh (*editor*)
REGENERATION OF WAR-TORN SOCIETIES

Bhaskar Vira and Roger Jeffery (*editors*)
ANALYTICAL ISSUES IN PARTICIPATORY NATURAL RESOURCE MANAGEMENT

Simon M. Whitby
BIOLOGICAL WARFARE AGAINST CROPS

Global Issues Series
Series Standing Order ISBN 0–333–79483–4
(*outside North America only*)

You can receive future titles in this series as they are published by placing a standing order. Please contact your bookseller or, in case of difficulty, write to us at the address below with your name and address, the title of the series and the ISBN quoted above.

Customer Services Department, Macmillan Distribution Ltd, Houndmills, Basingstoke, Hampshire RG21 6XS, England

Consumption, Jobs and the Environment

A Fourth Way?

Roy Carr-Hill
Professor in Health and Social Statistics
University of York, UK

Research Professor in Education in Developing Countries
Institute of Education, University of London

and

John Lintott
Senior Lecturer in Economics
South Bank University
London, UK

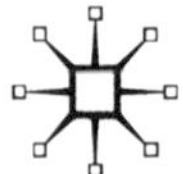

First published 2002 by
PALGRAVE MACMILLAN
Houndmills, Basingstoke, Hampshire RG21 6XS and
175 Fifth Avenue, New York, N. Y. 10010
Companies and representatives throughout the world

PALGRAVE MACMILLAN is the global academic imprint of the Palgrave Macmillan division of St. Martin's Press, LLC and of Palgrave Macmillan Ltd. Macmillan® is a registered trademark in the United States, United Kingdom and other countries. Palgrave is a registered trademark in the European Union and other countries.

ISBN 0–333–80009–5

This book is printed on paper suitable for recycling and made from fully managed and sustained forest sources.

A catalogue record for this book is available from the British Library.

Library of Congress Cataloging-in-Publication Data
Carr-Hill, R. A. (Roy A.), 1943–
Consumption, jobs and the environment: a fourth way?/Roy Carr-Hill and John Lintott.
p. cm. – (Global issues)
Includes bibliographical references and index.
ISBN 0–333–80009–5
1. Economic development – Environmental aspects. 2. Consumption (Economics) 3. Full employment policies. I. Lintott, John. II. Title III. Series.

HD75.6.C373 2002
330.12'6–dc21 2002072311

10 9 8 7 6 5 4 3 2 1
11 10 09 08 07 06 05 04 03 02

Printed and bound in Great Britain by
Antony Rowe Ltd, Chippenham and Eastbourne

Contents

List of Boxes, Figures and Tables

Preface

Our reasons for writing this book stem from twin concerns: with the pattern of economic and political development in the rich countries – epitomised by the 'Third Way' politics of Bill Clinton in the US and Tony Blair in the UK – and with the (quite inadequate in our view) response of many of their critics. Continued emphasis on ever-increasing production and consumption, irrespective of social and ecological costs, has been met, all too often, by demands that this growth be somehow reconciled with social objectives and ecological limits. We do not believe they can be reconciled, and much of this book is concerned to examine the choice that must be made between two alternative principles of development: welfare and profit.

Our interest and involvement in the topics of this book go back much further, however, to a period in the 1970s when we both worked at the Organisation for Economic Development and Cooperation (OECD), in their Social Indicators Development Programme. This programme had its origins in a declaration by the OECD Council of Ministers in 1970, that 'Economic growth is not an end in itself, it is a means to a better quality of life' (OECD, 1970).

In practice, if we judge the OECD by its entire range of activities, it, like many others, treats narrowly defined economic growth as an end in itself; and social indicators – and, by implication, the quality of life – have been relegated to a minor role. The decline of interest in social indicators has often been attributed to theoretical shortcomings, in particular the lack of general social scientific theories on which to base measurement of such theoretical constructs as 'welfare', and the tendency for social indicator systems to became divorced from the policy context, focusing on the measurement task, often to the exclusion of the political and institutional one. But, as we have argued before (Nectoux *et al.*, 1980), this analysis ignores the context in which social indicators were developed, in which government policies based on economic growth and income redistribution were confronted with, and attempted to assimilate, new forms of protest, concerned with such issues as the family and sexual politics, nuclear war, pollution, consumerism and the work ethic. By the late 1970s, however, for a variety of reasons, governments were abandoning the strategy of 'growth plus welfare' for a more robust, not to say authoritarian, defence of economic growth at all costs. With the arrival of Margaret Thatcher in the UK and Ronald Reagan in the US, concern with welfare on the part of government became a purely rhetorical matter, and developing social indicators to measure it was of little interest.

With the collapse of the Soviet Union (the 'Second Way') in the early 1990s, a path has been reopened for unhindered further development of Western-led, economic growth promoting, capitalism (the 'First Way'). Two problems stood in the way of openly acknowledging this situation however: on a rhetorical level, some concessions had to be made to social and ecological concerns; and on a political level, 'centre–left' politicians had to find a new role (or face unemployment!). It is in this context that the 'Third Way' was invented, a marriage of business as usual with 'caring' rhetoric, adopted initially by politicians of the left, but increasingly by those of the centre–right as well. Yet since these policies, without their Third Way packaging, amount to little more than continued promotion of economic growth and consumerism, they do nothing to address the real problems. We need to find a 'fourth way'.

Many argue that economic growth policies can be separated from concerns about environmental damage to a sufficient extent that growth can continue while its ecological impacts decrease. In part, therefore, our book addresses those who are persuaded of the importance of ecological arguments but believe that the problems can be contained, with relatively modest changes in policies and lifestyles. Instead, we argue that ecological concerns lead logically and inevitably to a concern with alienating employment, consumption and inequalities.

While this is an 'academic' publication, in the sense that we have fully referenced our arguments, it is not in the mainstream. Its potential academic readership is more likely to have a multi- or inter-disciplinary orientation than simply an interest in traditional economics. But, at least as important, this book is also aimed at the interested 'lay' person. As environmental and development concerns have come to occupy centre stage in more forward-looking social and political debates, huge numbers of people have become interested, and in a variety of ways involved, in these issues. We hope the ideas in this book will contribute to these debates and interest those people.

Several people have been kind enough to read and comment on various drafts of this book: Blake Alcott, George Carr-Hill, Elizabeth Currie, Luise Harland-Lahusen, Raymond Illsley, Jocelyn Kynch, Jean-Paul Lambert, Robert Moore, Christer Sanne, William Taylor. Two secretaries have done sterling work: Elizabeth Ingham and Sal Wilson. We are very grateful to them all.

Roy Carr-Hill and John Lintott

1
Introduction: the Purpose and Structure of this Book

Growth of output and consumption while maintaining (nearly) full employment remains the major stated target of government policy in nearly all rich countries. Yet, even by its own criteria, the pattern of growth of the last 25 years has been a failure. It has been less than in the previous 25 years; it has been more sporadic, and at various times and places negative; it has failed to generate full employment; and it has led to increased poverty and inequality, within and among countries, and especially between North and South.

In addition, the traditional view of growth as desirable has been increasingly questioned, particularly on environmental grounds. Unsustainable resource-use and environmental damage may mean that the uncounted costs of growth outweigh any benefits. Moreover, the benefits are themselves questionable given the failure of the 'trickle-down' approach from the rich to the poor.

The purpose of this book is to analyse how these problems have arisen in rich countries and, among other things, to propose a change in the criteria by which we judge policies. This latter essentially involves refocusing on the extent to which different forms of activity actually generate benefits in terms of human welfare. Few would argue against a welfare-maximising approach for both poor and rich countries, at least in principle, although that is not obvious from the behaviour of many international agencies as well as multinationals. But we see the problems of the environment, growth, inequality and unemployment as arising among the rich *rather than the poor* countries so that the book is concerned with economies in the North rather than the South. Note that, in our critique, although our examples tend to be based on the UK, we are talking in principle, about rich societies in general.

Given the inter-relatedness and relative complexity of the argument, we set out a one-sentence summary of the argument in each chapter by means of a diagram (Figure 1.1). Many will share some or all of our critique of the current situation – and in particular environmental damage,

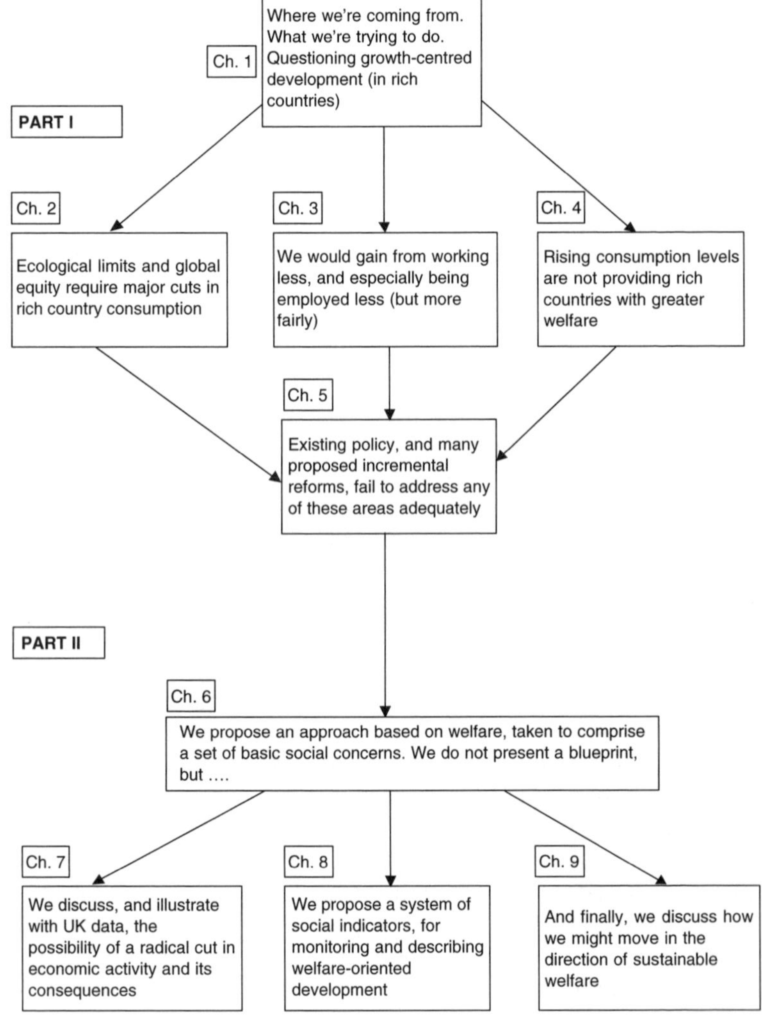

Figure 1.1 The flow of the argument

alienating and precarious employment and obsessive over-consumption – laid out in the first part of the book (Chapters 2–5). But it is easy to criticise, and exhortations to somehow 'do it differently' are unlikely to be effective. Instead, in the second part of the book (Chapters 6–9), we argue that in order to adequately respond to this complex of inter-related problems, the whole framework has to be changed in order to focus on welfare and equity. We propose a possible framework and explore its implications in terms of current policies as well as a possible scenario for substantially reducing environmental damage, involving considerable reductions in employment and consumption without loss in welfare, defined in terms of the quality of life that people lead.

Figure 1.1, above, shows the linkages between the arguments in Part I, and some of the implications of the reformulation proposed in Part II. The remainder of this chapter provides a little more narrative for each chapter to explain how the argument develops.

1.1 The failure of growth policies

1.1.1 The environmental problems

The impact of economic activities on the natural environment is often 'hidden' from economic accounting since no one pays directly for it, and it is 'external' to the economic transaction in the sense that those suffering the impact are generally not the ones gaining from the activity. But, over the last 30 years, the impacts have become greater and externalities more pervasive.

The concerns uppermost in the public eye have varied, from dependence on non-renewable fossil fuels for energy in the 1970s, to climate change, biodiversity and other 'global' problems in the 1990s. But, overall, the perceived environmental crisis has become more serious, with the focus shifting to the threats to quality of life in the short term and to survival in the long term. One sign of this is the development of an 'establishment environmentalism' from 1987 (the Brundtland report) onwards, which seeks to preserve growth and profits while minimising environmental damage, which we see as a totally inadequate response (see Chapter 5).

Nevertheless, while the ecological costs of present growth trajectories are probably very large, they are not *so* large and *so* certain that we can ignore other costs and benefits; and, in particular, the disutility of labour and the supposed benefits of consumption.

1.1.2 Employment and work

In Chapter 3, we argue that much of current employment is 'useless' in terms of contributing to human welfare and, inasmuch as it is labour directed by someone else, inherently dissatisfying and/or frustrating. We also query whether paid employment is an appropriate way to carry out many socially necessary functions (for example, caring).

Of course, many people fear unemployment, even though their current job generates stress and ruins their lives. But while avoiding unemployment has been a major concern since the advent of industrialised societies, the post World War II emphasis on *full* and *full-time* employment is a new invention. Indeed, in the first half of the century, at least until the 1930s (and its frequently recalled recession), the emphasis was more on how new inventions and technologies would allow us to develop the leisured utopia. In fact, there were major reductions in overall annual worktime in most countries during the inter-war period.

At the same time, for many theorists, work has been seen, for a very long time, as alienating (with Marx being the obvious referent). To understand how the emphasis on 'full employment' has arisen, we examine how notions of work have changed through the centuries; and how the present ideology is supported by very questionable research claiming to show how terrible unemployment is and how wonderful employment is.

1.1.3 Consumption and welfare

For mainstream economists, theory dictates that consumers choose freely what to buy. Presumably therefore – on that view – what people buy contributes to their welfare, because people are the best judges of what will improve their welfare.

On the whole, we accept that welfare is whatever people say it is and whatever they prefer, *provided* the procedures for revealing those views (the ballot box) and preferences (the market) do not distort or mislead. The increasing disaffection with elected 'dictatorships' is a signal that the ballot box is not recognised as a wholly legitimate way of obtaining views; and, of course, while mainstream economists recognise that there are market failures – from externalities to information failures and perverse subsidies – they are seen as rare and exceptional. Individually and collectively, we need to be able to take a broader (and more long-term) view than those mechanisms permit.

But there are serious grounds for arguing that increased consumption is, of itself, generating less consumer benefit in terms of welfare. In particular, there are many types of goods and services where there can only ever be limited consumer benefit, however much is spent: an obvious example is houses in sought-after locations. There is also a large amount of empirical evidence that suggests that increased consumption does not increase welfare: for example, from opinion surveys, from historical and cross-cultural studies, and from studies of how markets fail to reflect preference adequately. This is the subject of Chapter 4.

1.1.4 'Joined-up' thinking[1]

Of course, we are not the only ones to write about these kinds of issues, and much of what we argue in the following chapters has been discussed by other authors (and they are referenced in the chapters that follow), but our particular approach is to link the three problems of environmental damage, employment and over-consumption. Indeed, the basis for the argument in this book is that all these three issues are inter-related and that we have to consider them all together. Our arguments about the three themes in Chapters 2, 3 and 4 reinforce one another. If ecological risks are negligible, perhaps we should continue on the present path, given that it is politically easier. If (paid) work is so good for us, we should probably just look for more labour-intensive patterns of production. If ever greater consumption is essential to our well-being, then the ecological and employment costs may well be worth suffering, or at least we should focus on efforts to mitigate those costs, without reducing consumption.

On one level, therefore, we are doing a kind of cost-benefit analysis of alternative development paths: the benefits are welfare (Chapter 4) and the costs are ecological damage (Chapter 2) and unpleasant (largely employed) human labour (Chapter 3). But the problem with the standard approach to cost-benefit analysis is that too often welfare is measured solely in terms of (often imputed) monetary valuations, and technocrats then rely on its spurious precision to make (often rule-of-thumb) decisions. Instead, we argue that the whole framework of thinking about policy in terms of purely monetary valuations and output growth is misguided: policies and trends need to be assessed according to their contribution to welfare measured in human terms, and trade-offs, between different dimensions of welfare (and thence decisions) need to be made democratically.

1.1.5 Inequalities at home and abroad

Not only are these three problems inter-linked, their impact on the rich and poor in society tends to be cumulative. Those who suffer most pollution tend also to have the worst and/or insecure jobs and can barely meet their basic needs. The sporadic economic growth that we have experienced has not 'trickled down' from the rich to the poor: instead, further liberalisation is generating greater income inequality, with the poor finding themselves obliged to work at low wages for those who are better off (and sometimes only slightly), travelling further in degraded public transport and having even less time for life outside work.

Moreover, while this book is primarily addressed to fellow members of rich societies, a global approach to ecological problems is necessary if we are to understand and appreciate the limits that these place on the expansion of economic activity.

The fact that various ecological ills – for example, deforestation or soil erosion – are experienced most often in poor countries (or at least the consequences are most serious there), is taken to mean they can be blamed on the activities of people in those countries. In a further twist, since some of these ills may also have consequences for the rich countries, this can be used to justify dictating policy to the poor countries concerned. Never mind that the real ecological disaster zones are the rich countries, nor that most of the damage stems from satisfying the customers of the rich countries.

This is all rather obvious and well documented (see for example Sachs, 1993). Along with many others, we therefore reject the globalisation of ecological issues which consists in giving the rich the right to decide how the poor are to 'solve' ecological problems. The solutions we propose are addressed to those in the rich countries who are responsible for the problems in the first place. In other words we agree with the need to 'think global, act local' – in contrast to establishment environmentalists, whose motto seems to be exactly the opposite.

1.2 The role of economics

Much of the argument in the following chapters goes against prevailing ways of thinking about ecological issues, employment and consumption: the view that consumption brings welfare, that employment is fulfilling as well as necessary, and that ecological damage, even if troublesome, does not mean we have to abandon economic growth. These ways of thinking, while very widespread, are expressed in their clearest (and most extreme) form in orthodox economics. Much of this book is therefore (explicitly or implicitly) critical of economic theory and its most basic assumptions.

Orthodox, and particularly neoclassical, economics[2] has been subjected to a variety of fundamental criticisms over many decades. At the level of theory there are reasons to question its most basic assumptions (see Keen, 2001 for one exposition), and there are also of course many reasons to deplore its practical effects. Nevertheless, in spite of devastating criticisms, neoclassical economics marches on, and, even more strikingly, ideas rejected as nonsense a generation ago have made a reappearance since. Perhaps its strength lies in its ideological power – its use in justifying market capitalism – rather than any scientific content.

We agree with many of the criticisms made of orthodox economics. These include for example its static quality – its neglect of how economic institutions have come about – and its assumption that individuals are inherently motivated by self-interest. But we also have particular quarrels with it, something which this book highlights.

At a general level, we strongly disagree with the support of orthodox (and much unorthodox) economics for policies which promote economic growth. This is, growth of output and income; with its neglect – or at best, its failure to resolve satisfactorily – ecological issues; and with its quite ambiguous, even contradictory, attitude to work, employment and free time.

Much of our criticism relates to the role of consumption, which for most economists is closely related to welfare. Moreover welfare, as well as decisions about what to consume, is seen almost entirely in terms of the individual consumer, as if she or he led their life independently of others. There is a more general emphasis on the individual, and a neglect of results from other disciplines, which might help correct this emphasis. There is an acceptance of enormous inequalities in consumption levels as well as support for a global trading system which is making these inequalities greater. The political and social system associated with a market economy is neglected.

Perhaps even more important are the criticisms which stem from economists' neglect of ecological problems, something which results from ignoring the whole material basis of production and consumption: the role that nature plays in providing energy, materials, and waste disposal is taken for granted. As ecological damage on a vast scale has become impossible to ignore, economists have proposed various remedies, based however on completely unrealistic views of how markets work, how far substitutes can be found for natural resources, and the miracles of which technology will be capable. Even on an optimistic view of these factors, the solutions proposed are inadequate.

Regarding employment and unemployment, economists are inconsistent, or at least divided. For the neoclassical theorist, work is a source of disutility or welfare loss, compensated of course by the gain in welfare which results from spending the income. But in practice, one of the main stated targets of economic policy has been to minimise the level of unemployment without any consideration of welfare.

The above is merely an outline of the type of quarrel we have with orthodox economics. More detail will be found in the chapters which follow. In some key respects, however, this quarrel is not with economics as such, but with the continued domination of a particular kind of economics. We have nothing against the classic view of economics as 'the science which studies human behaviour as a relationship between ends and scarce means which have alternative uses' (Robbins, 1932), only against some aspects of the way it is conventionally interpreted. In particular, the costs of production in terms of natural and human resources must be fully allowed for; and the gains of economic activity in terms of welfare cannot (and indeed should not) be equated with the quantity of goods and services that are consumed. A much broader view of both the means and ends of economic activity is required; and this is what the second half of the book is about.

1.3 How do we move forward?

1.3.1 Will current approaches work?

We turn in Chapter 5 to examine current orthodox approaches to finding solutions to these problems. Although our examples are biased towards the UK, most of what we say applies equally to other rich countries. A variety of conventional possible solutions that have been tried, which presume (usually implicitly rather than explicitly) ever-increasing consumption, are considered and are shown to have mostly failed. In particular, connections and contradictions inherent to this kind of approach are often ignored.

While environmental problems will get more urgent, pressure for increasing consumption, and current conventional 'solutions' will continue to make things worse. This will be evident, at least symptomatically, in the social disorder – and the response to it in terms of increased security – consequent upon increased inequalities; and in the increasing pressure from migrants and poorer countries to share in the wealth of the richer countries. So pressure for change will intensify.

We argue that the problem is the ever-increasing consumption and output-oriented growth itself; and that, instead (macro-economic), policies should be evaluated in terms of their contribution to welfare. This means, among other things, that we have to focus instead on the extent to which production contributes to quality of life, without damaging the environment, paying specific attention to those people currently at the bottom of the heap. In other words, we have to focus on how welfare can be maintained and improved while having fewer (or fewer resource-using) goods and services.

It should be stressed that we are not talking about 'economic policy' in the usual terms. In particular, we are not talking about fiscal tools (interest rates and money supply) for managing growth; we are searching for a different development path.

1.3.2 Back to basics: defining welfare

The problem is what is meant by 'welfare'. We argue that welfare is inherently multi-dimensional and that apart from the elimination of absolute poverty in terms of basic education, food, unnecessary risks to health, shelter and water (both in our own countries and in those we exploit), the diversity of people's circumstances must be respected. Beyond those absolute minima, therefore, we take the position that people have the right to decide for themselves what their welfare means. We do not believe, however, that either the market or the ballot box allows them to do that adequately. The former only allows for a very crude one-dimensional (monetary) expression of relative preference and is inequitable (because of income inequality), while the latter is not only an alienating form of participation but also provides hardly any choice. While we empathetically prefer local referenda on every issue of substance, we realise there are all kinds of problems; and the examples that do exist do not encourage us (see Chapter 9). At the same time, consumer tastes are not as idio-syncratic as economists often imply; there is a core of social concerns, around which, surveys suggest, there is widespread agreement.

We show that a wide range of approaches to identifying the various components of welfare (that are apparently very different) actually lead to rather similar lists of components or dimensions. In the absence of an effective mechanism to reach a collective consensus about these dimensions, we have suggested an eclectic list of criteria based on earlier work on social indicators. This places more emphasis on minima, rather than more being necessarily better, and on collective rather than individual well-being. We do not expect everyone to agree precisely with our definitions of 'basic needs' for consumption, and we recognise that monitoring inequalities and human rights is notoriously difficult, but we think most will agree with our general approach to defining 'welfare'.

Our operational definition of welfare is therefore the set of social concerns and indicators as described in Chapter 6. These should be used as the basis for judging any proposed changes in policy. We illustrate the implications of adopting such a welfare framework for current policies in a number of sectors; they are substantial. This leads on to the next question: what should we aim for and how would we monitor progress?

1.3.3 Moving on from the rat race

In Chapter 7, we explore the implications for both ecology and employment through identifying a set of reductions in consumption of goods and services which: (1) make little or no contribution to welfare; and (2) whose production is labour intensive; or (3) environmentally damaging. We use these criteria to make some preliminary assessment of the impact of reducing consumption (without reducing welfare) upon current damaging levels of environmental emissions and jobs. To do this, we use the Environmental Input Output tables and the Annual Employment Survey. Clearly, the precise percentage of reductions we have chosen are debatable but we believe that we have demonstrated the orders of magnitude involved in what we are proposing, and we provide sufficient information for anyone else to recalculate, based on a different view of what counts as an adequate level of consumption. In the same chapter, we also demonstrate that our proposals are not utopian; countries with much lower levels of GNP per capita than those pertaining in the West have similar levels of welfare, at least on some dimensions.

Clearly, we do not expect our prescriptions to be adopted by everyone. In particular, we realise that many of the changes we propose require a rather substantial shift both in institutions and in value systems. While we are not proposing a political programme, we suggest that one essential element of the infrastructure for that shift will be an agreed set of indicators by which we can all assess the implications for ecology and employment of what is happening. We believe that the set of indicators that are developed in Chapter 8 would be broadly acceptable to most people. But they are only suggestions: the criteria that are finally adopted by any community would have to be fully debated and discussed before being adapted locally. We also realise that the implementation of such a structure requires vibrant local communities; and we fully recognise the difficulties entailed in creating (or recreating) those.

In Chapter 9, we examine a number of short-term changes that could be made to current policies to move in the direction of sustainable welfare, some of which might well happen anyway under the pressure of existing environmental problems (the obvious ones being traffic reduction policies). But we recognise that such changes can go only so far: if we are to drastically reduce ecological damage, then we have to reduce economic activity and therefore the opportunity for profit. There is a fundamental conflict between a concern for welfare and the pursuit of profit, and any change therefore cannot happen without substantial shifts in people's values.

We also show in Chapter 9 that there are increasing signs that people are more environmentally concerned. Similarly, the traditional view that more consumption means better or more welfare, is also being challenged. The obvious marker is the growth of environmentally friendly consumption which has been phenomenal over the last 10 years and the growth – although not so phenomenal – in less exploitative consumption.

While people are clearly concerned about ecological damage, many do not know or do not realise the implications of trying to reverse that damage. The increasing number of health restraints on certain kinds of consumption, however, and the extent to which people are choosing types of consumption, has also been remarkable.

In addition, unlike many environmentalists, we are not calling, in general, for sacrifices to be made in the name of sustainability. On the contrary, we are presenting ecological crisis as an opportunity to rethink what the costs and benefits of consumerism really are, and suggesting that the costs far outweigh the benefits. Through much of the consumerist-dominated last 50 years there have been movements which rejected consumerism. The 1960s is the obvious example, but apart from religious sects such as Hare Krishna, there have been many groups concerned with the problems of recycling rather than consuming anew.

We end as we began: current policies have failed and have brought serious ecological damage in their wake. The proposals developed in this book aim at improvements. We invite you to reject inertia and fatalism and to reconceive our world in the making.

Part I

Three Major Unsolved Problems

2
Ecological Impacts and Risks

2.1 Introduction

The impact of economic activities on the natural environment has often been ignored: it is 'hidden' from economic accounting since no one pays for it directly, and 'external' to economic transactions in the sense that those suffering the impact are generally not the ones gaining from the activity. This has long been known, but with industrialisation such impacts became greater, as did pressure to reduce them. National legislation against air pollution in the UK for example goes back to the 1820s. More recently, the emphasis has been on taxes designed, at least in principle, to reflect the full pollution impact of activities.

Such attempts to limit environmental damage may lead to some modification in the pattern of consumption, but they do not generally affect the overall level. That has not been the intention, nor in any case has there been any attempt systematically to create a situation where all costs and benefits are allowed for in deciding whether or not to consume.

Over the last 30 years, as impacts have become greater and externalities more pervasive, environmental concern has become much broader, more widespread and more urgent, focusing not only on local nuisances and resource shortages, but also on threats to quality of life in the short term and to survival in the long term. This has resulted in a huge increase in debate and in activism. There has been an expansion in the academic literature across a wide range of disciplines, and a variety of inter- and transdisciplinary projects have set out in search of new paradigms. Thus in economics, for example, there is both the more established 'environmental economics', a subdiscipline which applies mainstream (neoclassical) economic ideas to 'the environment', and a newer 'ecological economics', which starts from the premise that ecological factors pose a fundamental challenge to the economics mainstream, which needs to be radically reformed. Other social sciences, philosophy and, not least, business studies, have turned their attention to ecological issues, while most ecologists looking for practical solutions have accepted the need to take into account social factors, so that a variety of approaches cutting across traditional disciplines have flourished. From modest beginnings on the political fringe in the late 1960s, debate has moved to centre stage with the development of an establishment environmentalism, particularly since the late 1980s (discussed in Chapter 5).

This chapter is concerned with the implications of these issues and debates for consumption levels in the rich countries. The likely scale of present impacts and future risks does lend support to limiting consumption in these countries, especially when the basic needs of many people in lower income countries (presently unsatisfied) are taken into account. On the other hand, we recognise that we cannot be precise in any of the predictions set out here of the likely impact. Indeed, for a variety of reasons uncertainty is inevitable and its bearings on our general argument are considered in section 2.5.

Briefly, the argument in this chapter is as follows. There are ecological limits to economic activity and these are of two kinds. There are limits to how far nature can be used as a *source* of materials; and to how far it can be used as a *sink* for wastes. In addition, where the sink is also the source, of air to breathe or water to drink (for example, we have 'pollution'), human health may be affected long before the ecosystem is threatened. Since there is only limited scope for producing goods with less ecological impact, ecological limits translate into limits on production and consumption. This is true at the global level, and given the desirability of abolishing poverty, it translates into much *stricter* limits for rich countries.

Nevertheless, the uncertainties are crucial. We need some idea where the limits are: if they are far enough away they might as well not exist. Where there is reason to think that limits are close, but nevertheless there is some uncertainty about them, it may make sense, as many 'Greens' suggest, to adopt some form of 'precautionary principle'. However, what this actually means in practice depends on what benefits (if any) we derive from the activity which leads to the ecological impact, and thus on how much we are giving up in return for some reduction in risk. However, it is usually impossible to assess with any accuracy.

2.2 The limits debate

2.2.1 The argument

All living species face ecological limits: a given area can only support at most a certain population of a species, and any attempt to exceed this 'carrying capacity' will lead to food (or other essential resource) shortages and population decline. Even more seriously, it may lead to decline in carrying capacity itself, if for example the food species becomes extinct.

Humans are no exception to this argument, although in the human case the notion of carrying capacity is very much less clear since the demands placed on an area by different people varies so much: the carrying capacity of a given area depends very largely on how its inhabitants live.[1] Any attempt to arrive at some kind of concrete estimate of human carrying capacity for a particular country has to leave out entirely (or make arbitrary assumptions about) factors such as income inequality, the existence of a wealthy elite, and the proportion of land and other resources which is diverted to export. This does not of course mean that ecological limits don't exist, merely that they are better expressed in terms of the total amount of resource use (and thus, for a given technology, output and consumption) that the world can support rather than the number of people. In addition, it means that wastefulness and unequal distribution of resources and of consumption can cause the limits to become apparent very much sooner.

Experience of ecological limits is an inherent part of human life throughout history. Much of history, in particular the development and decline of societies, can be largely explained in terms of ecological factors such as the destruction of the existing natural resource base and the search for new resources (Ponting, 1991, especially Chapter 5). Awareness of limits is reflected in many philosophies and religions. Marshall (1992, Part I) for example shows that a sense of the dependence of humans on nature plays an important part in the thinking of all major religions. At an individual or small group level, ecological limits have been more obvious through most of history than they are now, particularly in rich countries, where resource supplies are a matter of global trading and socio-political factors rather than local and observable natural conditions. Even in a globalised world, individuals are rarely completely insulated from an awareness of limits; direct experience (of air pollution, for example) and well publicised scandals (relating to pollution, health, food contamination, and so on) make sure of that.

Until very recently however the impact of ecological limits has been restricted in scope. There have been cases of ecological collapse which were sudden and catastrophic, the best known case being that of Easter Island. The fall of the Roman empire – or more to the point its rise – left the ecology of the Mediterranean region permanently impoverished.[2] But this is still some way from threatening the global ecosystem or even human existence. The issue of ecological limits became more urgent with industrialisation, which led to human activities which have much greater ecological impact, mainly because it consisted of replacing an economy mostly based on human and animal energy with one mostly based on non-renewable fossil fuels – and in much greater and ever-increasing amounts. As a result, ecological impact grew per capita and thus much faster than population.[3]

Correspondingly, awareness of ecological limits focused increasingly on global limits rather than local nuisances or access to resources. Concern among economists about running out of key natural resources goes back to Jevons and *The Coal Question* (1865). More recent debate over the existence and relevance of ecological limits has focused on a set of arguments expressed at their simplest – some would say at their most oversimplified – in the 'limits to growth' debate (Meadows *et al.*, 1972; revised edition 1992). The limits to growth authors put forward a computer model of environmental processes and attempted to estimate the impact of continued economic growth on resources and pollution. At the core of the model are two sets of factors which come into conflict: *exponential growth* of population, food production, overall national income as well as national income per head, energy use, waste and pollution. In other words, exponential growth in human activity and its ecological impact; and *fixed* limits to the stocks of non-renewable resources, especially fossil fuels, the flow of solar energy and of renewable resources, and the rate of absorption of pollutants.

Not only do these limits preclude unlimited growth, attempts to breach them narrow the limits further. Stocks of renewable resources, which could be used sustainably, such as soil, fish, forests, and many waste absorption capabilities, are destroyed. Meadows and colleagues state their argument in terms of population, and the limits to growth in terms of the maximum number of people that can be supported by the environment – its 'carrying capacity'. As explained above, we would prefer to restate the argument in terms of the maximum equilibrium level of output and resource use which the environment will support, and to

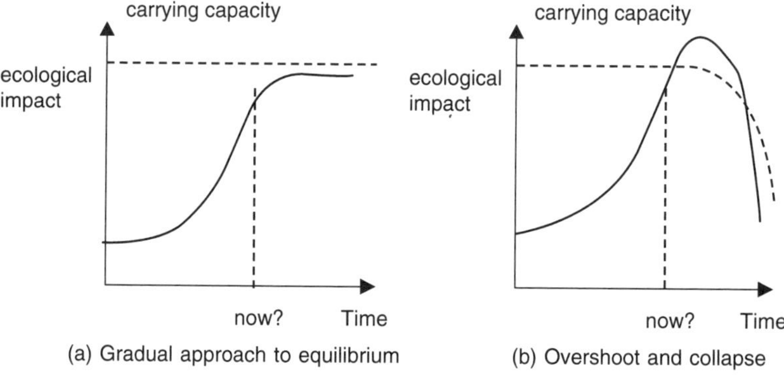

Figure 2.1 Limits to growth scenarios

Source: Adapted from Meadows *et al.*, 1992, p. 108.

understand carrying capacity as capacity to carry a certain ecological burden rather than a certain number of people. However, the nature of the argument is the same. The conflict between exponential growth and ecological limits has two possible plausible outcomes:[4] a gradual approach towards equilibrium, which requires that growth be abandoned; and failing that, an overshoot of ecological impact leading to a collapse in carrying capacity. Ecological limits will be respected, one way or another: see Figure 2.1.

The Meadows model was run with different sets of assumptions. The 'standard' run assumed continued growth and no policy change. It led to the 'overshoot and collapse' scenario, with world output (in the updated 1992 version) peaking about 2010, then both industrial output and food production falling due to lack of resources, leading to fast population decline. If a higher level of resources is assumed (the actual level of stocks of underground and underwater resources being essentially unknown), then growth continues a little longer but pollution increases so much that food production declines and the death rate increases anyway. And if this can somehow be avoided we still run out of land and population declines after 2070.

Such scenarios inevitably require us to make assumptions in cases where we are unsure or just don't know. Stocks of fossil fuels and other, largely hidden, resources are only one example; and we return to problems of uncertainty at the end of the chapter. However, the nature of the exponential growth, upon which the model is based, means that large changes in the assumptions usually make relatively little difference to the forecast (and perhaps even less to the practical and policy conclusions that can be drawn from it). It is in the nature of this type of (continuous) model – which projects existing trends – that it concentrates on limits which make themselves felt gradually and that we know something about (such as cultivable land or fossil fuels), where there are trends that can be extrapolated. It tends to ignore sudden catastrophes that we have some reason to expect but whose timing and consequences we know very little about (such as drastic climate change).

The original (1972) limits to growth model encountered a good deal of criticism, much of it from economists. Some of this seems to be the result of misinterpretation of what the authors were doing and perhaps misleading presentation on their part. The revised (1992) version makes it clear that their model was intended to be a 'what-if' exercise, rather than a forecast of what will actually happen. It was suggested that, once exponential growth and finite limits are assumed, the general results of the model are inevitable. The details of the forecasts can certainly be contested; in addition, the computer modelling was to some extent a concession to the then current fascination with the growing power of computers. But what really mattered was the logic of the argument. Much more significant was criticism of the model that claimed that limits to growth could be pushed back indefinitely, thanks to technology and market incentives. We return to this argument below.

At the same time, the model achieved a great deal in terms of popularising the notion of ecological limits, and setting the parameters of debate by challenging advocates of continued growth to show that the limits *can* be pushed back as fast as they can be approached, that is, exponentially. In the shorter term, the model acquired prestige as a result of the oil crises of the 1970s, which made the idea of essential natural resources running out plausible.

Perceptions of ecological limits have changed a good deal since the early 1970s. The existence of limits is now widely accepted in principle, though debate continues about whether, how far, how quickly, and by what means, the limits can be pushed back. In addition to, and largely directing, the intellectual debates, are various attempts by business to co-opt ecological concern, and milk it financially and ideologically (see Chapter 5). There have also been changes in *which* limits are most emphasised. As the price of oil and other non-renewable resources came down again in the 1980s and 1990s, there was less concern about their running out. On the other hand, there was increasing concern (and evidence) that renewable resources such as forests, soils and fish stocks were being used unsustainably (being 'mined' rather than 'harvested'), thus in effect becoming non-renewable. And, even more in the news, was concern with global pollution problems – acid rain, ozone depletion, bio-diversity loss – and especially global warming. Since the latter is almost entirely associated with fossil fuel use, we have, in a way, come back full circle to the 1970s and the problems of reducing fossil fuel dependence, with the ironic twist that this time the problem is that we might not run out of oil soon enough.

Acceptance of the logic of 'limits to growth' leads to quite a different approach from the mainstream economics one. The economy is part of an ecosystem which cannot expand and which (at least until we colonise space) thus limits economic expansion. The limits are physical ones which mainstream economics, generally dealing in monetary quantities, fails to capture. This is partly (and economists nowadays tend to acknowledge this in principle) because natural resources and waste absorption capacity are treated as 'free' and by implication, therefore, plentiful, so that prices fail to reflect their (generally increasing) scarcity. It is also because, as testified by the first macroeconomics chapter of every economics textbook, it misrepresents the economy as a circular flow of income which can grow indefinitely (provided the supply of money can do likewise). In reality, it is non-human processes which behave in a cyclical fashion (Figure 2.2(a)), as do the human processes which substitute for them, such as recycling. In contrast, most economic activity has a linear character – most waste is not recycled – with the implication that, at least beyond a certain scale, stocks of resources dwindle while stocks of wastes accumulate (Figure 2.2(b)).

From a more ecological point of view it is possible to derive a set of general rules which must be followed if an economy is to be 'sustainable', that is, able to continue operating indefinitely. This notion of sustainability is sometimes described as 'strong' sustainability. It requires: for *renewable* resources, that the rate of use not be more than

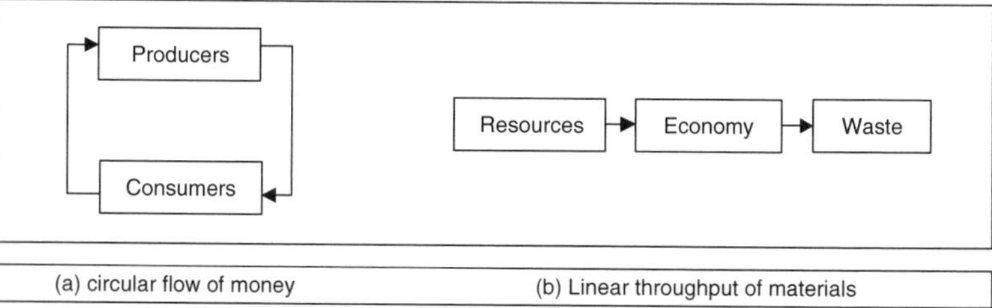

Figure 2.2 Two views of the economy

the rate of regeneration; for *non-renewable* resources, that the rate of use not be more than the rate at which renewable resources can be substituted; for *pollutants*, that the rate of emission not be more than the rate at which pollutants are rendered harmless, recycled or absorbed (implying, where this cannot be done, no emissions) (Daly, 1992).

Mainstream economists, while increasingly acknowledging that there is a problem and making certain concessions on policy (something we return to in Chapter 5), have generally rejected the view that there are effective limits to growth. Some of their arguments – that increasing production and consumption are essential for welfare or for eliminating poverty – are not really about ecological limits, but about the importance of circumventing them; these issues are addressed in Chapter 4. Doubts are also often cast on specific predictions of ecological doom, reflecting inevitable uncertainty (see below). The argument specifically about limits, the one considered here, centres on the role of technology and of markets.

According to this argument, technology can improve resource availability, reduce waste generation and achieve greater production with less of either. It can make it possible to replace resources in short supply with ones that are more plentiful. This makes shortages of specific resources irrelevant. Markets provide the necessary incentives for new technologies to be developed and adopted. Resource shortages lead to higher prices, which provide the incentive for a search for conservation possibilities and for substitutes. The result is more efficient technologies and in some cases new markets, as with recycled materials, bottled water or anti-pollution masks. Scarcities are always relative not absolute: they exist given a particular price and disappear when this rises sufficiently. Growth *ad infinitum* is therefore possible.

To be sure, there are market imperfections; in particular there is a lack of markets wherever there are no well-defined property rights. For example, no one owns the atmosphere and there is no market in clean air; there is thus no market disincentive to air pollution since there is no price to be paid to the air's owner. The solution is to establish, if not real then virtual markets: the state acts as owner of the atmosphere and either auctions pollution permits or taxes pollution. (The more traditional policy, simply prohibiting certain forms of pollution, is nowadays frowned upon as 'inefficient' and a gross infringement of market principles.) The 'strong' sustainability rules outlined above are unnecessary, given that substitutes can always be found for scarce resources. What is needed instead is a single 'weak' sustainability rule (one already followed by any textbook entrepreneur – though not by 'real life speculators' and fast buck merchants): the stock of capital needs to be maintained. However, given the problem of missing markets (that is, there are some features of the environment for which there are no markets), the definition of 'capital' must be expanded to include not only human-made capital, as now, but also 'natural capital', the total value of natural sources and sinks. As long as human-made plus natural capital does not decrease, we have sustainability. This in turn implies that natural capital can decline – perhaps to zero – as long as human-made capital grows sufficiently to compensate. It also implies that a way has to be found to measure natural capital in financial terms, if we are to calculate whether we are on a sustainable path. We return to this in Chapter 5.

There is no doubt that all sorts of technological improvements are possible, leading to improvements in ecological efficiency (less resource use and/or waste and pollution for a given output). This will be part of any solution to ecological problems, and some examples are discussed below (see section 2.4). However, as we shall see, even the most enthusiastic advocates of such technologies recognise that they will not be sufficient by themselves. Efficiency improvements themselves face limits. The direction of technological innovation will also have to change: technological development has largely been about reducing labour by *increasing* natural resource use (especially energy). And, not least, some resources (ones which are increasingly a focus for concern) have essentially no substitute, notably land (especially fertile land), water, the atmosphere and bio-diversity.

How successfully can markets be used to achieve substitution where possibilities for substitution exist? The evidence suggests that they may be effective in bringing about incremental but not structural change. A small tax incentive was enough to achieve change from leaded to unleaded petrol, in the UK and elsewhere; but very large increases in petrol prices in the 1970s led to modest improvements in car design rather than the abandonment of the car. Much of the direction of development depends on government decisions – for example, about infrastructure – not market incentives. Yet overcoming some of the 'relative' scarcities referred to above requires some very major structural change. For example, existing economies in the North are almost entirely (and, in many cases, increasingly) dependent on fossil fuels, which are both non-renewable and whose use leads to global warming.

There is considerable doubt about how effectively markets can be used to achieve even marginal improvements in ecological efficiency. Markets operate with delays and on imperfect information, take a short-term view and respond to demand only from those with purchasing power. In relation to natural resources, economists sometimes endow markets with god-like omniscience, as for example when they treat falling prices as evidence that resources are becoming less scarce (Simon and Kahn, 1984). But if those dealing on the oil market have no idea about the size of oil reserves, there is no way that the price which emerges when they do business can reflect this. At best, price movements will reflect short-term gluts and shortages, and speculation is likely to ensure that they often do not even do that.

Having said all this, the existence of limits by itself is not enough to justify worrying about them. Are they close? How fast can they be pushed back? And what do we do if we don't know?

2.2.2 How close are the limits?

Various people have tried to quantify both the current human impact on the environment and the various ecological limits, thus allowing some estimate of how close we are to those limits. Such exercises raise huge difficulties in view of all the uncertainties involved (a subject that is reviewed in section 2.5), but cannot really be avoided: no useful conclusion can be drawn from the mere fact that ecological limits exist 'somewhere in the future'.

Given the uncertainties and complexities involved it is perhaps easier to argue that limits have already been reached in some places and in some respects than to speculate about global limits. Thus it is sometimes argued that particular countries have overstepped their carrying capacity. Some authors have seen the clearing of forests in developing countries for cultivation or grazing as not only of global concern (notably because of the role of forests as carbon sinks, as well as loss of biodiversity), but also as an indication that those countries are running out of land and so reaching the limit of population they can support. Attempts at a systematic study of carrying capacity have been made. Foy and Daly (1992) for example have assessed the population of Haiti, El Salvador and Costa Rica in relation to carrying capacity, concluding that the population of Haiti is grossly excessive and in the other cases is getting quite close to carrying capacity. Yet such estimates are based on the existing pattern of production, where land and other resources are very unequally distributed, and where the best land is often allocated to export crops. They seem even more problematic if we consider that countries such as the UK or The Netherlands exceed their carrying capacity by a very much greater amount than Haiti. The Netherlands is estimated to have an 'ecological footprint' (discussed below) some 15 times its own area (Wackernagel and Rees, 1996). The notion of local limits makes little sense in a 'globalised' world; nor does the concept of carrying capacity in a world of inequalities.

A more promising approach to estimating how close we are to critical ecological limits is to consider our dependence on net primary production (NPP). NPP is the solar energy captured by plants through photosynthesis which they do not use for their own growth and reproduction, and which is thus the basic food source for all those – humans and other animals – who are not themselves capable of photosynthesis. The proportion of this NPP which is appropriated by human beings for their own use provides a good measure of the scale of the economy in relation to the ecosystem within which it is embedded, and of course it cannot rise above 100 per cent.

'Appropriation' includes both direct uses (for food or fuel for example) and indirect effects such as those resulting from deforestation or desertification, paving over, or introducing new patterns of plant growth, as with agriculture, which lower NPP. Vitousek *et al.* in 1986 calculated that some 25 per cent of net primary production was appropriated by human beings. Furthermore, average NPP is misleading since the scope for increasing maritime NPP appropriated by humans is small. More relevant is *terrestrial* NPP, and some *40 per cent* of that is (1986 figures) appropriated. Taking into account that some NPP must be left over for non-human use if ecosystem services are to be maintained, this would allow only at most a further doubling, taking 35 to 40 years at present rates of population growth, even in the unlikely event that per capita resource consumption does not increase.

In later work, Vitousek (1994) argued that there are (at least) three major components of global environmental change where we can be certain that large changes are happening, that they are due to human activity, and that they have important ecological consequences. These are: (1) rising carbon dioxide concentrations; (2) disturbance of the global nitrogen cycle; and (3) land use changes. Each of these has led us to a situation well outside our previous experience, and is known to contribute to global environmental problems, notably climate change and biodiversity loss. (This does not of course imply that the mechanisms are all well understood or the size of the effects known.)

Goodland (1992), reviewing the evidence that in a number of key respects 'the world has reached limits', argues that, in addition to Vitousek's NPP estimates, global warming, the rupture of the ozone shield, land degradation, and biodiversity loss, each suggest that we are close to, or overstepping, limits. Shortage of water and of cultivable land are also often mentioned as limits that we are fast approaching. Our current *level* of consumption, and not merely its rate of growth, may be unsustainable.

The variety of possible ecological impacts and risks may make it difficult to arrive at an overall assessment – although often any one impact would be enough to justify a radical change of direction – and a number of authors have tried to develop single summary measures. The mainstream economics approach is, of course, to impute a monetary value to everything and use this to assess the problem, as well as to evaluate policy. This approach, which has received a mixed response among ecologists, is appraised in Chapter 5. Energy use is sometimes used as a general indicator of ecological impact because of its association with a variety of major impacts (carbon emissions, acid rain, non-renewable resource use, local air pollution, and so on). Another approach, mentioned above, is based on the notion of 'ecological footprints' (Wackernagel and Rees, 1996).

Ecological footprints are an attempt to express the resource use and waste assimilation requirements of a population in terms of land area, providing a measure of the total land the population would require if it were to be self sufficient, given its consumption pattern. They allow comparison of at least some of the relative ecological costs of different countries' consumption (examples are: US 5.1 hectares/person; India 0.4; world 1.8), as well as estimating how different populations are using 'imported' resources (London's ecological footprint is 120 times its actual area). Globally, they suggest that we have already exceeded ecological limits: the estimated ecological footprint of the developed world by itself exceeds the global supply of ecologically productive land (Wackernagel and Rees, 1996, pp. 85, 91, 149).

Estimating current ecological impacts is not enough, however, since much of the concern is with the future. Duchin and Lange (1994) have attempted to test the Brundtland Commission's (WCED, 1987) hope that economic growth and environmental improvement can be combined, using a world input-output model backed up by case studies of the sectors which are responsible for the bulk of energy use, materials use and pollution. They investigated a number of scenarios incorporating various assumptions about technology, introduction of new energy sources, and rates of industrialisation. Their work goes beyond the relatively simple extrapolation of existing trends characteristic of much writing about limits, especially in the mix of economic, ecological and technological factors which are considered. They find that, even extrapolating current improvements in energy efficiency, recycling, and so on (as well as economic growth), large increases in resource use and pollution will continue. In addition, any attempt at 'greener' development worldwide – even more so than generalising the current less green development – would require a huge expansion (and change of direction!) in international credit. Moreover, even improvements in resource productivity are insufficient to deal with pollution: none of the scenarios considered, for example, stabilises carbon emissions at 1990 levels. With the Kyoto protocol of 1997 the rich countries undertook to cut emissions to 5 per cent below their 1990 level by 2010.[5] Overall, the conclusion is that growth – even in combination with any plausible assumption about technology – cannot continue if the environment is not to degrade further.

While (it seems to us) these attempts at locating and quantifying ecological limits make quite a persuasive case that growth must end, nevertheless there are reasons for being cautious. Some of the most pessimistic predictions of the 1970s – about population growth and its effects, or about running out of non-renewable resources, for example – have not materialised, or at least not yet. No doubt the reason is largely over-simple extrapolation of existing trends and neglect of structural change. Unfortunately the neglected structural changes are not, or mainly not, a matter of smoothly functioning markets ensuring conservation, substitution, and technological progress. Even if the oil price rises of the 1970s encouraged conservation and new discoveries, these in turn have only led to prices falling again and a return to more wasteful oil use – and rising carbon emissions. Some of the structural changes of the last three decades – such as the rise of the 'newly industrialised countries' – have made the limits more pressing. However the debate over ecological limits remains dogged by problems of uncertainty and competing claims, and we return to these problems later in the chapter.

2.3 The global dimension

Although this book is focused on the rich countries, the limits discussed refer to ecological impacts and risks *worldwide*. If low-income countries are to have the possibility of increased resource use, there have to be a much larger relative cut backs among the rich.

This is in contrast with the orthodox economics view which advocates abolishing poverty through higher growth. If no limits to growth are envisaged, and poverty is understood in terms of absolute income level,[6] then growth offers more possibility of making the poor better off than does redistribution, does so without making the rich worse off, and seems more feasible politically. Of course, this will not necessarily happen: if growth is accompanied by sufficient redistribution towards the rich, the number of poor people may increase (as arguably happened in the UK and US in the 1980s). But, more important for our argument, if the growth option is not available, redistribution of resource use (and assimilative capacity) from rich to poor is the only way to reduce poverty.

Though many economists take a relaxed view of ecological limits and argue that improvements in resource efficiency will allow present growth rates of output to continue, few argue that they will allow rich country levels of output to be achieved across the world, except perhaps on a time scale of centuries. This is not surprising given the magnitudes involved. Daly (1996), for example, estimates that a 36-fold increase in ecological efficiency (output per ecological impact) would be required for the world to achieve the same consumption per capita as the US – even without further consumption growth in the US or population growth anywhere. While, as stated above, we find the case for ending growth quite persuasive on ecological grounds alone, we consider that it is overwhelming if equity on a world scale is also adopted as a goal.

This raises the question of what place is reserved for the poor in the version of 'sustainable development' that has been embraced by establishment environmentalists, and which is intended to reconcile growth and ecology. Only too likely is an outcome where sustainability is regarded as a luxury, available to the rich only. Existing imports of natural resources from low-income countries, and of goods which are particularly dangerous or polluting to produce, are a sign of things to come. We return in Chapter 5 to the type of policies likely to promote the goal of sustainability for those who can afford it, and the various rationales offered for them.

One type of rationale however can be mentioned here, since it has to do with the (alleged) origins of ecological crisis rather than any proposed solutions, and amounts to little more than victim blaming. Ecology, from this perspective, becomes a stick to beat the third world with. The fact that various ecological ills – deforestation or soil erosion, for example – are experienced most often in poor countries, or at least the consequences are most serious there, means they can be blamed on the activities of people in those countries. In a further twist, since some of these ills may have consequences for the rich countries also – deforestation contributes to climate change, for example – this can be used to justify dictating policy to the poor countries concerned. This is in spite of the fact that the real ecological disaster zones are the rich countries, which long ago cut down their forests and transformed huge areas – from the former north African breadbasket of the Roman empire to the US dustbowl – into desert. It also ignores the fact that most of the damage stems from satisfying rich country customers – a process often controlled by multinationals based in rich countries – whether directly, as with tropical hardwoods or banana plantations, or indirectly, where export crops have driven production for local use onto marginal land. Indeed, large-scale ecological destruction seems to be particularly associated with the economics and culture of industrial capitalism (of both the free market and the command economy variety), and the poor countries' main crime is to be the victim.

This is all rather obvious and well documented (see for example Sachs, 1993). However, there seems to be one feature of poor countries which cannot be blamed – at least directly – on rich countries, and that is high rates of population growth. Not surprisingly, therefore, it plays a pivotal role in the eco-stick beating. High population growth is held to be the ultimate threat to ecological limits. In the US it has led to support by many ecologists for strict immigration controls. In a more liberal, even-handed version, rapid population growth in poor countries and consumption growth in rich countries are blamed equally, fostering an attitude of 'we're all in it together'. Yet, the situation is one where the per capita ecological impact of the richest billion is some 30 times that of the poorest billion (Durning, 1992, p. 28), based on income. Using energy use or various other indicators would give a different figure but a similar order of magnitude. The problem is, that while the world could support very much larger numbers of poor people, it apparently cannot support even the existing number of rich people (see also note 1). Of course, there is some maximum number of people that can be supported at any given standard of living, and at some point it may become necessary to trade one off against the other, but not while there are a billion people who could substantially cut back their consumption without (as we argue in the next two chapters) even suffering any loss of well-being. Meanwhile, to equate the right of the poor to have children with that of the rich to further increase their consumption (with demands for population control being, in practice, much louder than demands for consumption control) seems to lack all proportion.

A global approach to ecological problems is necessary if we are to understand and appreciate the limits that these place on expansion of economic activity. A *local* approach, applied to the rich countries, would only suggest that by and large environmental quality is getting better, and where it is not, the most politically feasible solutions are those at the expense of poor countries. However, we reject the globalisation of ecological issues which consists in giving the rich the right to decide how the poor are to 'solve' ecological problems. The solutions we propose are addressed to those in the rich countries who are responsible for the problems in the first place. In other words, we agree with the need to 'think global, act local'. Unfortunately, this is in contrast with establishment environmentalists whose mantra seems to be exactly the opposite.

2.4 Improving efficiency: the factor X debate

This section is concerned with the question, how far does the need to reduce ecological impact translate into a need to reduce production and consumption? There is now quite wide acceptance of the need to reduce or at least limit ecological impact; but this is often accompanied by one of two ideas. According to one view, it is possible to achieve sufficient impact reductions simply through greater efficiency, without reducing consumption – we will examine this claim here. According to the other view, reducing consumption – and thus according to this view welfare – is so far fetched as not to be worth considering – this we discuss in Chapter 4.

Certainly there are considerable opportunities for improving the ecological efficiency of production, that is for producing the same output with reduced ecological impact or risk: for example, using fewer resources or less polluting processes. An avalanche of proposals of this type occurred in the 1990s; here we mention briefly three books which attempt to gather these together into an overall assessment of the possibilities.

Factor Four (Weizsäcker *et al.*, 1997), as the title suggests, argues that a fourfold improvement in resource productivity is possible, allowing, as the subtitle puts it, 'doubling wealth, halving resource use'. It includes a large number of examples, with particular emphasis on energy use in buildings and on energy generation. While many of the examples are impressive, the book is less convincing when it comes to policy – based largely on modifying market incentives (see below and Chapter 5). Jackson's *Material Concerns* (1996) also provides a range of examples of how to reduce both resource use and pollution ('dematerialisation'), this time the major focus being on production methods. If reduced material flows can be designed into new production processes ('preventive environmental management'), in contrast with the earlier 'end of pipe' approach to pollution control (that is any environmental costs are borne by the consumer), not only are much greater reductions possible, but in most cases costs are reduced rather than increased. As a result there is a financial incentive to introduce such methods. Like *Factor Four*, however, Jackson's proposals for implementation (especially the 'new service economy' discussed in Chapter 5) are less convincing. Finally, *Greening the North* (Sachs *et al.*, 1998) has yet another major emphasis, on the role of infrastructure in determining what is produced and consumed, and at what ecological cost, notably in areas such as transport and energy generation. As a result, it is closer to the perspective of this book, in emphasising maintaining welfare, rather than consumption, while reducing ecological impact; and in achieving this it stresses collective decisions rather than the role of market incentives. We return to some of these proposals in Chapter 9, where we also review some of the arguments about 'delinking' growth and profits from resource use.

These and similar works are a rich source of ideas about both the opportunities for reducing ecological damage and issues raised by implementation. At the very least they suggest that there are considerable opportunities for improving ecological efficiency. However, they all agree, first, that such improvements may not be enough to prevent catastrophic ecological damage, even at present output levels[7] (and certainly will not be if poor countries are to match rich countries' output levels); and second, they will anyway be offset by increased production and consumption, unless something else is done.

But in any case we need to reconsider what the efficiency of an activity means. In general terms it can be defined as the ratio of benefits to costs. In a business context of course these are money quantities, and maximising efficiency is the same thing as maximising profit.[8] Ecologists have done an excellent job of pointing out that money costs ignore or distort the true costs, which consist of the *total environmental impact* of the activity. But, in addition, the monetary benefits usually give a completely misleading impression of the true benefits, the effects of the activity on *welfare*. (What we mean by welfare – as distinct from preference maximisation – is outlined in Chapter 1 and discussed in greater detail in Part II). Thus, 'efficiency' includes not only the efficiency of production (the output obtained from a given ecological impact) but also the efficiency of consumption (the welfare obtained from a given output). Box 2.1 illustrates this.

The intention of Box 2.1 is to suggest the range of ways in which ecological efficiency can be affected, and not to imply that it can in practice be reduced to a series of simple ratios. In reality of course welfare, environmental impact and related concepts are all multidimensional. Welfare is made up of a number of distinct aspects (health, relationships, security, and so on) and success in one aspect cannot simply offset failure

Box 2.1 Ecological efficiency and its components

Overall 'efficiency' can be defined and broken down as follows:

$$\text{Efficiency} = \frac{\text{Benefit}}{\text{Cost}} = \frac{\text{Welfare gained}}{\text{Total environmental impact}}$$

$$= \underset{(1)}{\frac{\text{Welfare gained}}{\text{Stock of consumer goods}}} \times \underset{(2)}{\frac{\text{Stock of consumer goods}}{\text{resource use}}} \times \underset{(3)}{\frac{\text{resource use}}{\text{Total environmental impact}}}$$

Examples:

(1)	(2)	(3)
Improving allocation and distribution	Durability, recyclability, repairability	Switching to renewable resources or more abundant ones, less polluting processes, avoid irreversible loss

Source: Adapted from Daly, 1992, Chapter 4.

in another; we expand this idea in Chapter 6. There is no way of aggregating performance in different areas, for example, in terms of money, in a way that makes sense and does justice to their distinctiveness. The same applies to ecological impacts and risks; we cannot compensate for a dismal score on climate change risk, say, by a better score on drinking water, and monetary valuation of the natural environment works no better than for welfare (see section 5.2.2, below). As a result, efficiency does not always, unambiguously, rise or fall; and decisions have to be made about which dimensions to prioritise.

The starting point for Box 2.1 is efficiency seen as the overall ratio of benefits to costs of all economic activity, the ratio of welfare gained to total environmental impact. Both mainstream economists and, in some cases, their green critics, have shown the perils of targeting a small part of that ratio, or even targeting only benefits or only costs. In the extreme case, the policies advocated by mainstream economists have amounted to maximising the flow of consumer goods, regardless of environmental impact or welfare gained; equally, some Greens have sometimes urged reduction in environmental impact even where this would inflict major welfare losses.

The overall ratio can be broken down into a number of sub-ratios. This could be done in a variety of ways, and the ratios (1)–(3) shown here were chosen because they provide a useful framework for looking at the various proposals for development which reconciles welfare and sustainability.

Ratio (1) includes the various ways in which more or less welfare can be obtained from a given quantity of consumer goods and services. It includes the effect on welfare of both the mix of goods ('allocation') and who gets to own or use them ('distribution'). Ratio (2) includes all the ways that goods can be made to last longer, and thus require less resource use for its maintenance. A good can be made to last; failing this it can be repaired easily and with a minimum of new parts; and failing that its components can be recovered and reused. The ratio therefore largely incorporates issues about how products are designed. Ratio (3) focuses on the ecological impact of a given level of resource use, including both characteristics of the resources used and whether once used they are allowed to become polluting.

Ratios (2) and (3) have been very much the concern of *Factor Four* and similar efforts discussed both above and in Chapter 5. These have suggested that very large improvements in efficiency are possible in these areas. But clearly there are dangers in focusing only on those areas: gains in efficiency under (2) and (3) may be offset by losses under (1).

Ratio (1) (but unfortunately rather a small part of it) has been the traditional focus of economics. Economists have generally avoided distribution issues, leaving them to philosophers and politicians. We attach importance to distribution on moral grounds, but in addition, the type of argument we present in Chapter 4, about the relation between consumption and welfare, tends to suggest that a more egalitarian distribution of income would increase welfare and thus ratio (1). If, as we argue in Chapter 4, increased consumption adds little to welfare once basic material needs are met, then redistributing consumption from the rich to those who have unmet needs will increase total welfare. Furthermore, economists have traditionally focused on allocation, but only in the limited sense of satisfying individual preferences expressed in markets. Issues about how preferences are determined, about the ways in which the preferences of different individuals depend on each other, about how far goods can satisfy certain preferences at all, and more generally whether more consumption increases welfare, are ignored. This is the subject of Chapter 4, where we suggest that most consumption, beyond what is needed to satisfy basic needs, makes little contribution to welfare while being costly in terms of labour and ecological impact. Here, independent of any efficiency gains, there may be scope for a double improvement in ratio (1): gaining welfare *and* reducing the stock of consumer goods.

To conclude this section, there are certainly opportunities for reducing ecological impacts and risks even without reducing consumption. Such ecological improvements would probably not be enough, and in any case would be undermined by increases in consumption. What we need is to look for opportunities to reduce consumption (and therefore ecological impacts) without reducing welfare – indeed, quite possibly improving it.

2.5 Uncertainty

While evidence of ecological damage suggests that changes in the direction of development are necessary, the whole environmental debate is pervaded with uncertainties. Furthermore, many of these uncertainties, by their very nature, are unlikely to be resolved as a result of further research. They undermine our ability to use ecological arguments, by themselves, as a guide to future development. These uncertainties are one reason why, in our view, these arguments need to be combined with others that are related to the welfare impact of work and consumption.

One source of uncertainty is simply that some resources are hidden. For example, the size of oil deposits, underground or under the seabed, is unknown. All we really know is that it is getting less, by the amount that we are extracting and burning. Of course we know about deposits already discovered, and geology allows estimates of probable deposits in surrounding regions, but since oil exploration and discovery never occur far ahead of consumption,[9] we will not have the whole picture until it is too late to act.

Another source of uncertainty is the situation where the effects are too complex to forecast on the basis of theoretical models, and where the phenomenon is new, so that there is no past history to guide us. A much-discussed example is that of climate change. There is now general agreement that emissions of greenhouse gases – mainly carbon dioxide from burning fossil fuels – have increased as a result of human activity. Substantial global warming seems likely as a result, taking average temperatures beyond anything experienced so far, though past experience of smaller temperature variations suggests the effects may be drastic. The complexities of climate are such, however, that it seems impossible to assess with any confidence how far tendencies to global warming will be offset or reinforced by various feedback mechanisms, how far different species will manage to adapt, and what the effects will be at a sub-global level. For example, will the Gulf Stream, on which the climate of Western Europe depends, stall altogether, or shift southwards, or merely get weaker? No one knows. An exact, definitive prediction of climate change is impossible.

Similar complexities, especially where long-term effects are concerned, seem to apply in the case of impacts on human health of exposure to various substances. Some 100 000 synthetic chemicals have been introduced in the last century (Gardner and Sampat, 1999). On average, three to five new chemicals are introduced into nature each day, 80 per cent of them not tested for toxicity (Meadows *et al.*, 1992, p. 91). Even where they are tested in controlled conditions, this provides no guarantee that they will be harmless when disseminated in an uncontrolled way. We remain largely ignorant about the effects of even common substances (Misch, 1994). In addition, with substances that have existed in nature for a long time, organisms have evolved to break them down and render them harmless, but with human-created substances, no such opportunities exist, and these substances may persist and accumulate indefinitely (Meadows *et al.*, 1992, p. 91).

In some cases, further research may help, but uncertainty is unlikely to be laid definitively to rest. As Giddens (1991, p. 21) points out, 'no matter how cherished, and apparently well established, a given scientific tenet might be, it is open to revision, or might have to be discarded altogether, in the light of new ideas or findings'.

Uncertainty is all the more of a problem because environmental concern about the future is even greater than concern about the present. To assess the future impact of resource shortages and pollution levels, we would need not only accurate information about resource availability and the effects of pollution, but also to be able to forecast structural changes in the world economy as well as future technological development. In all these areas more or less plausible guesses rather than accurate prediction are the rule, and those who debate the issues can choose from a range of conceivable scenarios, in accordance with their particular ideologies and interests.

Not surprisingly therefore there is a variety of conflicting claims. Within a particular discipline there may be no consensus, and the study of many environmental issues involves several disciplines. Meanwhile, the general public, while largely dependent on scientists for knowledge about environmental problems (including in many cases knowledge of the very existence of those problems), has some reason to distrust scientists' environmentalist credentials and competence. Thus there is all the more difficulty in deciding between the competing claims. Increasing commercialisation and politicisation of science in general and 'the environment' in particular, resulting in the 'greenwashing' discussed in Chapter 5, makes these decisions all the harder.

In answer to all these uncertainties, ecologists have often argued that we should adopt the 'precautionary principle', particularly where ecological effects are serious and may be irreversible. In a weaker form this means not waiting until we are certain ecological harm will occur before curtailing a possibly harmful activity. In a much stronger form it would mean not undertaking any activity until we are sure that no ecological harm will result. There is little consensus about what the precautionary principle really means in practice.

Taken too literally, in its strong form, this principle would imply the cessation of all activity, and thus be unhelpful as a guiding principle. Taken less literally the question is what degree of safety to require, and this seems to depend entirely on what is being given up in its favour. In addition, what other gains may be made by being cautious? – in other words the (net) opportunity cost. Few economic activities involve no ecological risks whatever, and it seems reasonable to accept greater risks the more essential the activity. Cutting down a forest may be reasonable if that is what it takes to provide warmth or cook food (although this is not how and why it usually happens) while cutting down a single tree is unreasonable if its fate is to be turned into disposable chopsticks.

2.6 Conclusion

Increased publicity and concern around a range of environmental issues is probably very largely justified, and especially so if we are also concerned with abolishing poverty and ensuring much greater equality. No technology is envisaged that would allow the whole world to match rich country consumption levels without much greater ecological damage. Equity as well as sustainability arguments therefore suggest that it is necessary to re-evaluate and reconsider the various economic activities which are responsible for the ecological damage.

But evaluating economic activity, even if the concern is only with its ecological impact, means re-examining *all* the costs and benefits, not only those environmental costs so far neglected by orthodox economics. This would include the costs in terms of labour, and not least the supposed benefits which are so often taken for granted. The need to reassess the latter two is all the greater given the uncertainties which are an inevitable part of the ecological argument, and we turn to these in the next two chapters.

3 The Employment Problem

3.1 Introduction

In this chapter, we ask what the impact is of working itself on welfare, that is, aside from any benefits derived from the products of work. Even if working conditions have improved since children were sent up chimneys, we have the modern equivalent in terms of widespread job-related stress and the incapacitated or sick of working age. Indeed, if jobs are so great, why are we paid to do them? The apparently *obvious* reason why we keep working is that, in the current 'work-and-spend' culture (Schor, 2000, p. 112), we all 'need' a job to get the income; and given that the current Western (but increasingly global) emphasis on economic growth presumes ever-increasing consumption, and therefore corresponding increases in the production of goods and services, we always will. But, as will become clear in this (and the following) chapter, rather than being a timeless feature of our societies, this is a recent post-Second-World War phenomenon. Indeed, in most free human societies – that is, those not based on slavery – the objective for most of the population has been to work as little as possible in order to enjoy life as much as possible (Sahlins, 1974). There is no evidence that the genetic make up of twenty-first century man or woman is any different in that respect.

But, in general,[1] there is no sign of a reduction in working time happening. Indeed, since 1960, in the UK, despite a significant increase in the population of working age,[2] the proportion in employment has hardly varied, staying between 70 per cent and 75 per cent, while working hours for those in full-time employment has certainly not decreased (this is also true for most European countries – see Box 3.1, A.). This is partly because, since the Second World War, providing full employment or near full employment has been an important part of most government policies[3] and this is also true in many other OECD countries (see Kalisch, 1998). It is also partly because, in nearly all OECD countries, the social insurance/security systems were integrated with occupational status so that having a job – or being a partner of someone with a job – gave entitlements. And surely the *coup de grâce* on the perspectives of employee themselves about the 'necessity' of working longer hours in order to retain their jobs has been administered by the impact of a flexible labour market and short-term contracts. At the same time, while most of those in jobs in 1960 were employed full-time, nearly a third of those in jobs are now on part-time contracts.

The problem is that none of these suggested factors are sufficient, even in combination, to explain why we have not reduced work-time. Of course, several arguments have been made during the century *against* reducing working hours: problems of selling increasing volumes of (largely unwanted) goods;[4] fear of what workers would do with their free time and the partial failure of various non-commercial schemes for controlling workers' free time. The only argument *for* reducing working hours is that it would help to redistribute work in the face of rising productivity and unemployment, but that would appear to work only with international agreement.

Instead, there have been many attempts to improve the conditions and quality of working life (apparently seen as a panacea); to create a surrogate community for those with full-time occupations. It is difficult to claim that those who perceive that the quality of their working lives is being enhanced in this way are suffering false consciousness and are in fact alienated labourers; but it is also obvious they have no free time that they can call their own. Moreover, there is very little concern, however, for those on short-term, contract employment.

Altogether this has led to increased income inequality: increased incomes for those who are employed, and at the same time increasing relative poverty for the unemployed. Moreover, those in work are finding that they have to work ever harder and longer (as well as often taking longer to travel to work) in order to maintain their relative position. Although this is more true in the UK and the US, working hours have increased in all European countries (see Box 3.1, B.). This in turn has led to an increase in 'stress-related' illness and the demand for 'quick-fix' leisure (see Chapter 4), the latter being something the unemployed are in general excluded from because of the cost.

Box 3.1 Activity rates and hours worked in Europe

Economic activity rates were higher in the UK than in other EU countries until the beginning of the 1990s; but now other countries are catching up (even disregarding the Scandinavian countries which have always had higher rates). Thus, the gap between males in the UK and the EU average was 8 points in 1991 but only 6 points in 1999; the gap for females was 9 points in 1999 but had been 10 points in 1991.

A. Proportion of population of working age who are economically active (%)

	1991		1999	
	Males	Females	Males	Females
Belgium	71.8	49.3	73.0	56.0
Denmark	–	–	85.0	76.1
France	75.5	58.9	75.5	62.2
Germany	80.9	61.1	79.3	62.9
Greece	76.2	41.7	76.9	49.7
Irish Republic	76.4	43.4	78.3	54.4
Italy	74.0	42.0	73.7	45.6
Luxemburg	77.6	47.5	75.7	60.2
Netherlands	79.4	55.3	82.6	64.4
Portugal	80.0	58.6	79.1	63.0
Spain	76.0	41.8	76.2	48.5
UK	86.3	66.8	84.1	68.4
EUR 12	76.5	57.0	78.1	59.2

Note: The table below gives the comparison of average working hours for employees in 1988 and 1992 and for full-time employees only in 1998. For full-time employees, it seems clear that UK full-time employees work longer hours than their European counterparts. But it is more difficult to interpret the comparison of all employees in 1988 and 1992 as there are many more part-time employees in the UK.

B. Average hours worked per week by employees, EU comparison

	1988		1992		1998	
	Males	Females	Males	Females	Males	Females
Belgium	38.1	32.5	38.3	31.8	39.1	36.9
Denmark	37.6	31.7	36.7	31.3	39.6	37.9
France	40.2	34.9	39.8	34.6	40.2	38.6
Germany	40.3	34.4	39.6	33.6	40.5	39.4
Greece	40.6	37.6	41.0	38.1	41.7	39.3
Irish Republic	41.0	35.5	41.1	34.4	41.3	38.0
Italy	39.4	35.3	39.4	35.0	39.7	36.3
Luxemburg	40.3	35.8	40.3	35.0	40.5	38.3
Netherlands	36.3	26.3	36.3	25.8	39.2	38.3

Box 3.1 (Contd.)

	1988		1992		1998	
	Males	Females	Males	Females	Males	Females
Portugal	43.2	38.6	42.6	38.2	41.5	39.4
Spain	40.9	37.2	40.7	37.0	41.1	39.6
UK	43.9	30.3	43.3	30.2	45.2	40.7
EUR 12	40.7	33.4	40.2	33.7	40.8	38.5p

Notes: 1988 and 1992: all employees; 1998: full-time employees only.
Sources: 1988 Statistical Office of the European Communities; 1992 EUROSTAT; 1999 Labour Force Surveys, EUROSTAT.

3.1.1 What we are doing

The purpose of this chapter is to ask how this situation has arisen, and what the obstacles are to drastic reductions in work-time. Why do people work such long hours especially when they don't need to when (for most) employed work is (at best) a waste of time? In large part, the reasons derive from ideologies and interests that have a long history.[5] For this reason, the approach in the first part of this chapter is rather different from that of the preceding and succeeding chapters where the current problems of the destruction of the environment and over-consumption are examined. While the focus here is also on the situation that pertains today and is likely to pertain tomorrow, we need to explain the options in terms of rather a long history both of ideology and entrenched interests.

First, we summarise the way in which ideologies of work have developed – from the classical Greek notion through to the Protestant ethic (section 3.2) – so that by the middle of the nineteenth century the idea of paid employment had became entrenched as a self-interested way of surviving and self-improvement (section 3.3). Since then, although the *nature* of paid employment has changed dramatically, with the collapse, first, of employment in the agricultural sector and then in the manufacturing sector, employment in a workplace has remained central to the lives of most households. However, a hiatus occurred in the middle of the last century when it appeared inevitable that, with increased productivity, work-time would indeed be drastically reduced; moreover, for many, this was desirable because of the alienating effect of most types of labour (section 3.4).

Returning to the (near-) present, we show how this potential threat to the hegemony of the work ethic was reversed during the last quarter of last century, with the creation of a marginalised part-time, short-term contract economy, often producing goods and services of doubtful utility (section 3.5). Finally, we examine the research claiming to establish presumed positive characteristics of employment, *any employment*, but in fact suggesting that many people do not want jobs (section 3.6); and discuss in the conclusion the obstacles to a drastic reduction in work time (section 3.7).

3.1.2 Definitions and ideas of work

First, however, we should be clear about what we mean by work. Work is directed activity. Variations in forms of work depend essentially on the answers to the questions 'directed by whom?, in what context? and for whom?'.

Historically, there have been four social forms of work: slavery, serfdom, wage labour and independent work. Slavery can vary from debt to domestic to economic slavery. Serfdom is only one of a number of forms of tenantship – others include conscription. Wage labour can be divided into proletarian and career wage labour, both of which exist in capitalist wage labour and in the command economies; and domestic work is a further sub-division. Independent work is found in community-based, family-based and guild-bound work and in production co-operations. The changes in ideology corresponding to these notions are illustrated in section 3.2.

Paid employment itself originates with the division of labour and the use of money in the exchange for its products. Thus, the first 'paid' jobs before the Industrial Revolution were 'simply' a result of the monetarisation of labour. Peasants transformed into tenant farmers still only produced what was necessary for them and their families to survive until the possibility of trading their market surplus arose. But, of course, the nature and kinds of employment developed over the centuries to include not only factory work and service jobs, but also the caring professions (see section 3.5).

The 'work ethic' is probably weaker now: most people nowadays would claim to subscribe to a purely instrumental view of work: people take jobs, where they work to provide goods and services, in return for money which they spend on goods and services, and they will generally work harder to get more. This has not always been the case and it does not explain the behaviour of everyone now, when, even at the high water mark of the culture of enterprise, work is regarded by some as a moral or religious duty. But, earlier last century, it was *assumed* that work was alienating:

> What is work? Work is of two kinds: first, altering the position of matter at or near the earth's surface relative to other such matter; second telling other people to do so. The first kind is unpleasant and ill paid; the second is pleasant and highly paid. The second kind is capable of infinite extension: there are not only those who give orders, but those who give advice as to what orders should be given. Usually two opposite kinds of advice are given simultaneously by two organised bodies of men: this is called politics. The skill required for this kind of work is not knowledge of the subjects as to which advice is given, but knowledge of the art of persuasive speaking and writing, i.e. advertising. (Bertrand Russell, 1935, p. 12)

3.2 Origins of the capitalist ideologies of work[6]

Most agree that current ideas about employment, jobs and work have been conditioned and produced by the industrial environment. But equally, most would also claim that 'work' (sometimes equated to employment/jobs) is a timeless role of crucial importance in the definition and nature of humanity (see, for example, the International Labour Office definition of Basic Needs – Chapter 6). But many who, earlier this century, accepted the necessity for 'hard work', assumed that it would eventually wither away, with machines replacing labour, and with technological advances – precisely the kind of conditions we are experiencing today.

3.2.1 Work – a necessary evil to be avoided

The greatest contrast with the current official attitudes to work can be traced to the roots of our own society. Plato promotes the ideal state where 'citizenship is frankly restricted to a class of privileged persons who can afford to turn over their private business – the sordid job of earning a living – to slaves and foreigners' (Sabine, 1951, p. 81). Aristotle is, if anything, clearer, showing 'far more than Plato's an actual contempt for the useful' (Sabine, 1951, p. 95), for, 'in the best governed states.... None of them (citizens) should be permitted to exercise any mechanic employment or follow merchandise as being capable and destructive to virtue [in order that they may] perform the duty they owe to the state' (Politics, 1328b).

Aristotle's contempt for the useful was extremely influential. It grew out of his distinction between proper and improper usage: '... it is not therefore proper for any man of honour, or any citizen, or anyone who engages in public affairs, to learn these servile employments without they have occasion to them for their own use'. (Politics, 1227b)

The distinction between 'proper' and 'improper' work was that to work for oneself was praiseworthy, whatever the nature of the work; *what mattered was the purpose of the task*. Mossé (1969) explains the contempt for labour: 'First the ties of dependence ... created by labour, and secondly the growth of a slave economy ... to work for another man in return of a wage of any kind is degrading' (pp. 27, 28). Arendt (1958, p. 31) writes that, in Greece '... even harsh painful labour was preferred to the easy life of many household slaves'; and Zimmern (1915, p. 27) specifically refutes:

> the false idea that the Greeks regarded manual labour as degrading. In truth, they honoured manual work far more than we do. But they ... objected ... against doing any more work than they needed when the joy had gone out of it.

This did not induce respect for work: in a society where economic values were subordinated to cultural and political ends, to be directed by others to work was to be at the bottom of the social hierarchy.

The transformation to tithed serf

Work as such – for most of the population – only began to be taken seriously as slavery declined. Scholars argue over the main cause for the decline of slavery. Some point to basic economic developments: 'the scarcity of labour of any kind and the rise in prices put a premium on free and individual labour' (Mossé, 1969, p. 22). Others point to the increasing influence of the Stoic group of philosophers who believe that both men and God were distinguished from animals by the presence of reason, creating suitable conditions for an anti-slavery ideology to develop (and for a partial rehabilitation of the idea of work). If all men are essentially equal, the older attitude to slaves would hardly be tolerated.

Medieval civilisation was founded on an agricultural economy and for the most part consisted of small, local, self-sufficient communities. The weak depended on the strong: a hierarchical system of land owning was reflected in a system of protective dependency and of obligation, service was performed in return for protection and the system extended from the monarch to the serf.

Economic relationships stressed neither effort nor zeal nor civilisation but the simple performance of obligation. Work was necessary in order to ensure the survival of the family, and as a kind of tax due to the Lord of the Manor. There was little point in working harder or more productively as with only a very rudimentary market economy, there would be nothing to do with a surplus. Sahlins (1974) makes essentially the same point about several 'economic' systems of production, distribution and exchange in the 'Third World' today.

The transformation of tithed serf to wage slave

It was a society which might have lasted for ever – as long as it did not change. But it did. Lords of the manor simply found that wage-labour provided them with a better deal than the services produced for them by peasants, and instead took annual payments from their tenants (rent). The monetarisation of labour obligations also affected the performance of other tasks that had previously been 'obligations' in the medieval system. For example, the obligation to serve in the lord's 'rapid-response force', wherein the peasant farmer-turned pillager/rapist/soldier would be clothed and fed from the lord's coffers, also disappeared, to be progressively replaced by the salaried soldier. It is interesting that the only feudal medieval obligation which has survived in European culture is the necessity for military service; it is even more interesting that it was first abandoned in possibly the two most warmongering nation-states (the UK in 1960, the US in 1973, but other European countries only during the last few years).

3.2.2 The development of markets

Eventually, nearly all the cultivation of land was left to the tenant in return for the payment of rent. It then became possible and worthwhile for the tenant to put more work into his own holding because increasing mobility made it easier to sell the surplus. There were other significant changes about this time concerning the tenure of the land, its eventual enclosure for sheep farming, and the introduction of usury for credit (Tawney, 1925). Together, these led to the breakdown of 'the whole scheme of medieval economic thought which had attempted to treat economic affairs as part of a hierarchy of values embracing all human interests and activities, of which the apex was religion' (Tawney, 1925, p. 106). Work, now less integrated into core social and individual needs, could begin to develop a dynamic of its own.

It would be superficial to suggest that feudalism simply gave way some time in the fourteenth century to the development of a market economy in preparation for the emergence of capitalism. But the extent of the shift from feudalism to the view of work held during the Industrial Revolution is clear: 'When the age of Reformation begins, economics is still a branch of ethics and ethics of theology, all human activities are treated as falling within a single scheme' (Tawney, 1948, p. 272).

As such, every class did its own 'proper work'. The social, political and spiritual systems were harmonious as long as each member played their allotted part. The worker might contribute to the mutual exchange of services for the sake of a good life (i.e. material comfort or general relief from hunger, poverty or war), but the good life was an end-in-itself and it was not to be measured in ergonomic or economic terms. The church developed a doctrine of the importance of work to support the system, but strictly as an instrument of spiritual purpose. Work was done out of necessity, because it was ordered so by a natural cycle and by God.[7] Although there was trade, this constituted only a fraction of the economy.

The emergence of 'economic man' during the Industrial Revolution therefore required an enormous shift in attitudes and beliefs. There is, of course, considerable dispute over whether the world changed first (see Marx) or whether men's understanding did (see Weber). Such chicken and egg arguments are always inconclusive but we examine Weber's account because an important part of his argument concerns the changes in the ideology of work. While, as we shall see, there were variations between capitalist and socialist doctrines, basic to both was a deep commitment to an ideology of work, that work should be undertaken willingly by those who are subordinate to superordinates whose authority over them is legitimate.[8]

Weber describes nostalgically the life of the old artisan who led a comfortable existence, worked from 5 to 6 hours a day, with moderate earnings, enjoying good relationships with his companions. This gave way to a harder frugality in which some participated and came to the top because they did not wish to consume but to earn (Weber, 1967, p. 68). Gaskell gives a parallel idealised account of the typical domestic manufacturer who 'lived to a good round age, worked when necessity demand, ceased his labours when his wants were supplied' (Gaskell, 1836, p. 29).

Traditional qualities such as these would not have facilitated the 'Spirit of Capitalism'. Calvin supplied the interpretation of a 'calling' that was essential to the development of capitalism during the seventeenth and eighteenth centuries. He believed that some are predestined into everlasting life, and others are ordained to everlasting death. In order to reduce doubts about salvation and as a sign to others of one's own goodness, the Calvinist was enjoined to a life of discipline and good works.

Religious ascetism, apart from enabling the businessman to make money with a good conscience, also provided him 'with sober, conscientious and industrious workmen who clung to their work as to a life purpose willed by God' (Weber, 1967, p. 177). The engagement of God as the supreme supervisor was a most convenient device; a great part of the efforts of modern management has been aimed at finding a secular, but equally omnipotent equivalent, in the worker's own psyche. The puritans stressed vocation thus: 'God honoured men as he honoured angels – in proportion to their serviceableness – that is their zealous application, their skill and their effectiveness. All men must work, gentlemen and commoners alike' (Walzer, 1966, p. 209).

But while religious asceticism may have motivated some, the majority of peasants would have to be made to abandon their self-sufficient lifestyle and forced off the land into factories. The Enclosure Acts were certainly a part of this process. Perelman (2000) shows that the origin of market capitalism is therefore in part the 'product of strategies pursued to take away from people the conditions for developing alternative ways to live and produce. [... Since] market capitalism was not inevitable, but a result of policies [...] the future is open' (De Angelis, 1997).

3.2.3 Implication for social organisation

Some of the consequences of this ideology of work would have surprised some of its proponents. Once work is dignified, it is a short step to dignifying the worker, hence admiration for the worker and contempt for the idle. Hill (1964) concludes that the emphasis on work was likely to lead to the final conclusion that property was justified by work and was not justified without it, so that idleness should be followed by expropriation.

Thereafter, the new doctrine could grow in two directions. The 'official' development during the seventeenth and eighteen centuries emphasised effort (in a calling), abstinence and thrift: it led to capitalist acquisition, and the spread of business enterprise. The alternative emerges in socialism and communism. Both depend on the same three characteristics as the Protestant ethic.

The first characteristic is abstinence from display and from self-indulgence. The moderation in consumption thereby permitting capitalist accumulation of savings becomes, in the alternative doctrine, the abolition of private property and the total negation of self-indulgence. The second, the ascendancy of 'rational' economic calculation by the individual economic actor under capitalism, is absorbed into the essence of state socialist central planning. The third, the primacy of work, becomes (in the alternative ideology), the central pivot of the conceptual system, carrying with it the idealisation of the worker. In capitalism, work and the worker remain an instrumental necessity. Socialist versions of the ideology are, in this sense, capitalism cleansed of its impurities. Subsequent conflict between incipient capitalism and incipient communism were but minor schisms within the new orthodoxy.

3.3 Motivating the anomic worker

The next stage in the development of capitalism was the developing division of labour which came with industrialisation. It posed a major problem: how to deal with the anomie resulting from the detailed division of labour by function and by task; and how to cope with the alienation resulting from the social division of labour by class and by interest.

3.3.1 Economic man

Adam Smith is, of course, regarded as the inventor of 'economic man' and as providing the justification for allowing full rein to 'market-forces'. In fact, he was deeply suspicious of manufacturers and he clearly regarded the people who do productive work as the chief foundation of any society: 'Labour is, therefore, the real measure of the exchangeable value of all commodities' (Smith, 1845, p. 64). But in using economic measurement to develop the theory, Smith helped to establish the primacy of economic rationalism over any (other) human rights.

In particular, as Perelman (2000) shows, Smith, together with Ricardo and others, realised that peasantry were being deprived of what was theirs: 'In that original state of things which precedes both the appropriation of land and the accumulation of stock, the whole produce of labour belongs to the labourer. He has neither landlord nor master to share with him' (Smith, 1845, p. 64). Indeed, Smith, Ricardo and their colleagues appeared to have deliberately obscured the nature of the control over labour under industrialisation, and actively supported policies attacking the economic independence of the rural peasantry that were essentially conceived to foster primitive accumulation.

Andrew Ure's 'satanic advocacy' was an extension of this process. In his view, one of the purposes of machines was 'to diminish labour's cost by substituting the industry of women and children for that of men; or that of ordinary labourers for trained artisans' (Ure, 1861, p. 23). He condemned the Ten Hours Bill (restricting working hours) by labelling it 'an interference with the freedom of the subject which no other legislature in Christendom would have countenanced for a moment' (Ure, 1861, p. 267). Similarly, the Factory Regulation Act of 1833 – forbidding the employment in textile mills of children under 9 and otherwise limiting child labour – was 'an act of despotism towards the trade and of mock philanthropy towards the work-people who depend on the trade for support. ... The Act ... will aggravate still more the hardships of the poor, and stop the conscientious manufacturer in his useful toil' (Gaskell, 1836, pp. 169–70).

At the same time as promoting the many advantages of economic freedom (for the benefit of employers), Ure recognises the inadequacy of economic theory as a motivator or controller of human behaviour. What is needed, says Ure, is a motive force which can cause 'self-immolation[9] for the good of others' (Ure 1861, p. 424). The answer was Methodism (derived from the Wesleyan revival in the Church of England) which came to serve as the religion of the industrial bourgeoisie, in direct succession to the Protestant ethic and the spirit of capitalism and, simultaneously, as the religion of the industrial proletariat. While this seems curious (Thompson, 1968, p. 391), there is no great contradiction in master and man sharing the same belief despite the wealth of one and the poverty of the other, if those same beliefs are held to lead to success.

But the main point is how did the (relatively new) concepts of respect for work and for economic values survive in the face of conditions which, as they were the more clearly perceived, must have made those notions appear ridiculous?

3.3.2 The role of self-interest

The resolution was and still is simple. Self-interest is to be seen as a moral principle: Victorian business ideology was distinguished by its promotion of self-regard to a moral duty. While Adam Smith recorded, often scornfully, that men do behave selfishly, we end with the conclusion that men *should* behave selfishly.

Theory had destroyed ideology by extracting its moral content. Manufacturers needed a new ideology which could explain existing conditions not only to employers but also to those they employed, which could provide a satisfactory reason for work, and which could motivate the employee to carry out his master's instructions with zeal and serve his interests with enthusiasm. Perelman (2000) provides evidence that employers had to enforce both presence at work as well as working hours very harshly at the beginning of the Industrial Revolution.

One of the essential preliminaries was a concerted attack upon traditional working-class habits and outlooks, including drinking, weekend leisure and swearing (Pollard, 1965, p. 195). Terms such as 'idle' or 'dissolute' were taken 'to mean strictly that the worker was indifferent to the employers' deterrents and incentives'. This labelling was overlaid with a tradition of paternalism stemming from medieval society, from the network of obligatory and dependent relations established under the control of God.

One of the most successful attempts to follow up the ideology of *laissez-faire* with a more or less consistent ideology to bridge the gap between wealthy and poor was made by Samuel Smiles in *Self Help*, published in 1859. Smiles elevated work to a position of absolute importance and made the willingness or ability to undertake it the only proper dividing principle between rich and poor, those who were successful and those who were unsuccessful. He was not prepared to defend traditional privilege and the advantages of birth and inherited wealth; his appeal appeared to be essentially democratic and egalitarian. Success is open to all who try ... 'Steady application to work is the healthiest training for every individual ... Labour is not only a necessity and a duty, but a blessing; only the idler feels it to be a curse' (Smiles, 1908, p. 33).

Smiles filled, and still fills, a serious gap in ideology: 'Help from without is often enfeebling in its effects, but help from within invariably invigorates. Whatever is done for men or for classes, to a certain extent takes away the stimulus and necessity of doing for themselves; and where men are subjected to over-guidance and over-government, the inevitable tendency is to render them comparatively helpless' (Smiles, 1908, p. 33). This principle of self-help provided some prospect of hope for the poorest: it both stimulated the search for increases in productivity (which provided individual success), and contributed to the docility and discipline of those who, by hard work, would fail. There are echoes of this in the current Welfare to Work approaches: as a Solidarity tract recently remarked:

> For all those temporarily denied a career but not oblivious to the gratifications of Exchange, we propose Local Authority grants for the following occupations:
>
> Eradicating graffiti from walls, municipal buildings, churches and toilets;
>
> Voluntary work as soldiers or policemen in seaside resorts;

Mime classes to teach individuals to mimic work while at home;
Extension of Time and Motion principles to all sexual acts;
Moral re-education for absentee workers;
Haircut and alternative comedy competitions;
Poverty sharing, voting practice and cycling lessons.

Of course, to some extent, ideology was unnecessary. Workers were attracted by high wages or recruited by poverty. Once workers were recruited, effort was assured by supervision, and by the conditions and hours under which they worked. Religion contributed significantly to the maintenance of a work ethic. But an additional exhortation was felt to be necessary. Smiles' homilies fitted the bill.

3.3.3 Were there dissenters?

There is a puzzling similarity between some early socialists and classical economists. This is because they both admire industrial processes and believe in the benefits they will bring; they both aspire to a 'steam-age intellect', although the socialist believes that economic relationships have to be transformed before realising the potential benefits of industrialisation. So were there no dissenters?

The 'radical' view

At one extreme, we have the political economist, Sismondi, who subordinated notions of economic progress to the ultimate test of whether or not it improved or worsened the condition of men. He was concerned about mechanisation because workers did not share in the benefits:

> The earnings of an entrepreneur sometimes represent nothing but the spoliation of the workman. A profit is made not because the industry produces more than it costs, but because it fails to give the workman sufficient compensation for his toil. (Sismondi, quoted in Gide and Rist, 1948, p. 197)

In contrast, Saint-Simon idealised industry and work: '... the whole art of government in civil society would become the application on a universal scale of the truths of political economy. ... The doctrines of work and progress were the driving ethical concepts of the new society' (quoted in Manuel, 1956, p. 240). Saint-Simon's 'radicalism' comes from his demand that society should be rid of all archaic survivals such as the royal family, thousands of unproductive churchmen, functionaries and military men (quoted in Manuel, 1956, p. 210). Instead, Saint-Simon proposed that 'industrials' should be the new elite: it was natural for those who organised work to organise social life because work was social life. The new technical order of things points to a world in which communist or syndicalist alternatives will differ in every respect except their common complete subjection of man to the economic and technical machine which (s)he has constructed. The only criteria which can be applied to the activity of our 'industrialists' are technical criteria, any other reference is to some traditionalistic mystification.

The anarchists

Even for some anarchist groupings, work could be fruitful and fun. Thus, for Proudhon (cited in Edwards and Fraser, 1970), if labour is properly organised with the necessary conditions of variety, health, intelligence, art, dignity, passion, and legitimate gain, then it can 'even as far as pleasure is concerned, become preferable to game and dancing, fencing, gymnastics, entertainments and all other distractions which man in his poverty has invented as a means of recovering from the mental and physical fatigue caused by being a slave to labour' (Proudhon in Edwards and Fraser, 1970, p. 82). However attractive this sounds, unfortunately it is not happening (see the following section).

3.3.4 Chasing one's tail

We can therefore separate two traditions of political theory: those which support an economic emphasis that stresses work and authority, and those which emphasise non-economic values and which do not value work in and for itself. The latter tradition was originally a European one, established in Greece, but resonant with many other groupings around the World (see Sahlins, 1974); it was maintained by a variety of anarchist groupings throughout the last millennium and for a time was well represented on the West Coast of California. The former, currently the official tradition, was established with the Protestant ethic and, entrenched with the spirit of capitalism, was (until recently) divided into a Western and Eastern orthodoxy. The Western branch, represented by American managerialism, recognises that an effective ideology of work can only be realistically maintained if work itself is changed. Work must be rehabilitated before anyone can be persuaded to take it seriously. Hence team work and continuous education/lifelong learning improve on performance, all of which activities generate even more work. The Eastern branch, confronted by the same problem, demanded changes in society in order to maintain the reality of work. Society had to be rehabilitated (an example being *perestroika*) before anyone could be persuaded to take work seriously. While the latter system was slightly less ridiculous overall, they were starting from a much lower level of 'needs satisfaction' and so fell apart first.

Basic to both is a deep commitment to an ideology of work, and in the communication of appeals that work should be undertaken willingly by those who are subordinate to superordinates whose authority over them is legitimate. This convergence is occurring at a time when the 'problem' of work (i.e. how to increase production) begins to recede. As empires are said to build their most magnificent monuments when they are in decline, so the ideology of work reaches its most refined state when it becomes redundant.

3.4 The contested growth of paid employment

Although paid employment at the beginning of the Industrial Revolution was nearly all in the (subsidised) private sector, one of the main spurs to the growth of employment subsequently has been the expansion of the role of the state. There were goods and services the private sector could not adequately provide (the so-called 'public' goods). The state broadly speaking takes general responsibility for 'repair and maintenance' of the system: education and health (care) services, care of older people – as well of course as maintaining a standing army and internal security. This responsibility has expanded rapidly as the task has become more difficult.

The growth of government is important for our argument, because – thinking in terms of private sector jobs – the consumer usually has to be persuaded to consume (and thence create or maintain employment). The consumer cannot be forced, although the means of persuasion have become steadily more persuasive, and some would say more oppressive. Instead, in the public sector, there is no obvious limit to job creation, at least in the short term; and indeed, there are 'natural' pressures to maintain or even expand the volume of public sector employment. Parkinson was one of the first in modern times to vocalise that service employment – much of which, at the time was in the public sector – was inherently capable of mopping up far more workers than manufacturing because the services provided are consumed each day and then have got to be provided all over again (cf. Smith, 1845). Gabor (1964) saw 'Parkinsonianism'[10] as a natural defence mechanism by society against the psychological threat posed by technological advance and the unwelcome prospect of an age of leisure. For example, in the UK, during the Thatcherite period of privatisation, public sector employment fell hardly at all; and, of course, it has increased substantially under New Labour, along with the re-centralisation of authority. As we illustrate in Chapter 7, it is not (entirely) clear what purpose many of these jobs are serving, other then providing a high income for the post-holder.

War production

Finally, the growth of war production has remained peculiarly immune from the rationalisations of economists, given that the eventual purpose of war production is destruction of other goods. The only economic 'rationale' is that of Mandel (1975) who argues that the major function of war is the destruction of old-capitalisms and the generation of new ones. This seems rather too far-fetched: war is principally about the search for power, which may indeed have economic motivations, but not the reification of capitalism (since that was never destroyed in the first place).

3.4.1 Socialist (and liberal) utopias in the nineteenth century

At the same time as the exhortations towards an ideology of paid employment, described in the previous sections, and despite the spread of paid employment, many intellectuals were looking for further emancipation. Thus, a dream of the Enlightenment at the advent of the Industrial Revolution, was to liberate people's time from the necessity of work. But many eighteenth-century political economists worried that prosperity would reduce the willingness of labourers to sacrifice time for work; the demand for leisure would increase with the meeting of basic needs. In the first part of the twentieth century there were many who rejected this classical notion of a 'natural' level of needs, arguing that the desire to emulate others would spur additional effort and so avoid the anarchy of undisciplined time, for others, however, lusting after these unnatural wants undermined community and a rational use of free time.

With spreading industrialisation, previously rural populations, now in the urban areas and lured by self-interest, began to work much longer hours. The conditions and nature of the work they had to perform were very quickly exposed as awful. Indeed, the original thesis of Marx's *Das Kapital* (English translation, 1801) was based on his argument in the

Economic and Philosophical Manuscripts (1844) that work was alienating; that idea, in turn, being based on Engel's analysis of the dehumanising nature of work at the beginning of the Industrial Revolution (1841). But, for both of them, there was an end in sight, and when the productive potential of the economy had multiplied, workers would take control so that work itself would be transformed into autonomous activity and then reduced to a minimum.

Of course, Communism itself – at least in the official version – was a failure: in the actual historical context, mostly because that system found it unable to compete militarily with the economic engine of Western capitalism, without emiseration of a large fraction of its population. But, in the long term and probably more seriously, it had failed to transform waged work; as Andy Brown (1983) put it:

> Both Western and Economic systems function so as to absorb people's lives in struggles which have no meaning. The one system eggs on to work in order to consume, without ever establishing the meaning of work or the products we consume, while the other functions so as to break people's spirits and to teach them the value of obedience and conformity even at the cost of economic efficiency. (page 9)

Marxists and their fellow travellers were not the only ones who were concerned that the division of labour had generated an economic system in which most workers were condemned to carrying out boring repetitive jobs. At around the same time, many others such as J.S. Mill (1848) looked forward to a new democratic leisure society where a learned class of educators would counteract the egoistic commercial spirit. For Bellamy (1886), work could become merely 'a necessary duty to be discharged before we can fully devote ourselves to the higher exercise of our faculties, the intellectual and spiritual enjoyment which alone means life'. Ruskin (1985) also rejected a fixation on jobs that produced unnecessary material waste for the rich and dependency and oppression for the labourer; Marx's son-in-law went further in proclaiming the right to idleness (Lafargue, 1907).

3.4.2 The technocratic solutions

Equally, many writers during the first half of the twentieth century celebrated likely innovations in technology as leading to the elimination of drudgery. In the inter-war period, the mass production economy promised both time and money. John Hammond (1933) wrote that mass production was creating an era of 'Common Enjoyment': soon leisure rather than work would be the core of personal experience for all. Of course, employers were resistant to any democratic debate about the balance between work and leisure, time and money (Cross, 1994); they were even more concerned that prosperity meant an erosion of incentives to work. But, both sides of the debate were convinced that new productivity meant that needs would be very quickly satiated.

In fact, given the way in which capitalist competition led to the proliferation of very similar products, and that 'needs creation' was becoming a new industry (see section 3.5.4, below), the employers probably had little to fear.

The real problem, however, was that few technocrats then (and probably few now) or labour leaders would concede that a democracy of free time and goods could replace paid employment as the organising principle of personality and community. When Tugwell (1927, p. 258) said that 'our social groups are consuming groups. We have almost completely divorced our producing lives from our consuming lives', he was concerned to revive the work ethic, not to bury it.

Work had to have intrinsic meaning. But that was the rub – no-one expected that (assembly line) work could be meaningful in the way that artisans had experienced work. The solution for many intellectuals was to share the benefits of increased productivity in substantial reductions in the time spent at alienating labour, with progressive disengagement from the pain of work for a society built around personal autonomy and renewed social solidarities in leisure. However, uncertainties about how to achieve social solidarity and personal integration in the realms of free time and consumption and an inability to articulate workers desires with these forms of 'democratic' leisure meant that, on the whole, these movements failed. Instead, there was an attempt to construct an ideology of work embracing the new technocratic values of service, the promotion of efficiency and the elimination of waste.

3.4.3 Work (and consumption) without end

Governing elites have always been concerned that idle hands would become unruly, or worse, politically involved; indeed, taking a cynical point of view, the 1929 slump was very useful in changing perceptions. By the middle of the 1930s, the notions of satiated needs and democratic leisure becoming the core of personal experience had been almost everywhere universally abandoned, to be replaced by the notions of limitless work and consumption (see also section 4.1.2). In particular, there are two categories of production that have developed over the last 150 years, on top of those goods and services that at least appear to have obvious utility. These are outlined below.

'Diversification' of output

The first is a logical consequence of the development of capitalist competition. In order for an entrepreneur to capture a market, he (it's usually a he) has to 'vanquish' other producers, something which involves producing the same thing in a slightly different form: and there is no obvious limit to the proliferation of products and services.[11]

There are many examples of this phenomenon, ranging from dog food to political parties; in the later argument (Chapter 7) we concentrate on only a few examples to make this point, for example, in the proliferation of equally useful or useless models of car, and of planned obsolescence of many 'durables'.

Conspicuous consumption

Medieval society required 'surplus' (non-marketed) production for the conspicuous consumption of the powerful. The lord's retinue of liveried servants provides one example. While some feasts, of course, were an occasion for general celebration and involved everyone (for example, the end of a successful harvest or Thanksgiving), many were symbolic demonstrations of the power and wealth of the victorious Lord of the Manor, or of the Court. Such conspicuous consumption, not only of food but also of clothing, furnishings and other 'household' goods, required protection from enemies and jealous friends and so the two original categories of what we might call useless production – war and conspicuous consumption – were, and are, self-reinforcing: the lord shows off his spoils of victory which in turn require (military) defence.

Conspicuous consumption continues, of course, in its original form – ostentatious behaviour by the rich and powerful – which now serves a dual function: it not only remains a symbolic demonstration of power and wealth, but also provides a powerful image of what can be achieved by competition and hard work (cf. Smiles, 1908). But 'keeping up with the Joneses' also requires conspicuous consumption and, of course, a large part of the advertising industry focuses on this sort of conspicuous consumption, rather than on competition between competing brands of a useful product.

Where there are no competing goods, the entrepreneur does not have to struggle to distinguish their product where there is no difference. Indeed, they do not have to innovate in order to respond to an already expressed demand for a product (that may not exist) but they are often in the position of generating demand for a 'new' product of doubtful utility (see also Chapter 4).

3.4.4 A life of work – or play?

Although the movements for meaningful 'democratic' leisure failed, time spent at work has been steadily eroded. Thus, at the beginning of the Industrial Revolution, working hours rose drastically and new employees – previously peasants used to an informal pace and duration of labour – had to be dragooned into work (see Perelman, 2000). But the corollary of employers imposing a standard (and intense) workday was, not unnaturally, a demand by workers' organisations (and, secondarily, by liberal intellectuals) for an equally uniform and uninterrupted period free from work. From the end of the nineteenth century until the Second World War, there were continuous pressures to reduce worktime, with successful movements for an eight-hour workday and for paid holidays as a right of industrial and social citizenship and, more mundanely, as the workers' share of productivity increases.

The working day

Almost immediately after the First World War, in 1919, the legal working day was eventually restricted to 8 hours (or a 48-hour week), after revolutionary agitation throughout Europe followed the Bolshevik uprisings in Russia. During the 1920s, labour organisations on both sides of the Atlantic campaigned for a 40-hour week. In Europe, this tended to be seen as a way of work-sharing; in the US, while originally on the grounds of 'over-production', it became a trade-off for intensified monotonous toil and for 'recreation and recuperation ... necessary to sustain vigour'. Moreover, in 1932, the American Federation of Labour (AFL)[12] seriously advocated a 30-hour week, although this was also more a way of sharing the misery of the depression than a push for more leisure. In 1933, there was an attempt to introduce an international 40-hour standard which failed, and it was only the Popular Front in France that introduced the 40-hour working week in 1936, and that was, of course, reversed with the advent of World War II.

After the Second World War, although the French 40-hour standard was restored *en principe*, up to 20 hours of overtime was tolerated so that working weeks had reached an average of over 47 hours by 1963. The 'distributiviste' movement, however, still survives (Lambert, 2000). In Britain, in a series of labour contracts between 1964 and 1970, nominal hours were reduced to 40 hours, but average hours for those in full-time employment in 1999 were 45 for men and 41 for women, compared to 39 and 37 respectively in Belgium (see Box 3.1, B., above).

Paid holidays

Prior to 1919, although the affluent took vacations, there was little demand among (ex-peasant) wage earners for extended paid leave, probably because they no longer had any land to use even as a smallholding, but also because there were no outlets such as packaged holidays for concentrated bouts of leisure. The only 'holidays' people had coincided with traditional religious celebrations or communal fairs and sporting events. However, during the inter-war period, European workers won the right to a one- or two-week paid vacation, and this expanded to four or more weeks during the growth periods of the 1950s and 1960s. In contrast, vacation rights of Americans scarcely improved, so that by 1989, they worked nearly 2000 hours a year compared to, say, 1650 hours in France.

3.5 The nature and productivity of current employment

Currently, of course, we do not have an age of leisure but a culture of 'work and spend' (Schor, 2000). But while the numbers in employment have remained roughly the same over the industrial era and despite the work-and-spend culture/ideology and the resistance of employers to change as described above, the total time a person spends at work has decreased substantially. Delors (1992) summarised the situation in France as follows: in 1946, a 20-year-old wage earner could expect to spend a third of his waking life at work; by 1975, the figure was a quarter; by 1990 it was less than a fifth. Even these figures hold only for workers employed full-time over the whole year. The issue, as raised in the 1920s, is who decides how these relatively large amounts of free time are spent. While not quite so dramatic in the UK, the trend is the same.

Most of this change, of course, is because of the lengthening of schooling and the increase in life expectancy, extending the number of life years in retirement; but the fact is that we are no longer living in a work-based civilisation. Nevertheless, Gorz (1994) argues that, while the chief consequence of the drive towards efficiency and economic rationalisation should be that it frees us from work, the actual emphasis is on the transformation of the nature of work brought about by the information revolution and on the prospects for an 'employment-rich growth'.

3.5.1 The information revolution

It is true that, with the introduction of microelectronics, repetitive and mindless jobs are tending to disappear from industry, although they often reappear in the service sector – see below. The argument is that in the 'New Economy', work is steadily becoming more absorbing and responsible, organised by the workers themselves, requiring self-motivated individuals with initiative and communication skills who are able to acquire and master a wide variety of intellectual and manual disciplines. According to this argument, a new class of craft worker is taking over from the old working class and realising the old dream of the producers holding power at the point of production and organising their own work there, answerable to no-one.

Gee, Hill and Lankshear (1996) suggest that, while the new work order stresses a vision of fully informed workers who participate in the decision-making process of the organisation and who take responsibility for the jobs that they do, the language is one of social intervention and control. The international management literature has developed a language centred on such notions as communities of practice, the knowledge economy, and the mutual appropriation of skills, where the presumption is that individual workers adsorb management values and goals, preserving management control. In fact, ethnographic data indicate that, in training these new workers, organisations pursue a very traditional transmission pedagogy that allows little worker discretion. On the shop floor, talk of 'non-authoritarian work structures' and 'work democratisation' in training sessions thereby disguises more traditional management worker-power relationships. There is an inescapable tension because the purpose of the new humanist discourse is to generate profits, not to empower workers. At the same time, manufacturing sectors are employing fewer and fewer people. While the UK and the US are leading the pack in deindustrialisation,[13] other OECD countries are not far behind (OECD, 1999).

What happens to this labour that is 'released'? In France, most of the new jobs created are 'atypical': temporary, casual, part-time, often with the illusion of being 'independent'. In Great Britain, 90 per cent of the jobs created over a five-year period during the 1980s were casual or part-time. And many of those jobs – for example, in a call centre – have exactly the same mindless repetitive characteristics that were being criticised in the first place and that were to be eliminated! Stable, full-time year-round employment – the supposed 'norm' – is becoming restricted to a minority; for around half the active population, paid employment no longer involves them in an absorbing occupation that 'integrates' them with their fellows (remember that the industrial working class was a mainly male one).

3.5.2 The new servant class

One increasingly popular way of creating a large number of jobs in a liberal economy is that of personal services, transforming activities which people usually perform for themselves into acts of paid service. Of course, this has been the nature of much economic growth: tasks which people had performed in the domestic sphere were progressively transferred to industry and to service industries where there were machines more efficient than those to which a household could efficiently have access. Hardly anyone spins their own wool any longer or weaves their cloth because those processes are carried out much more quickly and sometimes better by machines. For the same reasons of efficiency, only a few make their own clothes, bake their bread, make their jam or build their house, for example. Nevertheless, the home-made product has not been completely eliminated since some prefer it and are prepared to pay extra, either in terms of their own time or by paying higher prices.

The over-riding principle, even in the latter case, was of 'productive substitution': everyone can, in the end, buy more goods and services with the wages for one hour's work that they would be able to produce by and for themselves in the space of one hour. But the new personal service jobs will increasingly be of a different character than those which have been created in these previous periods of economic growth. Many of the new jobs involve the 'equivalent substitution' of 'service-providers' for time-consuming domestic activities. With few exceptions, they cannot be carried out more quickly whoever does them. Buying someone else's time to increase your own leisure and comfort is merely to purchase the work of a servant (Gorz, 1994).

Of course, the last few decades have seen the explosion of the 'caring professions' where the argument is that there are special skills involved. Caring professions developed only slowly in the late nineteenth century as conduits of charity from the rich to the poor, but have grown rapidly with the break-up and decreasing size of the Victorian family of myth. Hence almoners, followed by social workers; although a substantial part of the growth in the medical and teaching professions should also be included here. But, at the same time as there are some attempts being made to demonetarise the activity (there are moves towards community care, and so on), or devolve the costs, many of the privately rich are moving in the other direction by employing paid personal service.

Personal services are able to develop because a growing mass of people are excluded from the stable labour market where incomes are high. Social and economic inequality between those who provide personal services and those who purchase them has become a major factor in employment growth. Hence we are reproducing the conditions prevailing at the onset of the industrial era (when the rich also had servants). In that period, too, at the height of rampant market economy, perhaps over a third of the population were either domestic servants or surviving on occasional work (Gorz, 1994). But then we did not have the illusion of democracy and there was no right to education or a rhetoric of equality of opportunity.

Nowadays, for reasons of global competitiveness, governments want the majority of young people to leave school with an ever higher standard of leaving qualification. But at the same time – in order to maintain an ideology of 'full' employment – they are encouraging, through reducing taxes on higher incomes, the growth of an underclass of servants to ease the lives and leisure of the better-off classes. Fiscal transfers to the poor will increase the consumption of current industrialised products and services, the labour content of which is low; increasing the disposable income of the rich will increase the consumption of luxury goods and of personal services which have a high labour content.

3.5.3 What next?

On one view, there is a trend towards the self-servicing economy. In this view, there will be an absolute increase in the total amount of unpaid work as households 'invest' in domestic capital goods and shift their labour resources into the increasingly productive 'informal' sphere. Gershuny (1983), comparing data over 30 years, comments that since the early 1960s all social classes have shown a similar fall in domestic work time. But this latter fall is due to an enormously increased *productivity* of domestic work – in other words, the total value (whether evaluated privately or social) of domestic work has almost certainly increased.

Gershuny and Pahl (1980) predicted that there might be a shift from the formal to the domestic economy, as a reaction to high unemployment, new technology and government policies. They also forecast a great increase in informal work since the relative autonomy, personal fulfilment, self-direction and self-pacing it implied would, of itself, encourage its growth, despite the lower financial rewards involved. Similarly, Clemitson and Rodgers (1981), Clarke (1982) and Dauncey (1983) write of the potential benefits to be derived from a positive approach to unemployment, for example, lifelong education, occupational pluralism, community projects, 'sabbatical' schemes, developing hobbies, and so on. To this, we would add caring, some decision-making, perhaps some creative/artistic activities, some service occupations, where the nature of the job itself means that it is better carried out outside the market. This argument is the basis for some our estimates of the potential for reductions in consumption discussed in Chapter 7.

Instead, as Gorz (1994) has shown, we have a return to personal service again. The function of current job-creation is really to waste time in employment that has been artificially created for the greater comfort of those who have money to spend; the aim is now to reduce productivity and maximise the quantity of work by developing a tertiary sector that does not create wealth. The alternative is to redistribute work and consumption. But this will involve a substantial increase in people's free time that is out of control of the elites; yet earlier arguments that people do not like leisure are now difficult to sustain. Indeed, the only serious arguments that against reducing employment-time drastically are based on the view that unemployment is 'bad' for you, and these arguments are examined in the next section.

3.6 Research purporting to show that employment is 'good' for you and unemployment 'bad'

Common sense tells one that, even if conditions at work are wonderful, being in paid employment – being told what to do for most of your active life – is probably bad for one's self-esteem (see discussion of Maslow in Chapter 6) and is likely to induce stress. Indeed, at least in the UK, there are rising levels of sickness absence leading in some cases to withdrawal from the labour market (Webster, 2001). Whether one calls such a situation hidden unemployment or not, that group are reporting their sickness prior to unemployment and so, if anything, are demonstrating that it is *employment* that is bad for you. But in addition to the nineteenth-century apologists for hard work such as Smiles, and those earlier in that century saying that the lower classes wouldn't know what to do with free time, there have been many academic voices pronouncing a non-monetary justification for employment.

3.6.1 Unemployment and health

Research on the nature and impact of unemployment is extremely extensive. Although it appears to be thorough, the theoretical underpinnings of most of the research are, in fact, thin. For example, it is often claimed that unemployment is bad for one's health. But this seems to be based more on a fear of idle time on the part of commentators. The following quote gives an idea of the fear with which 'respectable' commentators view the prospect of substantially reduced time in paid employment.

> In order to argue that unemployment does not damage health, one would have to postulate some beneficial effects of unemployment to outweigh those damaging aspects. The postulated benefit would presumably be absence from the damaging health effects of work. Thus, if it was found that unemployment did not damage health that would be an even greater challenge to our social organisation, suggesting that work damages health even more than being poor, stigmatised or lonely. The Ecology Party could have a field day. (Watkins, 1982)

There is, however, a wealth of historical evidence that many occupations are bad for your health and that idleness is good for you. In the former category, we can start with Engels (1841), cite countless studies of fishermen, miners and soldiers, and refer to dozens of sociological studies (more frequent during the 1960s and 1970s than during the last 20 years) or to any report of the UK Health and Safety Executive. In the latter category, the fact that many social elites, such as the British (or European more generally), aristocracy, are rarely engaged in any active gainful employment and yet had longer life expectancies than the rest of the working population, seems to be a convincing argument in favour of unemployment in the shape of idleness being conducive to good health.

Of course, there are rather widely disparate relative income levels associated with being an aristocrat (or city financier) and being unemployed (and, while perhaps more evident recently, this is *not* just a recent phenomenon caused by monetarism or 'Reaganomics'/Thatcherism).

However, it is very rare to find a study that controls for income levels when assessing the relationship between unemployment and health.

3.6.2 Other 'impacts' of unemployment

Gershuny (1994) contrasts those who argue that the major source of distress produced by unemployment is financial, because it leads to chronic insecurity about whether the household budget can be balanced, with those like Jahoda (1982) who suggests that the implications of unemployment for personal stability are much wider ranging. Thus, Jahoda (1982) develops the following argument: that involvement in a paid job provides not only an income but also access to five socially important categories of experience (physical activity, social contact, collective purpose, a time structure and social status); she claims that these are crucial to the maintenance of psychological integrity. Peter Warr (1987) and Stephen Watkins (1982) make a similar point. But the social importance of physical activity, social contact, collective purpose, a time structure and social status are, in large part, *defined in terms of employment status*. For example, to take the dimension of social contact: if two-thirds of your waking life is spent in a job, then you are going to make friends there. According to this argument, stereotypical housewives should be totally friendless. In fact, the reverse often is true. Perhaps the late-lamented Charlie Brown would have understood the problem! We would like to separate the argument between job insecurity and the structure of meaning provided by work, and what the unemployed themselves say.

Job insecurity arguments

According to Jahoda, when employed, one has a time structure and control over one's day-to-day activities and that these are lost when facing insecurity over one's future. Although unspecified, this presumably refers to income insecurity. Indeed, the reactions of those in insecure jobs and presumably experiencing *both* Jahoda's categories of experience from being in a paid job *and* reduced well-being is not explicable from within Jahoda's model; instead, the threat of job loss could/is probably equated directly with the threat of poverty. Gallie and Vogler (1994) say that 61 per cent of unemployed found it difficult to make ends meet, followed by insecure non-active (58 per cent) and 32 per cent of insecure low paid, compared to 15 per cent of the secure higher paid. Burchell (1989) considers this to be only a 'possibility'. Instead, he (and Fryer and

Payne, 1984, 1986 and Fryer, 1986) says the data are compatible with 'agency theory' (Fryer, 1986) in which it is the interruption to the actor's plans and strategies which causes the negative psychological consequences. But, surely, that is only because they do not have the income with which to formulate forward plans in the first place! The current plethora of literature on the social psychology of job insecurity is simply replacing the previous literature on the social psychology of unemployment.

Providing a structure of meaning

Gershuny (1994) argues that other institutions may structure time and activity in our societies. In their research programme, questions were introduced into their Household and Community Survey to tap the five components that were meant to correspond to Jahoda's categories of experience:

1. I had time on my hands that I did not know what to do with;
2. Most days I met quite a range of people;
3. I was doing things that were useful for other people;
4. I had certain responsibilities at particular times most days of the week;
5. I felt respected by the people I met.

The way they were phrased, however, seems to us biased. It is difficult to see how one could agree to category 4 *without* acting within a framework; and difficult to see why one would want to impose such a structure on oneself (although some people engaged in creative activity might) unless one was a parent of young children, a carer, or had some medical condition which required regular attention. In addition, one does not necessarily *want* to meet a range of people *most* days (category 2). Thus, if housewives with children at a nursery group are *not* included, one would expect at least a one point difference in the score of non-active and unemployed versus those in some kind of paid employment. Why didn't Gershuny ask, 'Sometimes I had to do things I didn't want to do?'; or 'Sometimes, I would rather have been doing something else'. But perhaps that would have spoiled the story!

Jahoda's basic findings are given in Table 3.1. Although there are substantial differences between unemployed and non-active men and women in categories 1, 3 and 4, the general pattern of responses, in terms of the comparison with the self-employed and employed, is similar. However, Gershuny then analyses these data to show that the

Table 3.1 Categories of experience by employment status (Jahoda items)

	Category		Self-employed	Employed	Unemployed	Non-active
Men	1	Time on hands	9	10	58	39
	2	Meet range of people	69	59	42	44
	3	Doing something	69	62	36	44
	4	Responsibilities	83	77	51	53
	5	Feel respected	59	49	43	50
Women	1	Time on hands	17	8	31	19
	2	Meet range of people	69	66	40	38
	3	Doing something	66	69	56	51
	4	Responsibilities	90	83	75	74
	5	Feel respected	59	51	37	43

Source: Gershuny, 1994, Table 7.1, p. 217.

Jahoda categories account, at most, for 2 per cent of the variance in GHQ scores (based on the General Household Questionnaire, see Goldberg, 1978), after allowing for income and employment; and that even if one includes employment, the variance accounted for does not reach 5 per cent. Gershuny concludes that Jahoda is correct in saying that her categories are associated with paid employment; but, given the ambiguities in interpreting the items noted above, and the almost insignificant level of statistical association, we could take the results as showing almost the reverse!

What Jahoda, Warr, Watkins (and many others) seem to be trying to do is to promulgate a form of 'good' unemployment as against 'bad' unemployment. For example, the implications of Jahoda's argument are that new forms of activity and social organisation which improve unemployed people's access to the (five) categories of experience could have beneficial effects. Warr's ten characteristics of acceptable employment are: money, striving variety, goals/traction, decision latitudes, skill use and development, lack of psychological threat, security, interpersonal contact, valued social position. Watkins (1982) admits that 'it is probable that poverty contributes to the health damage of unemployment'. But 'probable' is only his third category of likelihood and he obviously thinks that the matter is not resolved because he concludes that 'more research is needed'. In contrast, he argues that the health damage of unemployment is clearly related to the importance of social support, the strength of the work ethic, self esteem and time structuring and he proposes a series of measures for 'sustaining the unemployed'.

Clearly, if Jahoda (1982), Warr and Watkins are right in claiming that the non-monetary characteristics of a job are more important (for health; for psychological well-being) than the *derived income*, then this would have important implications for the organisation and viability of 'alternatives to employment'. First and foremost, there is nothing like full-time employment; and second if you can't be employed then you should make unemployment as much like full-time employment as possible[14] through improving 'unemployed people's access to the categories of experience'. The argument would be that, even if categories 2–5 in Table 3.1, above, could equally well be provided by a much shorter day than the 'conventional' $7\frac{1}{2}$-hour day – at the same time as the presumed downsides of employment could be avoided – people would still have too much 'idle time'.[15] And because category 1 ('idle hands') generates problems (for whom?), then the best policies are to continue with the (fictional) notions of full, and full-time, employment.

As Garraty (1978, p. 5) puts it: 'unemployment presumes a curious mixture of freedom and dependence ... only those who work for wages or salary, who are at liberty to quit their jobs, yet who may also be deprived of them by someone else, can become unemployed'.

What the unemployed say

Extensive surveys have shown that the most essential characteristic of a job is the level of earnings and that, over time, there are signs of a greater stress on the importance of pay and income security. Other surveys have explored the extent of 'work commitment'. This scale asks people whether or not they would wish to continue working (or work somewhere) if they were to get enough money to live as comfortably as they would like for the rest of their lives. In the early 1980s in the UK, about a third already preferred this option (Gallie and Vogler, 1994, Table 4.4, p. 125). The commitment to employment was lower:

- for older compared to younger;
- for the less schooled compared to the more schooled;
- for those living with an employed partner.

Some have argued that absenteeism and sabotage disappear in the face of rising unemployment (Reeve, 1976). But, even in periods when unemployment was growing, there are contrary trends; first, workplace crimes, including absenteeism and theft, remain rife (for England, see Mars, 1983, but similar stories could easily be found for other countries).

Second, as in many other European countries, the UK Department of Health and Social Security? (DHSS as it was then) recently 'gave in' to the rising levels of sickness claims by allowing employees to *declare themselves sick*, without loss of benefit, for up to a week.

Turner, Bostyn and Wight (1983), in a case study of work ethic in a situation of declining employment, asked respondents to define 'work' or 'job'. The most common use was to describe an activity done in return for money, or which involves effort, or which is unenjoyable or which is something that has to be done. Parker (1982) suggested that £10 more than the benefit rate per week was the absolute minimum to offset the disutility of unemployment; many people Turner and colleagues interviewed suggested £20 as their minimum.

Nevertheless, Turner and colleagues (1983) concluded that:

> the values relating to work and consumerism are very persistent, even when a large proportion of the population lack prestige exactly because of this ideology. Very few of the unemployed come to terms with their situation by altering that attitude towards work, and most attempt to maintain their previous levels of consumption. (1983, p. 8)

However, the case histories they quote do not really confirm this. RT wants a job 'so long as it would be for what he considers a decent wage'; 'when MS discusses work, it is usually in terms of the money it brings'; JO 'does not want regular formal employment so much that he would accept a low paid job' and he would not take a very monotonous job (unless well paid); TM 'would take nearly any job – as long as it gave her at least £20 above the amount she [now] gets and as long as she found it enjoyable' (all taken from the Appendix to Turner, Bostyn and Wight, 1983, pp. 9–16).

This evidence shows that household activities have not substantially changed. The principal things that most people seek from work is consumer power *within their social milieu*: drinking in the pubs, going to bingo and other forms of gambling, buying clothes and household gadgets. Comparing this study with Marsden (1975), they find that, even though many more were out of work in the early 1980s than a decade previously, the social pressures to live at an accepted level of consumption were still as strong. However, they also suggest that any declared 'urge' to work may simply be a desire to conform to the 'normal' pattern of life, to attain full adult status; so that as increasing numbers are unemployed then the desire for work may decline.

3.6.4 Summary

In this brief tour of the research on the supposed links between unemployment and work and other valued dimensions of life, we have been arguing that it is a distortion for research to concentrate on a narrow examination of how the unemployed fare or what they do independently of their change in income. We should, of course, be concerned with and do appropriate research on the basic issues of poverty and of unequal shares which, with the present *contingent* economic, political and social arrangements, are linked to being in or out of paid work. Thus, in our stratification system, employment status is one, temporarily very visible, way of sorting people into rich and poor, high and low status. In fact, the dominant characteristic for the disabled, those excluded from paid jobs, the low-paid, the sick (and the unemployed) is their poverty, and hence their exclusion from leisure opportunities. Instead, the present direction of research on the impact of unemployment wrongly emphasises the content of the work rather than the wage and the waste of time, and thus draws attention away from the fundamental problem of the distribution of income, time and wealth in our society.

Equally, there are many for whom paid employment is irrelevant. Taking the UK example, three-quarters of the population were neither employed nor unemployed (these and other figures in this paragraph are from Social Trends 1999). While most of these are either children of school age (the under-15s constitute 23 per cent of the population) or over retirement age (males 65+ and females 60+ constitute 17.5 per cent of the population), there is also a large category of house-persons and others (the remaining 34.7 per cent of the population). Are all these groups permanently depressed? Lazy? Suicide prone? Obviously not – but neither are they in paid employment.

Apart from these definitional points, existing research on the effects and impact of unemployment is somewhat myopic. Should a future government decide to intervene with new job creation schemes, whether in the state sector or through state fiscal intervention, what would the likely effects of such hypothetical jobs be on the present long-term unemployed? What exactly would they be producing (and then consuming) in such a scenario – more personal services?

3.7 Conclusion

A positive ideology of work was unnecessary during times when the labour force could be conscripted and coerced at will. In conditions of a *fair* labour market, an ideology had to be developed in order to recruit labour and then, in order to motivate it, by persuading it that its tasks were important. This process had reached its apogee in advanced capitalism and in state socialism.

Nevertheless, there have been a range of sane voices arguing for a drastic reduction in employment time. While there has been some success, in that working hours are now much shorter, and, as Gorz says, we no longer live in an employment economy; the current trend is, if anything, upwards. What are the factors influencing these trends both in negative terms (the 'fear of idle hands') and what can be done to develop a more positive attitude and moves towards reducing work time?

Fear of 'idle hands'

Keynes talked about technological unemployment, on the basis that 'mankind is solving its economic problem'. He then says:

> Will this be a benefit? [...] I think with dread of the readjustment of the habits and instincts of the ordinary man, bred into him for countless generations, which he may be forced to discard within a few decades. Man will be faced with his real, his permanent problem – how to use his freedom from pressing economic cares, how to occupy the leisure ... won for him, to live wisely and agreeably and well [...] everybody will need to do some work if he is to be contented. We shall do more things for ourselves than is usual with the rich today, only too glad to have small duties and tasks and routines. But beyond this, we shall endeavour to ... make what work there is still to be done to be as shared as widely as possible. (Keynes, 1930, pp. 366–9)

While it seems to us quite possible that people will switch their energy and imagination to domestic work and the informal economy, this does not necessarily imply that people need to be involved in apparently productive activity all day. Indeed, there is little evidence that people will 'expand the work to fill the time available' (Parkinson, 1958, p. 4) if there are no clear benefits resulting for them.

The obstacles

The productivist vision of shared fruits of leisure and goods in the first half of the last century depended upon three factors: an effective alliance of labour and humanistic engineers; an ability to find an alternative to the traditional work ethic and the cooperation of business and policy makers. However:

(a) the attitude of trade unions towards productivism was (and still is?) ambivalent; not only did unions fear job and skill loss, but they had no reason to agree to a ceiling on 'high wages, as they had no clear doctrine of limited needs'. Meanwhile some engineers clearly saw a distinction between real needs and false wants. Thus, for Dahlberg (a systems engineer) the 'work ethic', by distorting 'efficiency' with needlessly long working days, was creating a culture dominated by frivolous consumption.
(b) At the same time, few technocrats or labour leaders would concede that a democracy of free time and goods could replace work as the organising principle of personality and community. How could a moral community be created out of division of labour and the atomising effects of social emulation? And who was to say who were to be the educators?

The underlying problem was dissatisfaction with the indeterminate social classes created, not by the production process, but out of the world of leisure and consumption. It did not appear possible to create a popular language of alternatives to mass consumerism.

The real 'fourth way'

We agree with Hakim (1982) when she says:

> As long as paid work is a financial, social psychological and moral imperative (for all men and for the great majority of non-married women), unemployment must necessarily be an unwelcome, damaging and degrading experience carrying negative and deleterious consequences for those who are caught in it. (Hakim, 1982, p. 461)

But we cannot agree with her policy recommendations:

> to make it a more positive experience, by removing the social stigma attached, by breaking down the rigid distinctions between paid employment and other productive or useful activities, by removing the stigma and suspicion attached to benefits provided for those not in paid employment, by removing perhaps the distinction between unemployment benefits and other social security benefits for those

> unable to work, or even moving towards a single maintenance scheme for people both in and out of employment. (Hakim, 1982, p. 462).

She goes on to claim that:

> such change might make it socially acceptable to share out more equitably available opportunities for paid employment and opportunities for other types of productive activity, be they voluntary work, child care, community work, education or training. (Hakim, 1982, p. 461).

It will not. The logical conclusion from Hakim's (and Jahoda's and Watkin's and Warr's) kind of argument is that we should carry on creating useless and alienating employment. Instead, we argue that we should move towards a situation where the income we receive must be more or less independent of the work we do, if we want to reach a situation where it is thought of as equally valuable to spend one's time painting at home, or being involved in voluntary work, as to be in paid employment.

The second half of this book argues for a very different approach that takes advantage of the large increases in productivity to increase enjoyment of life.

4
Consumption

4.1 What relation is there between consumption and welfare?

This chapter is concerned with how far consumption is linked to welfare, and therefore with how far it is possible to reduce consumption while maintaining or perhaps improving welfare, even leaving aside the ecological (Chapter 2) and employment (Chapter 3) costs of consumption. As Schumacher puts it, '... since consumption is merely a means to human well-being, the aim should be to obtain the maximum of well-being with the minimum of consumption' (1973, pp. 47–8).

The first half of the chapter looks at some of the empirical evidence for such a relation, and suggests that, beyond the level of consumption required to meet basic needs, increased aggregate consumption does not seem to improve aggregate welfare. However, any argument that consumption does not improve welfare has to answer the question why, in that case, people seek increased consumption. The second half of the chapter looks at the forces that – in the absence of improving welfare – might underlie rising consumption.

4.1.1 The link between consumption and welfare

Lewis Mumford characterised the prevailing consumer values thus: 'There is only one efficient speed: faster; only one attractive destination: further away; only one desirable size: bigger; only one rational quantitative goal: more' (Mumford, quoted in Sachs 1992, p. 120). Clearly, a society which adopts these values is one whose members will always feel deprived. That it *has* adopted these values does not need labouring. Much of the media exists for the prime purpose of promoting them.

Consumption is studied across a range of academic disciplines. Economics takes the crudest view of the consumption-welfare relation: the main indicator of economic progress, Gross National Product, is essentially a measure of potential consumption.[1] For this, economists are often criticised, but other disciplines largely join in the defence of consumption and, inside and outside academia, expectations of rising consumption – with time, with age (at least up to retirement), with experience – are almost universal.[2]

Nevertheless, economists lead the way. The traditional economics view equates welfare with preference satisfaction. As suggested in Chapter 1, in a sense we accept this view. Our quarrel is with the idea that these preferences can be adequately expressed in 'free' markets (or in parliamentary elections), and therefore also with the view that observed market behaviour demonstrates that everyone prefers greater consumption, so that their welfare improves as a result.

But the word 'consumption' can be used in different ways; this can be illustrated by using the chain of (possible) links from resources to welfare given in Figure 4.1.

In its dictionary definition, consumption is associated with 'destroying' or 'using up'. This certainly describes what consumption involves and what it is doing to the natural environment, and natural scientists, who are concerned with the material basis of economic activity, tend to think in terms of 'consuming resources' (Kåberger, 1996). Mainstream economics, on the other hand, defines consumption quite differently – as consumer expenditure, a flow of money, specified and measured in the national accounts. Resource use tends to be ignored, and the other links go unquestioned. In effect, the whole chain is collapsed into one item, consumer expenditure, which is identified with welfare. Clearly there is no scope within this perspective for examining how we can have more welfare for less resource use.

But there is also a more maverick tendency within economics, one which has existed for a century (Fisher, 1906; Boulding, 1949; Daly, 1996), and which regards consumption as a (regrettable) using up of resources. According to this line of thought, it is people's stock of assets which is a source of welfare, rather than the flow of new consumption

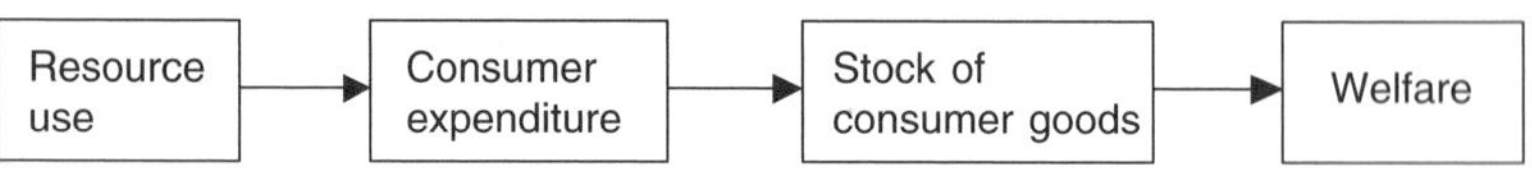

Figure 4.1 The resources-to-welfare chain

goods which is regrettably necessary to replenish the stock when it is depleted through wearing out of old consumption goods. In terms of our chain, there is a partial collapsing into two items, resource use, identified with the term 'consumption', and the stock of consumer goods, identified with (economic) welfare. This view is popular among ecologists since it recognises the value of durability, and it corresponds more closely to the natural scientist's perspective. From the point of view of the argument in this book, it is better than the mainstream view, since it allows for the possibility of the same or a larger stock of consumer goods with less resource use: as a result, for example, of better design leading to greater durability or repairability. It does not however allow for the possibility of greater welfare for a reduced stock of consumer goods, which is the subject of much of this chapter (but see also the discussion of ecological efficiency in Chapter 2).

We think it is simplest and clearest to use the word consumption to mean consumer expenditure, as in the mainstream view (but without making the same assumptions about its link to welfare). In practice it seems that national income, and therefore consumer expenditure, are quite closely linked to resource use (Costanza, 1980), although there is considerable debate about this and we shall return to the issue. The other links in the chain however are potentially very flexible. Improvements in design and production may lead to large reductions in the resources and consumption required to provide a given stock of consumer goods (Weizsäcker *et al.*, 1997, discussed in Ch. 2); improvements in the way we consume (our 'lifestyle') can lead to large reductions in the stock of consumer goods required to attain a given level of welfare (this present chapter and Chapter 7).

For our purposes, *all* the items in this chain, and the links between them, are important. The end terms, resource use and welfare, are the ultimate cost and ultimate benefit of economic activity, respectively. But the intermediate items in the chain are also important. The stock of consumer goods allows us to keep separate possible improvements in technology (which would mean requiring fewer resources), from possible improvements in lifestyle (which would mean providing greater welfare). Consumer expenditure is what we have reliable data about, and is the source of the profits that drive the existing system of production (we take up this subject in Chapter 9).

However, our discussion of consumption, in this and other chapters, is not confined to *private* consumption – of goods supplied via the market. Our arguments apply equally to many goods supplied, free of charge or at a commercial price, via the state. And the interaction between state and market provision is of some importance for our argument since the consumer 'sovereignty' which (so the theory goes) rules the market, is in practice largely constrained by the state-provided (or at least state-regulated) infrastructures within which the market operates.

4.1.2 Consumerism

Orthodox economics encourages us to see the wish to consume as much as possible as almost part of human nature. Broader, more historical and comparative analyses of how consumerism – an economic system based on continuous expansion in the production of consumer goods – has come about make it clear, however, that it is historically specific. Sahlins's (1974) analysis of the 'original affluent society' documents the situation of stone age hunters and gatherers who, even in the marginal habitats which they are nowadays restricted to, only require a few hours a day to meet their needs, and thereafter stop work. Moreover, hunting and gathering societies have inevitably been relatively egalitarian – since they had no means of storing and transporting substantial wealth – as well as being broadly sustainable.[3] The collapse of these societies has almost always occurred either as a result of environmental impacts or constraints or through outside aggression, rather than internal weakness (Gowdy, 1994, Ch. 2). This type of economy, while only possible at low population densities, is a vivid demonstration that consumerism does not necessarily stem from human nature.

Gorz charts the transition from 'enough is enough' to 'the more the better', the roots of which he sees in production for the market rather than for oneself. Without a mechanism for expanding needs, people are inclined to work less rather than earn more, as demonstrated by the need for early industrialists to cut pay in order to force workers to work a 'full' working day (Gorz, 1989, Ch. 9). Or, as Sismondi expressed it in the early years of the industrial revolution, 'Luxury is not possible except when it is paid for by the labour of others'; self-employed artisans chose leisure over luxury (Smith, 1993, p. 188).

For consumers, such a notion of 'enough', simply represents a kind of poverty. Sachs (1999, Ch. 1) suggests that poverty is applied to three very different situations, to refer to: (1) the *frugality* which is characteristic of non-consumerist societies, where needs are satisfied, but private wealth is discouraged and any surpluses are spent on the community; (2) the *destitution* which results when the basis (social and environmental) for need satisfaction is removed; and (3) the *scarcity* which is inevitable in consumer society, where needs are held to be insatiable, but which consumer society nevertheless attempts to overcome. The futile attempt by some to overcome scarcity is responsible for much of the destitution of others. While from a perspective of 'the more the better', all three are forms of poverty (and in fact from that perspective poverty is inevitable); from the perspective of 'enough is enough', only (2) destitution really qualifies. However, along with this 'absolute' poverty, conditions of scarcity (3) promote the creation of 'relative' poverty, and this we return to later in this chapter.

In fact, consumerism only really became established during the post-World War Two period (Cross, 1993). Until then, the finiteness of consumer wants – and therefore the likelihood that productivity growth would increasingly result in leisure rather than consumption increases – was largely taken for granted. The Victorian and inter-war periods saw the popularity of ideas about leisured utopia – and discussions of the problems it might generate (this was explained in greater detail in section 3.4). At the same time, considerable fears were expressed by the elite about how and how far they could control the process of democratising free time. There was fear, not so much of undermining work discipline, as of what people would do with their free time and whether it would threaten social order (see section 3.7). Nevertheless, large increases in public provision of education and culture were for a long time seen as a way of solving the problem by turning (male) workers into gentlemen.

But there were other problems, such as selling an increasing volume of goods, increasingly unrelated to needs, and redistributing available work in the face of rising productivity and unemployment. The 1930s slump undermined the desire for free time, and led to a 'solution' based on engineering increasing demand for consumer goods. Suburbanisation was the key, and, after release from the war effort, women found new roles as housewives – specialists in consumption (Cross, 1993, pp. 38–9). Working hours were to be somewhat shorter, though still far longer than they need be, thus providing both the time and income required for bouts of concentrated, commercialised leisure. Although there have been further changes in the pattern of work time, and especially its distribution between men and women, the overall quantity of employment remains very high compared to what had been envisioned by many in the 1920s and 1930s.

4.1.3 Empirical evidence

Clearly, some consumption adds to welfare, in a way that no one would contest: for example, consuming food adds to the welfare of the hungry, but not, obviously, for those who are already well-fed. But, equally, in rich countries, such a straightforward link is the exception rather than the rule. The lack of any simple relation between consumption and welfare seems to be widely acknowledged among non-economists (and even off-duty economists), whether in folklore ('can't buy happiness') or in sociology or psychology, where the motives for consumption are investigated more critically than in economics.

The following sections suggest that, in so far as welfare is related to consumption at all, once basic material needs are satisfied, it is an individual's relative, not absolute, consumption that counts for his or her welfare. It follows that, in rich countries, increases in consumption do not, in the aggregate, lead to improvements in overall welfare. Redistribution, on the other hand, may well improve welfare, to the extent that resources are switched from futile attempts to raise everyone's relative standing, to meeting any unsatisfied basic material needs.

Evidence from basic indicators

Commonly used indicators of basic welfare (such as life expectancy, literacy, adequate diet) tend to stabilise at much lower levels of consumption than those of present-day Western Europe or North America. Indeed, there is now a concern with over-consumption of food (and lack of activity) in terms of the resulting obesity and there are other areas (family and community life; urban environment) where welfare may decline as consumption rises. A recent attempt to estimate the Index of Sustainable Economic Welfare (ISEW), which is intended to 'correct' GNP for social and environmental costs (Daly and Cobb, 1990), for the UK showed a steady decline since 1970 (Jackson and Marks, 1994). Estimates of the ISEW for other countries have yielded similar results (Cobb and Cobb, 1994).

Survey evidence

There is a good deal of survey evidence, both about how happy people are and about what factors they consider important for their happiness. Perhaps best known are the findings of Easterlin (1972), based on surveys of self-reported happiness. Easterlin found that, although in a given country at a given time the rich are happier than the poor, there is little correlation among countries between average income and happiness, and there is some evidence that happiness does not increase with income over time. Easterlin concludes that it is principally *relative* income which determines happiness. A number of mechanisms may account for this (Abramovitz, 1979): the income-relativity of aspirations, habituation, rising prices of space and time, and (dis)satisfaction at work.

Other research on the relationship between income and happiness since Easterlin has largely supported his findings. Summaries of the evidence can be found in Myers (1992, especially Ch. 2), Frank (1997) and Oswald (1997). Myers suggested that the income-well-being correlation, even within one country at one time, seemed weaker than earlier thought. There is some conflicting evidence about whether people in the US since the 1970s have become slightly happier (Oswald) or slightly more miserable (Myers). But the change, in either case, has been so minute compared to changes in income that neither author really provides support for a relationship between income and happiness. Myers does suggest (1992, Ch. 3) that income, relative not only to others but also one's own previous experience, may have some importance for happiness. But equally there is strong evidence that pay rises (and indeed both 'good' and 'bad' events in general) have only a temporary effect. Frank, discussing the interpretation according to which happiness depends on relative income, suggests that some 'goods' escape this logic: but he does not mean consumer goods; rather he means things such as time, shorter commuting, avoiding stress, social networks – things which become *scarcer* as consumption increases.

Equally, there has been a considerable literature recently on income inequality, health and the psychology of stress (Wilkinson, 1986; Kawachi and Kennedy, 1999) arguing that an important cause of stress – and thence illness – is the unhappiness and felt lack of control associated with income inequality (see, for example, Elstad, 1998).

Other, more general, empirical studies of 'subjective well-being' (such as Campbell, 1981; Diener, 1984; Abrams, 1973) have tended to confirm Easterlin's findings and interpretation. Diener, for example, reviewing empirical evidence about what influences subjective well-being, concludes that, '...the influence of income is largely relative; it is not the absolute level of goods and services that a person can afford' (1984, p. 553). Such studies raise many methodological problems of course. Where people are basically asked what the most important determinants of their well-being are, and how satisfied they are with each one, the findings must be treated with caution. It is unclear how far self-reported well-being reflects true well-being rather than, say, social norms about putting on a brave face, especially to strangers. It seems significant nevertheless that there is no clear relation between absolute levels of income and happiness, and that a number of factors other than income are more important in determining happiness. In particular, health and social relations come top of most lists of important factors. This is supported by more general studies of factors influencing happiness (Csiksentmihalyi, 1992; Argyle, 1987).

The various types of empirical evidence on consumption that we have, tend to support each other. Together, they suggest that the goal of ever-increasing consumption, far from being universal, is a feature of post-WW2 industrialised societies. But even where consumerism rules, factors other than consumption are more important for welfare. And (most important for our argument) in so far as consumption does affect welfare, it is consumption relative to others and not consumption *per se* which seems to matter (once the minimum required to meet basic needs is obtained).

4.2 The forces underlying consumerism

This section is concerned with three related questions: how does consumerism come about? What factors maintain it in place? Why do people apparently freely choose to consume if consumption does not (in the aggregate) apparently improve welfare?

Views about why people consume as they do vary largely according to the academic discipline reviewed. Traditional (neoclassical) economists consider it none of their business: people who buy cars, for example, simply want to have cars, and that is the end of the story (the 'axiom of exogenous preferences'). Less traditional economists have suggested that it is certain characteristics of goods which consumers seek: people buy cars because they are the best means of access to desired locations – to 'get from A to B'. Although these two views may lead to very different conclusions about the relation of consumption to welfare, they both look at consumption in terms of the overt purpose of the good consumed. They are discussed in the next section.

Others, particularly anthropologists and psychologists (but also 'consumer researchers' interested in marketing and the role of business), have looked at explanations for consumption in terms of psychological or social benefits which are unrelated to the overt purpose of the good consumed. Such explanations focus on factors such as constructing identity, marking status, and group participation. From this perspective, car ownership has very little to do with transport as such. This type of explanation is discussed in section 4.2.2.

Of course, consumerism may result from a number of causes, and the different explanations don't necessarily exclude one another. Moreover, once consumerism becomes established, additional mechanisms may develop which reinforce it. For example, car use may become established as a result of deliberate policies of subsidising roads, running down public transport, and building suburbs, and be subsequently reinforced by becoming an indispensable status symbol. It may be quite difficult to distinguish the original causes, and not all that important, given that our main concern is with exploring whether and how far consumption can be reduced without loss of welfare.

4.2.1 Service benefits of consumption

The orthodox economics view of the benefits of consumption is based on a framework of welfare as preference satisfaction (see Chapter 1), 'rational' consumers pursuing their self-interest, and unrestricted markets responding efficiently to consumer wishes. Consumption, from this perspective, can only reflect preferences and add to consumers' welfare; more consumption can only mean more welfare. Income, as a measure of potential consumption, is thus also a pretty good welfare indicator.

There are various situations in which the market may fail to deliver the expected welfare. This may be as a result of marketing and advertising, information deficits, monopoly, public goods, income inequality, externalities, and so on. The orthodox view treats these as exceptional cases of 'market failure' and (though with little enthusiasm) prescribes a variety of remedies involving at least some degree of state intervention. They are not seen as inevitable and pervasive consequences of markets, or as constituting strong arguments for some other means of allocation. The relation between consumption and welfare has been questioned even less, perhaps because it is more central to the orthodox view.

That said, the importance of relative consumption has been recognised to some extent even in mainstream economics since at least the 1940s[4] and Duesenberry's 'relative income hypothesis' (1949). This suggested that consumption was influenced by others' consumption, and thus income relative to others, as well as its absolute level. There have been other attempts from within the mainstream to move beyond the view that preferences are simply given. Thus, in the 1950s, Hicks (1956) argued that consumers chose between different *objectives*, then decided among alternative means of reaching those objectives; and in the 1960s Lancaster (1966) launched the 'new consumer theory', which starts from the assumption that when people consume they seek certain *characteristics*, then choose the bundle of goods which provides these at least cost. Lancaster did not question the view that consumption increases welfare. However, his theory does invite questions about what the 'characteristics' that consumers seek might include. They may for example include characteristics that stem from social wants, or that are not satisfiable by any bundle of goods.

Advertising and need creation

If consumers seek certain characteristics of goods rather than the goods themselves, the question then arises what sort of relation exists between the two and how far it can be manipulated. It has been suggested for example (Schmookler, 1993, Ch. 10) that while advertising does not *create* needs or wants it does have a vital role in *transforming* them (the need for conviviality, for example) into desires for particular goods. This is necessary because 'it is the nature of the market that it is simultaneously exquisitely sensitive to some categories of our needs and wants and is virtually blind and deaf to others' (1993, p. 11). Advertising consists not only of overt, paid commercials, but also many other media products – soap operas, for example – which contribute to establishing social norms, including consumption norms. Advertising thus reinforces the pressure to conform, discussed below. The recent rapid growth of TV programmes such as 'Changing Rooms', 'Home Front', 'Ground Force', 'The Property Ladder', and so on, has taken home-decorating, gardening and house-purchase (as another 'consumer good') to new dimensions hitherto undreamed of by advertisers. Advertising 'colonises experience', is used to create new needs that can only be met by consuming, and in the process 'redevelops' human beings (Mander, 1978).

Endogenous preferences

Dissatisfaction with the view that preferences should be taken as given has led to considerable research on 'endogenous preferences' – the ways in which economic institutions, notably markets, influence preferences rather than just responding to them. Surveying this literature, Bowles (1998) attempts to draw out a number of conclusions that are '... plausible and consistent with substantial evidence'. Markets favour 'self-regarding' preferences. A non-market economy, on the other hand, may involve bartering favours, other-regarding or relational preferences: As a result, markets encourage the loosening of traditional community bonds. Markets reduce the enjoyment that people derive from activities, which is much greater where the rewards are intrinsic. Markets make people less 'nice', in the specific sense that they are less likely to exhibit traits, such as generosity, cooperativeness, trustworthiness, 'which in social interactions confer benefits on others'. The tasks we perform within the market economy influence how far we feel we are effective in influencing our fate, outside as well as at work (and thus in most cases will make us feel *in*effective). And finally markets favour the development of schools and other specialised child-rearing institutions which foster personality traits preferred by employers.

Reviewing the evidence from experimental economics, Gintis (2000) finds that, outside a market situation, in experiments where they are given a choice between cooperating and competing against others, '... economic actors are not self-regarding, but rather in many circumstances are *strong reciprocators* who come to strategic interactions with a propensity to cooperate, respond to cooperative behaviour by maintaining or increasing cooperation, and respond to free-riders by retaliating against the "offenders", even at a personal cost, and even when there is no reasonable expectation that future personal gains will flow from such retaliation' (p. 311). However, 'When other forms of punishment are not available, *H. Reciprocans* responds to defection with defection, leading to a downward spiral of non-cooperation. *H. Reciprocans* is thus neither the selfless altruist of utopian theory, nor the selfish hedonist of neoclassical economics. Rather, *H. Reciprocans* is a conditional cooperator whose penchant for reciprocity can be elicited under circumstances in which personal self-interest would dictate otherwise' (2000, p. 316).[5]

Much of this can be summarised by saying that the individualistic and mercenary 'homo economicus' which mainstream economics takes as a starting point, something which justifies the market and its consequences, is on the contrary – to the extent that they really exist – a product of the market. Other economic institutions create different people. These institutions must be evaluated not only by the consumer preferences they satisfy, but also by the preferences they generate (and often fail to satisfy). Bowles' conclusions contribute to our argument in this chapter in two ways. They provide reasons why people may consume even where this does not increase their welfare – in various ways the market has distorted their preferences. And they point to negative effects of markets on welfare – additional to the ecological and employment effects discussed in other chapters – which have to be set against any positive effects from the consumption which results.

Hirsch and positional goods

The relative nature (or relativity) of wants is inherent in a number of approaches. Of particular interest is Hirsch's discussion of the 'social limits to growth' resulting from increasing emphasis on 'positional' goods as societies become richer (Hirsch, 1977), since it is an attempt at an 'economist's answer' to the problem (although it has not had much impact on mainstream economics).

Positional goods are goods such as cars, higher education, cottages in the country, whose contribution to each person's welfare diminishes as others acquire them. Such goods are subject to 'social congestion': access to 'the good things of life' is 'restricted not only by physical limitations of producing more of them but also by absorptive limits on their use'. (Hirsch, 1977, p. 3). Positional goods have grown in importance but individual attempts to increase the welfare derived from them result in no overall increase. An increase in total welfare derived from positional goods is by definition impossible.

The force of this argument is widely recognised in the case of cars, for example. Increasing car use initially provides greater mobility and access since it leads to the appropriate infrastructure of roads, garages and other facilities being put into place. But beyond a certain point it merely leads to congestion, and mobility is reduced (Sachs, 1992). Meanwhile the collapse of alternative means of transport, as well as the relocation of homes, workplaces and essential services further away from each other, drastically reduces access for non-motorists, and locks motorists into car use. Attempts to restore mobility by 'improving' infrastructure merely aggravate the problem. But, although the result may well be lower speeds (Illich, 1974), and certainly less access than prevailed before the advent of the car – at huge cost environmentally and economically – the incentive to drive remains: indeed cars, for most people, may become essential.

A similar process is at work with other positional goods. Yesterday's suburbs become today's inner cities, and a master's degree may be worth the same to a job seeker as a school leaving certificate was a generation or two ago. But as long as the original 'good' – a suburban environment, more qualified employment – is still sought, the incentive remains to move yet further out of the city, or to study even longer.

Hirsch's argument is thus not that individuals' preferences are irrational, but that the expression of individual preferences, however rational, may lead to an irrational outcome. 'Consumers, taken together, get a product they did not order' (1977, p. 6). There is a 'tyranny of small decisions'.

Moreover, the problem arises from the nature of positional goods, not market allocation, and no other allocation mechanism will solve it. Positional competition in fact tends to lead to pressure for collective provision (for example, state education or road building), which merely makes the problem more acute.

How much consumption is positional? It is impossible to say with any accuracy since purely positional and purely non-positional goods are extreme cases, and most goods have elements of both. But, as the examples already given make clear, the positional argument applies with particular force to all aspects of transport (commuting and tourism, for example) and land use (especially suburbanisation). These are particularly relevant to the argument in this book since they are important sources of ecological damage. Transport in particular is now the main energy-using sector in the rich countries, and increasingly so. The other sectors, domestic and industrial, are in fact stable or declining). It also relates to the pattern of employment and leisure, which requires daily commuting and encourages multiple short holidays. We return to the question of how far the positional argument applies to different consumption categories in Chapters 6 and 7. But clearly, it is quite pervasive, affecting many of our everyday activities to a major extent: what we eat and drink, the clothes we wear, how far we turn up the heating in our homes, the technology we use to communicate, our leisure habits, and much else.

Underlying the positional problem, Hirsch argues, is scarcity in a much stronger sense than that which applies to other goods. The latter are scarce in the relative and temporary sense, in that other satisfactions must be given up for them and thus supply is fixed at any given time; but more can be produced tomorrow if demand is sufficient. Positional goods on the other hand are associated with absolute scarcities. For example, although more people can migrate to the suburbs, when the population density in suburbs increases, they lose the characteristics that made them desirable in the first place. Although Hirsch was scathing about the major environmental issue of his time (running out of oil and other non-renewable resources, which he saw as at most a distant possibility), increasing concern among ecologists with absolute limits makes the positional concept increasingly applicable.

Common experience suggests there are many situations where mechanisms similar to the positional one are at work, where each person strives to consume either more or the same as others. Cross and Guyer (1980) have created a taxonomy of 'social traps', focusing on the role of factors such as short-sightedness and ignorance that facilitate patterns of behaviour leading to immediate rewards but longer term costs. Their taxonomy includes types of consumption where both reward and cost is experienced by the individual consumer (addictive consumption or impulse buying, for example), as well as cases where the cost is borne by specific others ('externality traps') or the community in general ('collective traps'). Others, rather than attempting to explain the importance of relative position, have looked at how far it may account for observed economic facts for which orthodox theory has no explanation. Frank (1985), for example, seeks to explain high levels of wage inequality (after allowing for productivity) in this way.

In terms of policy, the waste involved in positional competition and similar social traps suggests that there should be collective action to limit consumption of positional goods, and ensure equitable sharing of inherently scarce goods. It also suggests that public policy should aim to reduce income differentials, so as to reduce the incentive to engage in positional competition, as well as shift consumption towards non-positional (or less positional) goods. We come back to this in Chapter 9.

The idea that welfare depends on *relative* consumption can be taken further, since it may be consumption relative not only to other people's consumption, but also to one's own previous consumption (itself influenced by others), that matters. Hirsch's argument can be extended: whenever it is the relative, not absolute, consumption level that affects individual welfare, attempts to improve welfare by increasing consumption are in the aggregate futile. Much, perhaps most, consumption takes place in a social context where factors such as socialisation, habits, imitation play a major part, where welfare derives largely from satisfying expectations, and where there is thus great pressure to conform. In fact, as the next section discusses, it is possible to view consumption as having very little to do with the functional characteristics of the objects consumed.

4.2.2 Social benefits of consumption

Consumption and community

Wachtel (1983) argues that in modern societies it is mainly the expectation of being better off than before which affects the sense of economic well-being. The desire for more arises from the attempt to compensate for loss of security derived from community and tradition. Wachtel emphasises the collective nature of consumerism as well as anti-consumerism:

> the concrete realities of our society ... make it difficult for all but the most extraordinary individual to extricate himself from the temptations and exigencies of the consumer life on his own. From street crime to a shortage of public recreational facilities to peer influences on oneself and one's children there are a range of forces that make

> individualistic and consumerist choices hard to eschew. Understanding how our present choices are self-defeating is a crucial step in the process of change, but so too is understanding how the social and political context makes such self-defeating choices seem almost inevitable. ... One of the reasons that for a short time in the Sixties young people could so radically alter their lives is that they did so jointly, with mutual support and within informal social structures that made it easy.[6] (Wachtel, 1983, p. xiii)

Consumerism requires people to be re-engineered, and it presupposes the death of community and the aloneness of the individual. 'Only when his or her life is emptied of a deep sense of belongingness to a community, family or tradition does the atomised individual begin to seek meaning in various pseudo-solidarities, one of the most important of which, today, is the solidarity of the consumers' (Nandy, 1995).

Scitovsky (1976) argues that consumer behaviour involves a search for comfort and for stimulation, with a balance between the two being necessary for optimum welfare. He suggests that the American way of life (in the US) involves excessive emphasis on comfort seeking. This is largely associated with habitual or addictive behaviour and with a search for belonging, which can be easily channelled into ever-more consumption. There is a need for both comfort and stimulation, but this can be satisfied with relatively little consumption. It is the attempt to compensate for lack of stimulation with greater comfort, and for lack of emotional comfort with greater physical comfort, which leads to ever greater consumption.

Much 'modern' stimulation also comes with a price tag. Recreation of all sorts, whether sport or leisure, is increasingly a costly behaviour: membership of clubs and sporting facilities, specialist equipment and clothing, games of all kinds. Indeed, shopping itself has now become a major modern leisure and recreational activity on its own (an example being the TV programme 'shop till you drop') and for some, an important way of 'relaxing' after work (hence the expression 'retail therapy').

Sometimes consuming takes on the character of a full-blown addiction. Elliott (1994), for example, studied a sample of 'addicted consumers' and found a pattern of compulsive buying, being attracted to the immediate pleasure of buying while ignoring later costs (pressure to pay off debts for example), use of shopping for 'mood repair' (an activity closely linked, of course, to 'retail therapy'), and features reminiscent of other addictions. Perhaps not surprisingly, the factors associated with addictive consumption were similar to those associated with shoplifting.

Consumption and identity

If economists have been largely silent about the question (central though it is to their subject) 'why consume?', other disciplines (anthropology, psychology, sociology, philosophy, ...) have tried to answer the question from their own perspectives. Within these perspectives, the physical nature of goods and services becomes less important, and if consumption (sometimes) meets a material need or want then that is a happy side effect of other motivations for consuming.

Thus consumer goods are 'signs' or 'sign values', and images or messages rather than commodities are consumed (Baudrillard, 1970). Goods are 'a system of communication' (Douglas and Isherwood, 1979; Douglas, 1982). For postmodernists, the focus is on such things as 'consumption sites', 'lifestyle shopping', and commodities' 'aura' of 'symbolic meanings' (Shields, 1992). The purpose of goods as a means of communication is to express identity and mark status (Douglas, 1982; Fine and Leopold, 1993), and people define themselves through messages transmitted by the goods they possess. Within the management of appearances, commodities act as 'props' (Warde, 1994).

This is of course a social, not an individual matter. People 'need goods in order to commit other people to their projects' and 'to involve others as fellow-consumers in ... consumption rituals' (Douglas, 1982, p. 23). The object of consumption is 'to enter a social universe ... matching goods and classes of social occasions' (p. 25) and there is a need for fellow consumers to 'mark' or grade different goods. Goods are endowed with value by the agreement of fellow consumers. 'An individual's main object in consumption is to help to create the social universe and to find in it a creditable place' (p. 26).

This view of consumption, as motivated by a need for identity and status, offers something that is completely missing from conventional economics: it puts consumption in its social context, and makes it possible to seek an explanation for what is consumed and why, in contrast to taking for granted individual 'preferences', as in mainstream economics.

Thus, Douglas starts from the study of various 'traditional' societies, extends the argument to modern society, and considers the logic of consumption to be universal. It is true that using commodities as symbols is not a unique or modern trait but is one found in many other cultures, and indeed is often considered to be an important way of creating or maintaining social bonds or expressing identity (usually elite) status. Many traditional peoples engaged in trade – often long-distance exchange – to acquire 'sumptuary' goods for personal enrichment or ornamentation, all the more valued because of their 'exotic' appearance.

The question remains, however: why the wish to consume and the amount consumed should be so much greater in our (Western) society than in others. As we have suggested, *consumerism* seems to be far from universal; other societies seem to work and consume far less than they could in theory. Theories of consumption need to explain why it varies so much. As we have seen, there seems to be no evidence of a universal desire to consume as much as possible, only held back until now by lack of technology and wealth, although some postmodern authors seem to distinguish a new role for consumption which is specific to postmodern society. It is true that hierarchical societies allowed some indulgence by the elite (which may also serve to mark their superior status) because others are bearing the cost; but the pursuit of ever-increasing consumption levels by a whole society is unique to our culture.

In part, this is because of the 'theoretical' spread of egalitarian societies in our present world (that is, the breakdown of traditional notions of the nature and role of old-world elites). As a result, everyone now aspires to a universal norm which is based upon standards set by the wealthy; in traditional societies, most 'ordinary' folk were (and are) discouraged (even prevented) from emulating their social superiors!

What is the bearing of these theories on our core questions and, specifically, do they support the view that welfare increases with consumption? In Douglas's terms, can consumption rituals be redesigned in ways that provide the same social universe-building and identity-formation services, using fewer goods, or, more precisely, using less labour and causing less damage to the ecosystem?

For Baudrillard, people can never satisfy their need for difference (in contrast with their desire for particular objects). For Douglas, there is a tendency to maximise the number of consumption events and of consumers taking part in them, and therefore consumption itself, since this activity will increase consumers' status.[7] In fact, there is more pressure to consume more than if goods existed primarily for meeting material needs.

On the other hand, if goods are primarily for constructing social universes, there seems to be even more scope for consuming more efficiently – consuming goods which require less labour or ecological damage – than if they are for meeting material needs. There are even more opportunities for replacing cars as status symbols than for replacing cars as means of transport.

In so far as the 'statuses' involved are scarce, higher positions in a pyramid-shaped hierarchy, there may be more of a problem. Goods that use scarce resources may be uniquely suitable for the marking of scarce social statuses. But here Hirsch's positional goods argument applies.

The race for higher status through more consumption is futile as others join the race. And by definition, a gain in status by some implies an equal loss by others.

So we conclude: there is no more a welfare gain from increasing consumption (in the aggregate) where consumption is for social reasons than where it is intended to meet material needs. It is therefore quite possible for consumption to be reduced without reducing welfare. Of course, there may be substantial costs of adjustment. But there is no reason to think that people cannot construct social universes that are just as good at lower ecological and labour cost. There's a possible problem of the resulting goods and services not being scarce enough to mark certain statuses appropriately – but that's really the problem of reducing hierarchy.

5
Orthodox and Green Solutions

The last three chapters have looked at the impact on welfare of ecological damage, employment and consumption. We conclude that continued growth in economic (or not so economic) activity may reduce rather than improve welfare. This chapter focuses on the policies which have been implemented or proposed, from orthodox or green perspectives, to influence the extent of this activity or mitigate the consequences.

From the perspective of promoting sustainable and equitable welfare, we have suggested that consumption by the relatively rich should be reduced, along with the associated costs in terms of employment and ecological damage. This is not the kind of approach that is envisaged by orthodox economists and politicians, however, partly because the problems are perceived in a completely different way; this we discuss in the first half of this chapter.

But in some respects policy may be changing under the influence of the environmental movement, and the rhetoric certainly has. The second half of this chapter is concerned with some of the greener solutions proposed, those that are finding favour among mainstream economists and politicians. We also consider work with market incentives and profit making, as well as those which pose more of a challenge to prevailing institutions and interests. There is now a large overlap between orthodox and green approaches, and many environmentalists argue for market-based policies, merely urging a faster rate of implementation. (Ironically, many Greens seem to take more seriously the virtues of the market than most businessmen.) But even those whose analysis departs quite radically from the orthodox view, and with whom in many respects we would agree, often end up advocating similar policies in an attempt to reconcile ecological goals with existing dominant economic interests. One of the themes of this book is to argue that this attempt is futile.

5.1 Orthodox approaches: solutions to what problems?

Our discussion of the last three chapters assumes that the aim of economic and social activity is to improve aggregate social welfare. Indeed, that is more or less implied by the way we define and use the term 'welfare' (see Chapters 1 and 6–8). But, in considering the policies adopted by government or advocated by its critics, it would be naive to assume that policy is motivated by the general good; a more plausible motivation is promoting the welfare of the elite, making maximum profits, and defending the economic and political institutions which make continuing (and preferably increasing) profits possible. The welfare and profit perspectives interact in various ways, outlined in this section and documented more fully in the rest of the chapter. Associating, or confusing, the two play an important role in defending profit making.

Conventional economic theory claims that the goal of economic activity is welfare, but argues that welfare will be greatest where (and only where) profits are maximised in a 'free' market, subject to certain assumptions which are approximated (or in a more realistic variant, *should* be approximated) in the real world. Broadly speaking, profit maximisation is a necessary and sufficient condition for welfare maximisation; policies aimed at profit achieve welfare and are the most effective way of doing so. We should be grateful to 'entrepreneurs' for their 'wealth creation'.

For mainstream politicians, from the 1950s to the 1970s, something like the converse was also true: policies that promoted welfare, specifically those aimed at full employment and the development of a welfare state, would create the best conditions for profit making. Then things changed: for mainstream politicians since the 1970s, welfare promotion – particularly if it guarantees economic security – has increasingly been seen as a liability, something that would interfere with profitability.

As a result, a huge gap has opened up between rhetoric, which still depends on associating profit with welfare, and a reality which is more concerned with maintaining an insecure and therefore pliant workforce. Greens and other critics cannot avoid this conflict either. But the reaction to it, on the part of Greens who are concerned with welfare and question its link with profit, is often nevertheless to see proposals that threaten profit as utopian and unrealistic.

5.1.1 Golden age or can of worms?

The view that markets (and the ballot box) are at least capable of maximising welfare (understood as preference satisfaction) was reinforced by the fact that for some 30 years after World War Two, policies combining output growth with full employment, welfare benefits and redistribution, were seen as providing the best foundation for social stability and profit making.

This 'golden age' has been explained in a variety of ways. At the time it was largely ascribed to Keynesian demand management and thought to have banished unemployment for ever. Others have explained it in terms of a bargain, more explicit (and successful) in some countries than in others, in which workers agreed to moderate their wage demands and accept a degree of flexibility in return for guaranteed full employment and a gradually rising standard of living. This ensured both peace between capital and labour, and, from the point of view of capital, a level of wages low enough to ensure high profits, but high enough to allow the development of mass markets. Whatever the exact explanation, the post-war bargain started to unravel in the late 1960s, with, it was variously argued, a profits' squeeze, increasingly militant labour, and internationalisation making national demand management unworkable (Marglin and Schor, 1989). Economic security, it seemed, brought by full employment and the welfare state, weakened work and social discipline, to the point where profits were seriously threatened.

As a result, the view that in essence stability will be ensured and profits will thrive if general welfare is guaranteed, was largely abandoned by business and government in the late 1970s.[1] Full employment and economic security were increasingly seen as a threat rather than a contribution to profits as workers resisted the job losses required for restructuring and put in for 'inflationary' wage increases (in reality, in many cases, merely resisting real wage cuts). To a large extent, government policy since then has replaced the welfare 'carrot' with unemployment and other 'sticks'. Provided it is not taken too far (so that people adapt to unemployment), a policy of allowing higher unemployment will reinforce not only discipline at work but also the idea that employment is desirable: a job may be all the more valued if it cannot be taken for granted, and is less likely to be given up if there are no other jobs in sight (see Chapter 3). The result is a political rhetoric that is increasingly at odds with the policies actually undertaken. This rhetoric – that policy aims to provide decent jobs for everyone who wants them, ensure that needs are met, and promote 'sustainable development' – has become increasingly implausible.

One further feature of conventional approaches to the problems we have discussed is that they are viewed separately; connections and contradictions are ignored. An example is the type of 'strategy' for sustainable development commonly adopted by governments, and which consists of two parts: (1) promote continued output growth; and (2) reduce environmental damage.[2] More generally, creating jobs is presumed to imply growth; this is, however, ecologically unsustainable. Meeting needs would imply that further growth is unnecessary, but unemployment would then result. And so on. On the basic issues whether to work more or work less, consume more or consume less, wreck the environment or save it, the implications of orthodox approaches and policies are in effect quite ambiguous.

In each of the three areas with which we are concerned here, conventional solutions – at least to the problem as conventionally stated – have failed, leading for many to a suspicion that the stated problem is not the real one.

5.1.2 (Un)employment

In the case of employment, the problem is usually stated in terms of ensuring enough jobs. This is seen as necessary for both financial and psychological well-being (see Chapter 3). A key feature of the 30-year post-war economic boom was the virtual guarantee of full employment (with benefits as a back-up policy) in the industrial economies. Since the 1970s, while full employment has remained the aim in principle, high levels of unemployment have become the norm. And the solutions which have been tried – demand management, direct job creation, wage and benefit cuts – have all failed to restore full employment. Where the unemployment *figures* have fallen, this has often been due to the adoption of new, more restrictive, definitions and measurement methods, rather than reduction in the underlying problem.

There are a variety of reasons for the failure of each of these attempted solutions. But one reason which applies to all of them is that progressively the goal of full employment has been downgraded, and policies to address it have been applied in a half-hearted way, with more concern for public relations and for putting the blame on the unemployed themselves, than for job creation as such. This has been accompanied by an increasing emphasis on keeping inflation low, and whenever unemployment (still very high by post-war standards) falls, financial markets panic and demand counteracting measures (notably higher interest rates). 'Creditors hate inflation, since it erodes the value of their stock-in-trade, money itself' (Henwood, 1997, p. 122), and they are worried that it will result from an inadequate level of unemployment: '... if the pool of skilled workers runs dry, then wages will rise as employers bid for the scarce resource and workers feel their power and turn more demanding' (p. 123). Industrialists, while less concerned about inflation, fear the dangers of full employment for other reasons, since 'employers in any industry like slack in the labour market; it makes for a pliant workforce....' As a result, 'while rentiers might like a slightly higher unemployment rate than industrialists, the differences aren't big enough to inspire a big political fight' (pp. 123–4).[3]

In other words, we are not getting solutions to unemployment because, up to a point, it is not a problem but itself a solution. It is a solution to the problems which resulted, and would again result, when employees had the relative upper hand in the labour market. Governments' true unemployment target is thus a great deal more than zero, and government is far more worried about undershooting than overshooting. For public relations purposes, both problem and solution are usually expressed in terms of fighting the threat of inflation rather than the threat of full employment; but this device becomes less convincing as the rate of inflation falls to a negligible level.

At the same time, unemployment is undesirable in terms of forgone profits, loss of work skills and discipline, benefit and social service costs, and the creation of an 'underclass'. Government faces conflicting arguments therefore in deciding on an optimal employment policy: how to ensure enough unemployment to enforce discipline and foster insecurity, but not so much that millions are permanently excluded, become used to it, and to consuming less.

Of course, as the next chapter argues, from a welfare perspective, the problem of unemployment looks quite different. It can be solved quite simply, through redistribution of available employment and income. And after 25 years of failure to ensure 'full employment' in the old sense, this solution may become more appealing.[4]

5.1.3 Consumption

To return to consumption, the conventional stated view remains that more is better, so that people's needs and wants may be satisfied. These behaviours are also held to be unlimited, however: as one set of needs or wants is satisfied another emerges. Rising overall consumption is also considered necessary for other reasons: to ensure full employment, and to increase the consumption of the poor, given the alleged political unfeasibility of achieving this sufficiently through redistribution alone. A high rate of growth of output and consumption continues to be the central aim of economic policy, even though the average rate achieved has been much lower in the 1980s and 1990s than in the earlier post-war period.[5]

As we have seen in Chapters 3 and 4, the view that consumption should increase indefinitely is essentially a post-World War 2 view. Until at least the 1930s slump, it was generally thought that as prosperity spread, free time would become most people's goal rather than further consumption increases. In contrast, the post-war strategy of modest work reduction (or none), combined with commercialised leisure, responds to the needs of sales and profits rather than welfare, and, as Chapter 4 argues, rests on factors such as positional competition and advertising (with new 'needs' resulting from environmental and social problems playing an increasingly important role).

This strategy becomes more difficult to defend as ever higher consumption levels are reached without any evidence that satisfaction is increasing. (In fact the contrary is the case – see Chapter 4, section 4.1.3.) Moreover, the fairly stable relation that seemed to exist in the 1950s and 1960s between output and employment of all kinds, has given way to a situation where growth may provide no jobs at all, or very low-paid jobs, or only highly skilled jobs which, while well paid, are only available to the well qualified (see, for example, Aranowitz and DiFazio, 1994). Indeed, such jobs as are generated are often not a result of output growth at all, but a device for redistributing time and money – low-paid service jobs which allow the chronically over-employed more time for spending their money. This is the 'service economy' – or servant economy – which, some argue, is to be the source of 'green growth'. Certainly economic growth in a more traditional sense is no longer a source of (relatively) reasonable jobs for all.

Finally, the view that rising overall output is needed to lift people out of poverty, is losing credibility, given the increasing inequality of income and consumption, within and among countries, which has accompanied growth in the last 25 years. This suggests that redistribution rather than growth is the key to improved material well-being.

5.1.4 Environmental damage

Environmental damage has been one result of human activity throughout history; but in terms of policy, until recently, it was seen as a *local* issue, involving such things as water and air pollution over a small area. In traditional economic terms it was a matter of externalities and missing markets (see the following section), market failures which made government intervention necessary. Systematic (national) clean air legislation goes back to the early nineteenth century in the UK, though local (informal) regulation presumably existed in earlier human settlements. Such intervention was essentially microeconomic and restricted in scope. There was no question of any modification in macroeconomic development strategy.

As damage has become more pervasive and concern more widespread (see Chapter 2), there has been a clear need to go beyond piecemeal correction of the regrettable side effects of industry under market conditions. This has led to a clash, and various efforts at compromise, between perceived ecological and economic goals. The situation has varied according to the interests of the different actors and sectors in the economy. In general, environmental issues have been absorbed into orthodox thinking only in so far as they could be used to reinforce growth of output and consumption (and profit), rather than undermine it, as much green thinking threatened to do.

Growth is to continue, but to become more environmentally efficient, thanks to technological change leading to less wasteful use of, and substitution for, scarce resources. Solving environmental problems will itself be a source of growth (waste processing, anti-pollution equipment, certain types of tourism – including, ironically, 'ecotourism'[6]).

Within this overall strategy, there are a variety of interests favouring different compromises or none at all. At one extreme there is denial and direct opposition. It is not in the interests of oil companies or investment fund managers to make more than token concessions, although much confusion arises since everyone nowadays has to engage to some extent in green public relations. Every sector defends its activities in terms of the positive contribution they themselves make to environmental quality. A notable example is the nuclear industry, which, completely discredited on grounds of both environmental risk and commercial non-viability, is now attempting a come-back on the basis that, at least, it does not contribute to greenhouse gas emissions in the same way as fossil fuel-based energy. Fake environmental pressure groups, which adopt green sounding names, images and rhetoric, and sometimes even fund genuine green activities, while promoting the benefits (or non-existence) of climate change, radioactivity, and other ecological problems, have proliferated. Their activities have been documented in some detail (Athanasiou, 1996; Beder, 1997; Tokar, 1997).

Some other industries have reacted to environmental issues in a way which appears at least to be more positive. Clearly, encouraged by fears of contaminated products, there are markets for 'cleaner' ones (organic foods, Body Shop cosmetics, ecotourism, ethical investment funds, ...), and thus opportunities for their producers. Yet other industries – notably insurance – are threatened by the costs of cleaning up environmental damage.

As a result, during the 1980s and 1990s, what can be described as 'establishment environmentalism' emerged. Key stages in this development are the Brundtland report of 1987 (WCED, 1987) and the Rio conference of 1992. The Brundtland report is notable for proposing and outlining the main features of a compromise between ecology and growth. This is well illustrated by its introduction, a mainstream discussion of the phrase 'sustainable development'. This can be used to incorporate the radical ideas of *ecologically* sustainable and *qualitative* development (see, for example, Daly, 1992). The famous Brundtland definition of sustainable development ('development designed to meet the needs of the present while allowing future generations to meet their own needs') carries the notion of keeping ecological impact within regeneration possibilities. However, it leaves open the questions of what and whose needs are involved, as well as at what level sustainability is to be achieved (that of a community, a nation, the world) (Sachs, 1999). As a result of these ambiguities, increasingly, 'sustainable' was used to mean 'everlasting' and 'development' was equated with growth, so that from being a zero growth slogan it came to represent the perpetuation of growth. The Rio conference was notable, particularly for bringing the business 'community' on board; its main result, as we might expect, has been the launching of public relations initiatives such as 'Agendas 21'.

This terrain is the meeting place of, on the one hand, establishment representatives whose motivation ranges from mild reform, through continued or enhanced profit making, to wrecking; and on the other hand, many environmental groups who, whatever their analysis or goals, see co-operation with business as the only realistic approach. Many of these groups in fact boycotted the Rio conference itself. In addition, the fake environmental groups mentioned above, of course flourish in this climate.

Brundtland and Rio introduced 'the environment' to the international stage, where it could be suitably reinterpreted, and blame and responsibility apportioned. Aspects of the resulting ecological discourse, Arturo Escobar suggests, include seeing 'sustainable development' in 'global' terms, that is in terms of the perceptions of global rulers. Poor nations, and the poor within each nation, are blamed for much ecological damage; economic growth and the natural environment are to be reconciled, so that it is growth, and not the environment, that is sustained; and 'nature' is redefined as 'the environment', to be regarded purely as a resource for humans (Escobar, 1996). Nicholas Hildyard

(1993) suggests some further aspects of this discourse. The rich countries distance themselves from past ecological destruction. Conflicts of interest are denied (the talk is of 'humanity's common resources'). Global rather than local aspects of ecological destruction are emphasised, opening the way for multinationals, rich country governments, and international agencies to dictate the 'solutions', which they alone are in a position to supply, thanks to their resources (capital, technology, expertise, markets). Finally a crisis-management mentality is imposed – stressing the need for action rather than debate about what action should be taken.

In other words, environmental problems are now too important to be left to local or national authorities. Everyone must take responsibility: the rich, who can afford to care about quality of life and therefore suffer most from threats to it, for bringing their expertise to bear on deciding how to solve the problems; and the poor for causing the problems in the first place, by breeding, by cutting down primary forest and by unrealistically wanting a higher standard of living – things the rich got over a long time ago.

In each of the cases we have looked at – ecological damage, work, consumption – orthodox 'solutions' have failed to address what, from a welfare perspective, appear to be the problems: excessive ecological costs, alienating labour, and consumption that does not meet needs. But that is because from a profit perspective the problems are quite different. They boil down to how to keep output, and thus the scope for profit, growing: how to keep people consuming, by devising new needs and introducing new ways to satisfy old needs (new ways that are more commercial and usually less effective); how to keep people working and, above all, wanting work; and how to reconcile ecology and growth, or better still transform ecology into a strategy for growth. But in the area of ecology at least, the orthodox solutions have come under attack. This is the subject of the rest of the chapter.

5.2 Green solutions

Discussion of these issues among many environmentalists over the last decade is in sharp contrast to debate in the early years of the modern environmental movement, in the late 1960s and 1970s. Concern with ecological damage was then very largely an outgrowth of a broader rejection of consumerism, alienating work and the profit motive (Schumacher, 1973; Gorz, 1983; *The Ecologist*, a magazine which has been published since 1970). More recent debate, especially in the UK and US, has generally been characterised by: (1) a narrow focus on the unrecognised environmental costs of growth, leaving the benefits of employment and consumption unquestioned; and (2) a welcoming, or at least ambivalent, response to the establishment environmentalism of Brundtland and Rio.

The result has been a variety of half solutions, sitting on the fence, and falling between two stools. Some have supported the view that a sustainable growth strategy is desirable, and to be achievable essentially through green taxes and green accounting. This relies on technology and markets to do the rest and assumes that this would be enough. Others have recognised the need for consumption cuts but have argued, implausibly, that the same kind of policies or other modest reforms would make these acceptable to profit maximisers in business and government.

5.2.1 The mainstream approach

The theoretical basis for the mainstream policy approach is neoclassical environmental economics. This is the point of view that carries most weight among economists, particularly among those that advise government and play an influential role in policy discussion.

Environmental economics differs from the rest of neoclassical economics in recognising explicitly that any economic system is embedded in, depends on, and cannot operate without an ecological system. While obvious, this tends to be ignored, or at least taken for granted, by other economists. For the latter, resource prices are taken to reflect what in reality are unknown long-term scarcities rather than only the known, short-term scarcities. At the same time, the capacity of the ecosystem to absorb pollutants is treated as effectively infinite; much of the environment is regarded as – in effect – not scarce, not subject to economic calculation, and zero priced. In contrast, environmental economists point out that resources, capacity to absorb pollutants, and other ecosystem services are generally both valuable and scarce and need to be integrated into economic calculation. Linked to this, human well-being cannot be expressed adequately by money flows, since the environment is a source of well-being in a number of ways which are not reflected in money flows.

This could be the starting point for a fundamental reappraisal, which would for example consider how far ecological damage is inevitable given the way economic activity is organised, and how far the benefits justify this damage. However, instead, environmental economists see neglect of the environment as calling for a number of repairs to what is otherwise a sound framework, one based on property rights and markets. Their focus becomes the design of appropriate taxes, subsidies and markets, to be grafted onto the existing economy (in contrast to the earlier, cruder 'command and control' policies enacted in response to 'market failure').

The earliest efforts of this kind were the classic taxes, first advocated by Pigou (1932), required to 'internalise' 'externalities', and applicable to many types of local nuisances. For example, suppose the decision of a firm to produce a good (or ultimately the decision of a consumer to buy it) results in dumping toxic waste in a river, and this imposes a cost on others ('externality') who otherwise would get their drinking water, swim or fish in the river. Then an appropriate tax would be one that required the firm to pay the full cost of the waste dumping, and financed compensation for those who bore the cost.

This type of approach can in principle be extended to global nuisances such as carbon emissions, for example, by taxing fossil fuels, and using the revenue to subsidise 'soft' energy development. In practice, the need for agreement among all the countries involved creates huge difficulties, especially as the countries most responsible for the nuisance are generally the richest and most powerful, and thus the best placed to sabotage or water down any agreement.[7]

Many environmental goods however, including some which are essential to sustaining life, are not currently traded in markets, so that another approach is needed. The answer, for environmental economists, is to create *new* property rights and markets. An example is a system of tradeable air pollution permits which in effect designate the state as owner of the atmosphere, with the right to auction pollution permits in line with whatever pollution level it considers acceptable. These permits can then be traded, ensuring, so the theory goes, that there are incentives both to limit pollution, and to do so in whatever way is cheapest.

More generally, it is argued that excessive ecological damage arises where property rights over resources are inadequately defined (the so-called 'tragedy of the commons'[8]), and that *any* allocation of property rights (Coase's theorem) will, in principle, eliminate such damage because the owner will have an incentive to maintain the resource. In practice, profit-maximising individuals and enterprises are considered the more suitable owners, since governments and non-profit making organisations are not subject to the same market discipline.

Where decision making cannot be wholly transferred to the private sector, environmental economists advocate cost-benefit analysis: government decisions should be based on full accounting, in terms of money, of all costs, including environmental costs, and benefits. In addition, they advocate environmental accounting, again in money terms, to provide a general framework for economic policy, including an overall target and measure of progress – a kind of green national income.

Environmental economists also envisage the abolition of what they see as environmentally perverse taxes and subsidies. These are huge and widespread[9] (Roodman, 1996) and there is no doubt that abolishing them would be a very worthwhile first step. Condemnation of these subsidies and tax breaks can give the impression that neoclassical economics is environmentally friendly, in spite of the fact that in other respects – by identifying welfare with consumption for example (see Chapter 4) – it helps to promote ecological damage.

This type of programme, if it is to lead to sustainable growth (see Chapter 2), requires the smooth functioning of markets together with continuous improvements in technology – and not the kind of technology which requires ever greater use of resources. Only then can ecological limits be pushed back indefinitely. Neither of these requirements can be met to a sufficient extent, as we argue in Chapter 2, given the present level and rate of growth of output, and especially if absolute poverty is to be eliminated and inequalities at a global level reduced. Moreover, evidence so far suggests that market instruments such as tradeable permits have been used to cut business costs rather than reduce damage (in fact there is much less trading than anticipated). Indeed, that seems to be their primary purpose (OECD, 1994, 1997). The effectiveness of all these measures depends on an idealised view of markets, and they are likely to have limited success in the real world.

In the 200 years since the start of the Industrial Revolution, both technological change and market incentives have favoured more profligate resource use and it is not clear how this will be changed by the policies proposed. More plausibly (as is already happening) markets will serve to shift the burden of environmental costs increasingly onto those who are less 'willing to pay' for high environmental standards: in plain language, the poor.

The effectiveness of market instruments also requires that a number of problems be solved, for example, enforcement problems, which would be enormous if environmental taxes were applied systematically; problems of international coordination, crucial given the transnational nature of many of the issues; and all the political and technical issues involved in designing new property rights.

It may be argued that these problems will occur, to some extent and in some form, even if other policies are chosen. But in addition, the neoclassical approach requires that monetary values be assigned to all ecological costs and benefits. Monetary valuation of all environmental costs and benefits is at the core of the whole project. Setting taxes which reflect environmental costs, carrying out cost benefit analyses in which ecological costs are subtracted from welfare benefits, estimating a Green Domestic Product, all require money valuation.

5.2.2 Monetary valuation

There are many criticisms of monetary valuation of ecological costs and benefits. Many critics focus on what they see as 'technical' issues – issues which will be resolved as a result of further research. In our view, the difficulties are not merely technical, they involve fundamental issues about the type of development which valuation is intended to serve; and many of the supposedly technical problems will never be solved. (Some of this is discussed in more detail elsewhere, in Lintott, 1996, 1999.)

Weak and strong sustainability

As was explained in Chapter 2, *weak* sustainability treats manufactured and natural 'capital' simply as sources of income, actual or imputed, in effect implying that it is always possible to substitute one for the other – environmental degradation can be offset by additional factory building, for example. It is then possible to envisage sustainable GNP growth in spite of apparent resource and pollution limits. Using some kind of 'Green National Income', based on deducting a monetary valuation of ecological damage from National Income as currently measured, as a policy target requires that one accepts the weak sustainability view, since Green National Income growth is consistent with continued environmental degradation provided investment in manufactured capital is sufficient.

Not only does monetary environmental accounting require weak sustainability; weak sustainability requires monetary environmental accounting if it is to be implemented. Only if natural capital, or at least changes in it, is measured in terms of money can one know whether environmental degradation is offset by manufactured capital formation, and so whether development is on a (weakly) sustainable path.

On a *strong* sustainability view, however, there is no particular necessity or advantage in monetary valuation. Implementing strong sustainability policies requires following a set of rules limiting use of the different natural resources and release of the various pollutants to what is sustainable

(Daly, 1996, Ch. 4). What is then needed, in order to monitor these policies, is separate measurement of the different aspects of the environment, which can be in appropriate physical units. We return to this in Chapter 8.

Willingness to pay

Most imputation methods proposed are based on estimating the 'willingness to pay' (WTP) of individuals for environmental services, most often through survey methods (the 'contingent valuation' approach[10]). The logic underlying WTP (and its twin, 'willingness to accept compensation') rests on the assumption of 'rational' economic people, spending their incomes in such a way as to maximise their welfare. In the case of marketed goods, the observed willingness to pay $1 for a good is taken as evidence that the good procures the buyer at least $1's worth of welfare. If we then aggregate over all purchases of goods (and services) and for all individuals, this gives a measure of welfare, and this is essentially the rationale for treating GNP or National Income (NI) as such a measure.

Attempts to construct a Green National Income or similar measure have thus all in effect been consumption based. They start from consumer spending, as defined in the National Accounts, and then apply various modifications both in terms of what is included and how it is valued; but consumption remains the major item. A close link between consumption and welfare is assumed. More generally, the rationale for monetary valuation of ecological damage relies on the view that consumption, and so the work required to produce the consumption goods, contribute to welfare. We have given a number of reasons for rejecting this view in Chapters 3 and 4.

In practice, the methods used to arrive at a valuation result in a wide range of estimates, even in relatively 'easy' cases. Comparison over time is quite unreliable: '... even small variations in approach and data availability may affect the indicator more than actual changes in what it purports to measure' (Bartelmus, 1994, p. 53). There is a risk that in practice the more 'difficult' cases will be left out altogether, or that arbitrary guesses will be introduced.

These issues are often seen as merely 'technical', that is, as simply requiring further research and improvement in techniques. But at the heart of the problem seems to be the fact that monetary imputation based on willingness to pay is a matter of invention, not discovery. Exchange values are created by exchange; they do not exist in the absence of markets. Willingness to pay imputations are an averaging of individual decisions taken in the completely different context of survey research, and sensitive to variations in that context.

Willingness to pay is also in practice usually limited by ability to pay. One result of this is that large discrepancies are found between willingness to pay for an environmental good and willingness to accept compensation for its loss, which is not limited in the same way and which in some cases leads to an infinite value (there may for example be no amount which will induce an individual to accept the building of a motorway next to his or her home). Even more seriously, environmental goods are systematically assigned a greater weight, the richer the people enjoying them or suffering from their loss, simply because they would be prepared to pay more. The result is that WTP valuation functions as a mechanism for redistributing ecological costs from rich (people, areas, countries) to poor.

Environmental accounting

Environmental accounting deserves particular attention because of the role of national accounting in directing government policy making, and in particular the role of aggregates such as GNP in setting the general direction of economic development. Environmental accounting encompasses a variety of attempts to apply accounting principles to environmental resources, and thus trace energy and materials through the economic system in much the same way that company accounting and national accounting trace monetary stocks and flows. There are a number of possibilities for accounts in physical units, based on the materials balance approach originally put forward by Ayres and Kneese (1969). A number of countries have constructed quite elaborate input-output systems where natural resource inputs and waste/pollution outputs are linked to the standard economic input-output tables via common industry or commodity classifications. Prominent examples are the Norwegian and Dutch systems (Lone *et al.*, 1993; De Haan and Keuning, 1996). This is also the approach followed by the United Kingdom (Vaze, 1998). It makes it possible to work out the resource use and pollution which results from producing each type of consumer good by looking at the impact of each of the industries which contribute to its production; thus the ecological impact of changing consumption patterns can be estimated, something that is illustrated in Chapter 7.

For most environmental economists, however, and many activists, accounts in physical terms are merely a first step. By imputing money values for environmental goods which currently have none, it is possible to construct accounts in money terms which complement, or even replace, the present national income accounts. As a result, concepts such as GNP or National Income (NI) are replaced by more realistic measures of economic success. National Income, as presently measured, includes two large categories which bring no increase in welfare. It includes defensive expenditures – that is, expenditures which offset declining welfare rather than providing a genuine increase in welfare. So, if people buy cars in order to maintain the same standard of mobility and access that they previously had, before the decline of public transport, or if they install double glazing to exclude increasing traffic noise, the cost of those purchases is included and NI registers a gain. NI also includes a large element of natural capital depreciation which, like manufactured capital depreciation, should be omitted.[11]

The problem is that such an approach fails to allow for the full cost of resource depletion and for environmental degradation. If, for example, increased production of a good involves greater pollution, the value of increased production is included in NI, but nothing is subtracted for the pollution. To arrive at a 'Green' National Income, these costs all need to be identified and expressed in money terms, and subtracted from existing National Income. In other respects, this approach leaves the traditional economics view of the environment unchanged.

The current pattern of economic activity is not seen as inevitably or irreversibly damaging to the environment, perhaps leading to environmental costs the money valuation (or 'willingness to pay' – see last section) of which is infinite, or at least to costs which outweigh any benefit from the activity. On the contrary, so the theory suggests, thanks to sufficient substitution possibilities, environmental damage per unit of output can be reduced to any desired level, provided the market is allowed to work. Environmental damage can always be side-stepped or repaired if individuals are 'willing to pay' enough (and if they aren't that can only be because their 'preference' is for experiencing the damage). As far as welfare is concerned, the traditional view is maintained, that consumption is closely related to welfare and should therefore be maximised. Economic growth and sustainability, on this view, can and should be reconciled.

There have been a number of scholarly attempts at modifying the national accounts to incorporate environmental costs in money terms. An early attempt was Nordhaus and Tobin's 'Measure of Economic Welfare' (Nordhaus and Tobin, 1973), a version of which was implemented by the Economic Council of Japan (1973). More recently, Daly and Cobb's Index of Sustainable Economic Welfare (Daly and Cobb,

1990) has gained some prominence and been implemented for a number of countries. Such efforts are mainly intended to challenge the picture painted by the existing national accounts, and succeed in doing so in spite of many failings and objections which might be raised against the methods used (Cobb and Cobb, 1994).

The purpose of the satellite accounts proposed by the United Nations, the 'Satellite System for Integrated Environmental and Economic Accounting' (SEEA), is different. It represents an international and official consensus about how the UN System of National Accounts might be extended into environmental accounts (United Nations, 1993). Such accounts are intended as policy tools, and the issues of how they are to be used, and what the implications of their use are for economic development, are crucial. The UN system is made up of a number of versions, ranging from environment-related disaggregation of the existing national accounts, through incorporating environmental factors in physical units, and on to increasingly ambitious proposals for monetary valuation of these factors. Not surprisingly, these also raise increasing difficulties. It is of course possible to stop short of the monetary version, but that is not what is intended by the accounts' authors. As one of them suggests: 'Introducing a monetary valuation for environmental goods and services facilitates choices between economic goods and services and environmental ones. This is what economics is all about' (Bartelmus, 1994, p. 45).

Environmental accounts, like other statistics, are a policy tool, and their merits can only be evaluated in terms of their uses. The uses envisaged seem to fall into two categories.

One type of use for environmental accounts is as a source of data for planning and modelling. From this perspective, there is a strong case for developing accounts in physical terms. Just as a complex money-using society is likely to want to trace money flows, as in the national accounts, so any society concerned with environmental damage is likely to want to trace resource and pollution flows and stocks. To the extent that there is a significant relation between the two flows it makes sense to connect the respective accounting systems. It will help, for example, to determine which economic activities are most responsible for which forms of pollution, and predict the environmental effects of expanding or reducing various consumption categories. But this type of use does not require environmental accounts in money terms; on the contrary, accounts in physical units are much more appropriate.

The other use for environmental accounts is as a way to construct a 'Green National Income' which would replace GNP as a target of policy, and would thus play a key role in guiding development. But the kind of development which would result from using the accounts in this way would involve the continued association of welfare and progress with increasing consumption, continued growth of output, and very limited concessions to environmental costs compared to what is required. It would thus achieve little in terms of promoting welfare in a sustainable way. The case for constructing environmental accounts in money terms is therefore quite weak, particularly since there is a better alternative. The development of social and environmental indicators, as we argue in Part II, seems more promising for evaluating policies aiming at sustainable welfare.

The mainstream approach to allowing for ecological costs in economic policy making is based on attaching a money value to everything, and putting it up for sale. This does not really appear to be feasible, at least not if it is to be applied in a serious way. Even if it could be implemented it would at best fall well short of what is required from an ecological, welfare or equity point of view. It is in fact likely to make things worse, on all three fronts, since there is no questioning of consumption or employment, and the result may even be a strengthening of the growth paradigm.

5.2.3 Departures from the mainstream

In this section we do not try to examine all the non-mainstream theoretical and policy viewpoints which have been proposed to deal with ecological damage. We have chosen to look first at work within economics that nevertheless differs from the orthodox theory. We look particularly at those that have regard to the nature of limits and the possibilities of substitution. Secondly, we look at some of the more empirical assessments that have been made in recent years of the possibilities which exist for improved ecological efficiency. In each case we look at the policy implications which are drawn and compare them to the mainstream view.

Herman Daly's work provides a particularly coherent example of the first approach (see Daly, 1992). In terms of theory, Daly emphasises physical limits that he claims cannot be overcome through markets, technology and substitution. Hence the scale of an economy in relation to the ecosystem must be limited. He rejects the notion of substituting manufactured for natural capital (the two are complements) and therefore advocates 'strong' rather than 'weak' sustainability – natural capital, not only total capital, must be preserved. Though there is plenty of scope for improving ecological efficiency, such improvement itself has its limits.

The policies which Daly advocates in order to arrive at a 'steady state economy' include some non- or anti-market ones: maxima and minima for income and wealth and restrictions on 'free' trade. The latter is used as part of an emphasis on national solutions and against economic internationalisation. But for the most part he advocates extension of markets, notably the auctioning of depletion quotas (for non-renewable resources), and transferable 'birth licenses' (to limit population growth). Moreover, he goes along with proposals such as ecological tax reform, and monetary environmental accounts. Overall, then, Daly's policy recommendations include reliance on the market to allocate resources, but in combination with policies to limit the overall scale of the economy, which are a mixture of market instruments and more direct government controls. Although we are sceptical about the use of market approaches and monetary incentives, it seems to us that Daly's work stands out among that of other economists for taking the implications of ecological limits for production and consumption seriously.

As we saw in Chapter 2, in recent years a number of studies which take technological innovation rather than economic institutions as their starting point, have argued that it would be possible to radically reduce the ecological impact of consumption (Weizsäcker *et al.*, *Factor Four*, 1997; Sachs *et al.*, *Greening the North*, 1998; Jackson, 1996). They all tend to emphasise the large improvements in material efficiency which are possible. These are indeed impressive; but, as they all admit, such improvements are not enough to ensure sustainable and equitable development, hence there is a need for consumption reduction as well.

Our concern here, however, is with how the proposals made by these studies, both for consumption reductions and for improvements in the material efficiency of existing consumption, are to be achieved. And here the proposals are problematic, in that they seek to work with (or at least not against) the profit motive, to create a situation where less production and consumption will inevitably reduce profit opportunities. The authors support the usual taxes and subsidies, in particular in the form of 'ecological tax reform', where taxes on what they regard as desirable things, like work and capital (income, employment and profit taxes), are replaced by taxes on undesirable things like damage to the environment. Apart from sounding like an opportunistic grab for the tax-cutting right-wing vote, this relies on dubious arguments about incentives to work and to offer employment, and of course again assumes that work is desirable.

Taxing pollution however is not enough. It is not obvious that there is money to be made, even with the taxes in place, by being more efficient. Jackson points out that, unlike end-of-pipe pollution reduction, which costs money, what he calls 'preventive environmental management' reduces costs and may thus increase profits. But the problem is that in a competitive market such a profit increase must be short lived as it is eroded by competition. On the other hand, if the market is monopolistic, there will be little incentive to reduce costs in the first place.

One approach, advocated by both Jackson and *Factor Four,* is a move to a 'new service economy', where consumers rent rather than buy, and pay for the service they receive from the goods (for example, renting rather than buying a house) rather than the goods themselves. Supposedly producers then have more incentive to cut material and energy costs because they can go on charging for the same service. But, just as competition will drive down the price of the goods, it will also drive down the rental price and hence the profits.

One example of this type of mechanism, emphasised by *Factor Four,* is the market for 'negawatts'. A small number of electricity utilities in the US have been allowed by their regulators to treat energy savings ('negawatts') as if they were equivalent to electricity generation for purposes of calculating the profit they are allowed to make. There is then an incentive to make such savings. However, this is very much the exception that proves the rule. Electricity utilities in the US are monopolies, and are closely regulated by state and local commissions who can, if they wish, set prices and thus profits in a way that provides an incentive to conserve energy. Generalising this type of approach across the economy would require detailed regulation and would amount more to overriding market incentives than to relying on them.

While supporting some of the above ideas, especially the idea of ecological tax reform, *Greening the North* puts more emphasis on changes in infrastructure, particularly in areas such as energy generation, transport and product standards, and thus on government regulation rather than on market incentives. This is more plausible, and we take up some of these ideas in Chapter 9.

In summary, within existing economic frameworks, even if modified in various ways suggested by Green economists, there is a little incentive for firms to introduce more ecologically efficient production methods. There is even less incentive for them to support lower consumption levels. It is difficult to envisage a profit-oriented society with less (though better) consumption and less paid employment; but that (as Chapters 2, 3 and 4 argue) is what a welfare-oriented as well as an ecologically oriented society implies.

At least to some extent, all the proposals discussed here have a contradictory approach to market capitalism. On the one hand, they accept its continued existence, in many cases advocating extensions in the market mechanism, and seek incentives for business to follow a more ecological path. But at the same time, they all accept the need to reduce consumption in rich countries, and thus, inevitably, profits; and there is no way that business will willingly accept such a version of 'sustainable development'.

Table 5.1 attempts to summarise the various policy objectives in a nutshell. Rows 1, 2 and 3 are concerned with the 'orthodox' view, as expressed by policy makers in their speeches (row 1), the indicators they point to (row 2), and in the policies they actually implement (row 3). Row 4 reflects what seems to us the perspective of many Greens: a concern with reducing ecological damage and risks, of course, but a large degree of acceptance of stated orthodox aims in other respects. Row 5, anticipating the discussion of the next few chapters, reflects the view that we are putting forward here.

Table 5.1 The policies: consumption, jobs and the environment

	1. Consumption	*2. Employment*	*3. Environmental damage*
1. Goal as stated by orthodox economists, politicians, media, etc.	The more the better, to satisfy unlimited needs/wants	Ensuring enough jobs	'Sustainable development' – understood as modified output growth
2. Main indicators	GNP	Unemployment rate	Emission rates stabilised at global level
3. The real objective – establishment point of view	Ensuring balance between needs satisfaction and needs creation for continued profitability	Maintaining work (and social) discipline – some but not too much unemployment	Continue growth and shift burden onto poor
4. A 'pale green' view (accepts 1, ignores 2)	More eco-friendly products	Create jobs that improve the environment	Eco-efficiency as key to sustainable development
5. A welfare – oriented view	Basic material needs satisfaction and redistribution	Job and income sharing	Reduce and redistribute

5.3 The argument so far: delinking welfare from economic activity

Debates about how sustainable development can be achieved, and the kinds of issues we have discussed in the first four chapters of this book, depend very largely on what links are thought to exist between economic activity and ecological impact, consumption of goods and services and welfare, economic growth and profit, and just how elastic these links are.

There is broad agreement that there are limits to the ecological impact of economic activity which is tolerable or feasible, although wide disagreement about where exactly these limits lie. There is much debate about whether this also implies limits to the size of GDP, assumed itself to be strongly linked to welfare. Can GDP (and welfare) grow indefinitely, even though ecological impact cannot, as a result of improvements in 'ecological efficiency'?

Until quite recently, the link between GDP and ecological impact, as measured by indicators such as energy use, was thought to be quite strong, at least within the same country (Costanza, 1980). However, differences between countries (especially between the US, and Western Europe and Japan), and reductions in the energy intensity of GDP since the 1970s, have suggested that the link can be, if not broken, then stretched somewhat.

Moreover, there are ambitious proposals to stretch the link much further. Some have suggested a move to a less material economy, and have pointed to apparent existing trends towards services as well as information products. Certainly it is possible to *conceive* of economic activities with little ecological impact. Back on planet Earth as it were (see section 2.4), it has been argued that a 'Factor Four' efficiency improvement is possible on the basis of existing technology (Weizsäcker *et al.*, 1997), with the eventual possibility of Factor Ten (Schmidt-Bleek and Weaver, 1998) to follow. Perhaps even more ambitious, is the 'zero emissions' approach (Pauli, 1998) which aims to mimic nature by creating clusters of industries where all wastes from each process are inputs into other processes (See also Hawkins *et al.*, 1999).

The proposition that GDP and ecological impact can be sufficiently delinked must be treated with some scepticism however. To begin with, what is required for GDP growth to continue indefinitely, without its ecological impact becoming more serious, is that ecological efficiency improve indefinitely as well. Yet all economic activity involves some degree of ecological impact, and increases in ecological efficiency themselves face limits. Even the various proposals for improved efficiency which have been discussed inevitably involve varying degrees of speculation. In particular, the technologies involved are often untested, and unforeseen practical difficulties may well yet emerge.

The reductions in ecological impact per unit of GDP which have been observed so far in some of the richer countries, and which some authors would use to extrapolate into the future, may result not so much from improvement in efficiency as from other changes. They may result from trade, for example, from importing goods which are polluting to produce, effectively raising one country's (apparent) efficiency at the cost of another's. They may also reflect the marketing of previously non-marketed services, as a result of the growth of the service/servant economy. A shift from cooking at home to getting prepared meals from restaurants or take-aways, for example, leads to no more meals being prepared or eaten than before, although it does redistribute both money and free time. However, even though essentially the same activities are carried out as before, the result is higher GDP.

Proposals for a shift to a less material economy, where we consume services and information products rather than objects, raise a number of difficulties. The statistics showing apparent trends towards consumption of services may be largely spurious and result from the same changes listed above as well as from reclassification of activities (for example, where service activities of manufacturing firms are 'hived off'). Moreover, where there is a tendency to consume more services, the reduction in ecological damage is often less than might be expected. Many service activities are capital intensive; construction costs and commuter journeys may be the same as for other activities; and computer manufacture, on which 'new economy' activities depend, is also environmentally damaging – even if not to the same extent as car manufacture. Furthermore, many service activities (for example much of the financial sector), irrespective of their own direct ecological impact, are inextricably tied to activities that are ecologically damaging. In other words, many services are complements of, rather than substitutes for, manufacturing, mining, and other seriously polluting sectors.

Finally, it is not enough for low ecological impact service activities to exist; there has to be a demand for them, and it has to increase indefinitely if overall growth is to continue without increasing ecological damage. Yet there is no existing trend at all towards consuming *fewer goods*; at most there is a trend towards consuming a smaller proportion of goods out of an increasing total amount of consumption.

Even if significant improvements in ecological efficiency are achieved, it has been widely recognised by those who see such improvements as the most promising solution (such as the *Factor Four* authors), that there is a risk that increases in output will more than offset any improved efficiency, resulting in an increase in overall ecological impact. That is what has always happened in the past. Increases in the miles per gallon/litre done by the average car, for example, have been dwarfed by increases in passenger miles. This is the well-known Jevons' paradox, where more efficient use of a resource leads to its wider use and to greater output, and thus to more, not less, use of the resource. In addition, at a microeconomic level, profit maximising means that firms need an incentive to improve efficiency, and that incentive is the prospect of increased production and increased sales as a result of consumer response to lower costs and prices.

Nevertheless, in spite of all these qualifications, for those who consider GDP growth essential, seeking improvements in ecological efficiency is essential. While recognising that GDP cannot ultimately be delinked from ecological impact, they can only hope that the link can be stretched a long way.

But, as we argued in Chapter 4, the link between GDP and *welfare* is virtually non-existent. In these circumstances, if the aim is welfare, there is no reason to worry about the GDP-ecological impact link as such. The real issue is delinking welfare, not GDP, from ecological impact. In achieving this, improvements in the efficiency of production (same output for less impact) may make a substantial contribution, but improvements in the efficiency of consumption (same welfare for less output) are the real solution. The problem then is how to know whether or not welfare has increased, and that is the focus of the next chapter. Of course, this assumes that the aim is welfare. From the perspective of profits, the prospect of abandoning growth is less attractive, and we return to the questions this raises in the concluding chapter.

Part II

Towards a Solution Based on Welfare

6
Moving from Growth to Welfare – a Conceptual Framework

6.1 Background

The overall aim of this book is to focus on the problem of how to increase or at least maintain welfare (the benefits) while reducing ecological damage and risks and alienating labour (the costs). We believe that the case for reducing ecological impact of economic activity is proven (see Chapter 2) so that the issue is how to reduce economic activity and what would be the consequences of so doing. We have shown in Chapter 3 that much of current employment has little measurable impact on welfare other than on the person's income which, *with current employment and income policies*, is nearly always higher when one has a job.[1] In Chapter 4, we showed that for a number of reasons, the consumption which is derived from income is a very poor measure of welfare.

In other words:

- Instead of using full employment as a mantra and creating useless jobs, we need to consider what tasks need to be performed, how these are distributed and how they improve the quality of life;
- Instead of costing environmental damage into the National Account, we need to consider it as a distinct resource, and source of utility or welfare, one that cannot be *exchanged* for other goods and services;
- Instead of presuming that increases in overall levels of consumption automatically leads to any improvements in welfare, we have to move away from the principle that 'more means better', towards focusing on what improves people's quality of life.

It is, of course, always easy to criticise; we need to propose some alternative ways forward (or backward). While we could focus on how to move towards alternative policies (and we do discuss this issue in

Chapter 9), we believe that this would lead into rather detailed fractional arguments. We believe that the important prior issue is to discuss the *criteria* by which policies might be judged and *demonstrate the implications* of adopting different criteria; in any case, we do not think there will be one single identifiable *process of political change.*

The crucial connecting question in all three of the above arguments is: what do we mean by quality of life or welfare? Thus, our analysis in Chapter 5 suggested that the root cause of many of the problems we discussed in Chapters 2, 3 and 4 was the policy framework and, in particular, the presumption that welfare is maximised when profit is maximised through growth in output. Together these lead to the fixation on a single measure of national output or national income (whether or not 'greened') to guide policy, to the virtual exclusion of other measures of welfare. As we shall show, if we take reasonably plausible definitions of what would count as welfare as the overall policy goal, then many of the problems identified in Chapter 5 appear soluble.

The focus is therefore on the criteria used to define and measure welfare. The current indices used to measure economic welfare, Gross Domestic Product and Gross National Product, are based on the systems of national accounts, which measure aggregate demand including both intermediate and final consumption. Apart from our critique in Chapter 4 which states that much consumption does not contribute to welfare, it should be emphasised that these measures were not originally intended as a measure of welfare or even of economic welfare. This was recognised by mainstream welfare economists, who therefore thought it 'natural' to search for ways of extending them so as to better reflect real welfare. As we have shown in Chapter 5 (see also Lintott, 1999), we don't think these attempts get us very far.

In this and the following two chapters, we explore an alternative welfare framework for evaluating policies. In this chapter, we set out what we see as the various dimensions of welfare and how these could be measured. In the next chapter we examine the implications of adopting such a framework in terms of the kind of changes in the level and pattern of consumption (and therefore production and employment) that we think are required to avoid ecological damage, and in Chapter 8 how progress towards those targets might be monitored. The issue of what could be done now is taken up in the final chapter.

6.2 Approaches: a thousand flowers bloom

We take it as axiomatic that a credible framework has to be as comprehensive as possible, including most aspects of welfare as judged by different interest groups in our societies. Where aspects of welfare are left out of the framework, they will not easily be taken account of in the decision-making; and this is especially important where there are likely to be contradictions between the components of the various proposed solutions that we have described in the previous chapter. There are a large number of candidates. Indeed, since the 1960s, there has been a 'florescence' of different methods of measuring the quality of life in industrialised societies, and those developing Social Indicators at the time talked of a 'movement' (Gross and Straussman, 1974).

There are many ways of categorising these approaches – for example, in terms of methods, theory and policy, or of policy relevance. For our purposes, however, in searching for an alternative to the GNP framework, the crucial characteristic is whether or not they advocate a uniform method of valuation.

There are those who emphasise the importance of a uniform method of valuing welfare. Of course, the majority of this work has been based on the financial nexus and have led to proposals either for methods of extending GNP to better reflect economic welfare; or for ways of valuing other, currently non-monetarised, components, using the measuring rod of money. This can entail including non-marketed production and other 'goods' such as leisure, making deductions for production which does not contribute to welfare or for social or environmental costs, reclassifying items among consumption and investment, or among intermediate and final production, and so on. We discussed the problems of doing this in the previous chapter (see also Lintott, 1999). Similarly, while there has been interesting work carried out using time as the basis for valuation (Stone, 1964) we see the basic problem as being one of forcing the assessment of welfare into one dimension. If we are not going to evaluate social progress on one dimension using something like output/GDP, then how *are* we going to do it?

Many have argued that we must escape from a system of data which is dependent only on the national accounts or of opportunity cost: either through developing a system for monitoring (minimum) living standards; or through constructing a different kind of composite based on a selection of key indicators; or through social surveys of the quality of life whether 'objectively' measured (the numbers of households without basic amenities, for example) or self-reported (happiness or satisfaction).

The remainder of this chapter explores some of these alternatives (focusing on those that influenced our particular choice) and proposes a general framework that is not, in fact, dissimilar from many others that have been proposed. In the final section, we use an example specification for this framework as a platform for assessing current government policies. These will provide the backdrop to some of our recommendations in Chapter 9, both because it shows us how much institutions and people have to change and because, although we have to move beyond the confines of what are currently considered sensible policies, in the short term, we have to start from where we are now. Chapter 7 attempts a quantitative evaluation of the potential for solving some of the problems discussed in Chapters 2 to 4, and specifically on the reduction in activity and energy consumption implied by this critique. In Chapter 8, we develop a possible specification of the social concerns in terms of social indicators and suggest how such a framework might be implemented.

6.3 Socio-economic reporting systems

We consider three approaches that have influenced our thinking: it is not meant to be a comprehensive review. The first is the postulate that there is a minimum set of basic needs, which should be satisfied for everyone which are then, unfortunately, usually aggregated into an index; the second is the investigation into people's happiness, quality of life and/or satisfaction via structured questionnaires; and the third is the compilation of usually administrative data according to a list of 'concerns'.

6.3.1 Theoretically based systems

There have been several proposals for a theoretical framework which could structure such a list. We consider the basic needs framework (derived from Maslow, 1954) proposed essentially in the context of developing countries, and its extension by Doyal and Gough (1991) to industrialised societies.

Basic needs

Abraham Maslow (1954) proposed that human needs could be put in a hierarchical structure from physiological needs (hunger and thirst), safety needs (for security and avoidance of anxiety), belongingness needs (desire for affectionate relations), esteem needs (the respectful evaluation of oneself); and that human beings would seek to satisfy these in ascending order.

There are difficulties with the hierarchical point of view,[2] because there are well-documented cases where people do not value survival above everything else. For example, the death of one partner in an elderly couple is often followed relatively rapidly by the death of the other; some choose, for a political cause, to die through starvation – for example, Bobby Sands in Ireland. First, despite Thatcher's claim that 'there is no such thing as society', most people value sets of relationships on different levels, including their relationship, however tenuous, with government. Even the residual welfare states (such as in the UK and the US) are based on the importance, for a sense of well-being, of taking care of the economically marginal – and, of course, there has been a resurgence of interest in 'community' through the discourse on social capital. Indeed, belonging may be essential if physiological and safety needs are to be met.

Nevertheless, Maslow's framework was taken up in the Basic Needs approach to development and was defined in the Programme of Action (Box 6.1) at the 1976 International Labour Organization (ILO) World Employment Conference. Basic needs were taken to include two elements:

- certain minimum requirements of a family for private consumption, as well as certain household equipment and furniture;
- essential services provided by, and for the community at large, such as safe drinking water, sanitation, public transport and health, educational and cultural facilities.

The conference argued (see Box 6.1) that the following needs should be satisfied for everyone:

1. security, food and water, clothing and shelter, sanitation (the survival needs);
2. access, knowledge, mobility and skills (to function in society);
3. quality, justice and self-reliance (to express a fundamental identity).

The importance of this approach was that, in contrast to previous emphases upon growth maximisation and industrialisation, the objectives were defined in physical terms; and that is the essence of poverty or wealth. Neither a certain money income per capita, nor full employment (the current means to such an income) can ensure that essential goods and services are produced in the right quantities at the right time and actually reach everyone.

The major problems are twofold: first, that while everyone needs/wants a certain minimum of several aspects, few can agree on what the optimum level of which combination is required; second, most of the authors, while nodding in the direction of consumer sovereignty, have not taken that position seriously in their subsequent elaboration.

Box 6.1 The International Labour Organization's programme of action for basic needs

1. Strategies and national development plans and policies should include explicitly as a priority objective, the promotion of employment and the satisfaction of basic needs of each country's population.
2. Basic needs, as understood in this Programme of Action, include two elements. First, they include certain minimum requirements of a family for private consumption: adequate food, shelter and clothing, as well as certain household equipment and furniture. Second, they include essential services provided by and for the community at large, such as safe drinking water, sanitation, public transport and health, educational and cultural facilities.
3. A basic-needs-oriented policy implies the participation of the people in making the decisions which affect them through organisations of their own choice.
4. In all countries, freely chosen employment enters into a basic-needs-policy both as a means and as an end. Employment yields an output. It provides an income to the employed, and gives the individual a feeling of self-respect, dignity and of being a worthy member of society (ILO, 1976, p. 1).

A theory of need for industrialised societies

The Basic Needs Approach was, of course, developed in the context of developing countries. Doyal and Gough (1991) have attempted to elaborate a theory of need which might be a more appropriate basis for industrialised societies, claiming that Maslow's list is full of internal tensions and that needs cannot be seen as real psychological 'drives' at all.

Doyal and Gough reject arguments that '... basic human needs are nothing but a dangerous and dogmatic metaphysical fantasy' and that only expressed wants (or demands) are 'real'; equally, they highlight problems of relativism which is bound to be heavily value-laden with presuppositions. They argue instead that, while there is large cultural variation, there is a rock-bottom set of needs defined by the following proposition:

> So you can need what you want, and want or not want what you need. What you cannot consistently do is not need what is required in order to avoid serious harm – whatever you may want. (Doyal and Gough, 1991, p. 50).

This is consistent with our view that people 'need' a minimum along several dimensions that correspond to aspects of 'well-being' (see below).

Avoidance of physical harm cannot be the only 'need', otherwise Huxley's 'Brave New World' allowing for some individual want satisfactions within a regimented system would be Utopian – and obviously it is not. They therefore argue for the importance of autonomous choices, 'to have the ability to make informed choices about what should be done and how to go about doing it' (Doyal and Gough, 1991, p. 53) even though this may result in some unhappiness. Like physical health, autonomy at its most basic level tends to be seen in negative terms – very much as a loss or lack of control. They argue – and we would agree – that what is crucial are real *opportunities* to act and change one's life and conditions, both in day-to-day things and in the political arena.

Thus they argue that democratic structures, in addition to basic income and output, are a prerequisite for optimising need–satisfaction; although in political terms, the extent of real democratic participation depends upon the flexibility of the state and its structures and the viability of other forms of participation. Equally, the organisation of society has to assure human rights and eco-sustainability. These societal preconditions must be fulfilled so that intermediate needs can be fulfilled, which in turn account for basic needs (health, autonomy, and so on) in order to achieve the universal goals of avoidance of harm and critical participation.

They show how their arguments can be integrated with those of Habermas (1984) for liberal democracy, of Rawls (1971) for maximised rights and goods for all; and of Sen (1992) for capabilities and entitlements. They then extend their theory to a discussion of minimum and optimum need fulfilment and of the preservation of the societal fabric and enumerate a set of what they call 'need-satisfiers' or 'intermediate' needs for achieving the first order needs such as health and autonomy. While they are anxious to acknowledge cultural relativity, they argue that there are some universal characteristics of these 'needs satisfiers'.

Their final list, one that seeks to account for: (1) basic needs; and (2) intermediate needs, appears in an abbreviated form below (Table 6.1). They also suggest possible social indicators to measure them. While starting from very different policy and theoretical premises, the hierarchical approach of Maslow, the ILO's Basic Needs approach or the more conceptual approach of Doyal and Gough to needs each appear to generate a rather similar set of components.

6.3.2 Empirical bases for measuring the quality of life

In contrast to a theoretical basis for the welfare criteria, there is an empirical approach. Consonant with the quantification of everyday life

Table 6.1 Universal satisfier characteristics based on a theory of need

Main headings	*Components*
Food and water	Appropriate nutritional intake
Housing	Adequate shelter
	Adequate basic services
	Adequate space per person
Work	Non-hazardous work environment
Physical environment	Non-hazardous physical environment
Health care	Provision of appropriate care
	Access to appropriate care
Childhood needs	Security in childhood
	Child development
Support groups	Presence of significant others
	Primary support group
Economic security	Economic security
Physical security	A safe citizenry
	A safe state
Education	Access to cultural skills
	Access to cross-cultural knowledge
Birth control and childbearing	Safe birth control
	Safe childbearing

Source: Doyal and Gough, 1991, Table 10.1, pp. 219–20.

(Marcuse, 1968), there has been a rapid growth in the numbers of surveys being carried out in EU member countries. Originally, some argued that social surveys of this type could be used as basis for systematic citizen reporting (Johansson, 1976); however, it again became clear that this approach would not work. In this brief section, we identify some of the reasons why surveys are of only limited use in defining or measuring the quality of life.

Subjective happiness/satisfaction

One group of surveys is concerned with deriving satisfaction measures. A systematic approach to measuring happiness and/or satisfaction has been developed in the Michigan school, the major exponents being Andrews and Withey (1976). They argue, on the basis of relatively small-scale survey work, that several domains contribute to the final outcome of happiness and that responses to questionnaires about satisfaction in respect of each of these domains can be used to generate a happiness scale. (The fundamental issue is whether or not one believes that happiness may be expressed in terms of a simplistic equation such as: adequate income + good health + rewarding social relationships = happiness.)

We think that such satisfaction surveys – and they are now even more extensive and sophisticated[3] – provide very good evidence that happiness isn't strongly linked to income. The problem is that subjective social indicators are just not robust enough to be used to monitor trends in welfare over time.

An example of the difficulty of using survey responses of this kind was an analysis of the aspirations and attitudes of relatively highly paid workers in industry. Goldthorpe (1968–69) showed how workers in the chemical, engineering and motor industries were taking on the then attributes of the middle class in terms of their concern with consumption and general lifestyle. However, his claim that they were 'happy' and/or 'satisfied' was somewhat marred in terms of policy implications by the observation that, immediately after the publication of his thesis, there was the longest car strike on record. Another example is the way in which, despite objective indicators of health status improving over the last 30 years, the proportion of those *reporting* a long-standing illness in the 16–44 age group in the General Household Survey has increased from 14 per cent in 1972 to 24 per cent today (see Walker *et al.*, 2001).

The halo effect

There is a problem in that people's general view about an institution tends to colour their responses about specific interactions with the services provided by that institution. For example, in the UK, recent shifts in the provision of welfare have led to more emphasis on the quality of service people receive from the state, as well as, of course, the concentration on service from private companies. But, while dissatisfaction with the quality of services can be assessed using relatively simple questionnaires, until relatively recently there has been a tendency for people not to complain about the services they received from the British National Health Service – even though there are well-documented inadequacies – although this does appear now to be changing.

Another problem is that there tends to be a 'halo' effect, in that people tend to respond in the same kind of way to quite different questions, whatever their objective situation. Empirically, it is true that a person's quality of life in one dimension tends to be associated with their quality of life on another, so that 'disadvantages' in respect of a whole range of indicators will be concentrated among particular groups in society. But the *extent* to which this happens is a very important question. Otherwise (if we take it as axiomatic that a person who is unemployed will also be ignorant and in poor health) we shall be falling into the same GNP trap that we are trying to avoid through distinguishing between different dimensions of well-being.

More generally, if direct questions about satisfaction are asked, nearly everybody responds 'satisfied', and a large proportion 'very satisfied'; this is partly because responses appear to measure social norms (of the 'can't complain' variety) rather than self-ratings of well-being.

6.3.3 The eclectic approach: a list of concerns

Rather distinct from either of these approaches has been the eclecticism of, for example, UNRISD (United Nations Research Institute of Social Development) in developing 56 indicators of the level of living in the 1950s (UNRISD, 1953). This was later developed into a more systematic schema for the observation of socio-economic conditions (McGranahan, Pizarro and Richard, 1985). But the major difficulty remains the quality of data typically available in developing countries.

The 'Ways of Life' argument

In industrialised societies, in the 1970s, the apparent difficulty when the social indicators movement was born was that there were several alternative visions of utopia which are very culture and time specific (Miles and Irvine, 1982); and several 'lists' had been proposed. Miles and Irvine (1982) argue that there has been a tendency towards 'cultural' bifurcation in modern technologically advanced industrial societies in that there are different Ways of Life (WOL) with different priorities and different value systems. They argued that a split was emerging between the Dominant Way of Life, involving over-consumption, with the attendant individual and social pathologies, and Alternative Ways of Life where small groups have withdrawn from consumerism (as far as they are able) to live communally, ecologically, lovingly and sensitively. *In extremis*, this argument leads to the claim that without such a shift to the latter Ways of Life, we, the human race, will not survive.

We consider the problems of value shift in Chapter 9. Here, however, the interest is more mundane: the issue is whether or not it is sensible to *develop* indicators along one dimension of well-being independently of another (leaving aside the empirical question of associations between dimensions mentioned above). The proponents of a WOL approach argue that tendencies in respect of one aspect of the quality of life can only be assessed in terms of an overall paradigm: a dominant WOL or an alternative WOL. On the whole, while we agree with Galtung *et al.* (1977) that there *is* a Dominant Way of Life in modern industrial societies, we do not think that it can be defined in terms of over-consumption and social pathologies. For us, the Dominant Way of Life is partly characterised by an over emphasis on technocratic relations between means and end, partly by a devaluation of the multiple ends that the individual can pursue. These tendencies can perhaps be illustrated in terms of the features they describe but the attempt to force all aspects of the quality of our life into either a dominant WOL or an alternative WOL does injustice to the complexity of the components of the quality of life.

Instead, we tend to the view that individuals' quality of life should be assessed not in terms of one or two overarching theoretical designs, but in terms which are both accessible and which reflect the variety of ways in which people order their lives. We do not want to deny that there are some overbearing constraints on the possibilities for individuals to play or to participate in projects – such as the threat of poverty or war. But, *within* those constraints, there are a variety of modes of living which give different emphases to different aspects of well-being. We have therefore preferred to argue that it is best to approach the definition and specification of the elements of well-being from a variety of perspectives and that, with certain limitations, each perspective is coherent in and of itself. Such an approach, naturally, will mean that some phenomena will appear in more than one area. On the whole, we would argue that these overlaps are not serious.

Social reporting

Around the same time, governments started to prepare 'Social Reports' (for example, Social Trends in the UK, Social Indicators in the US, Données Sociales in France and Social and Cultural Report in The Netherlands). Originally – but briefly – these were supposed to provide information about how the fruits of never-ending economic growth were being used. But these 'optimistic' motivations were rapidly submerged by the growing awareness of crisis in the development of capitalism. Not only were there some 'dysfunctions of growth' (for example, pollution, traffic, mental illness), but evidence began to accumulate that, despite increasing national prosperity, Marx's prediction of the impoverishment of the proletariat (Marx and Engels, 1848) was certainly true on an international scale and still worth debating inside developed countries. Moreover, many of the younger generation did not seem to automatically accept the promised 'Garden of Eden'.

These issues began to dominate statistical work in advanced capitalist countries. A number of administrative approaches to social reporting have been used by different governments:

- component based living conditions approaches based on objective statistical information;

- level of living surveys emphasising access to resources and inequalities of distribution. The presumption as that, given adequate resources, people will dispose of them wisely for their optimal need satisfaction as autonomous individuals. These also include some subjective evaluations of living conditions;
- quality of life research where the focus is on need fulfilment in relation to a predefined set of desirable goals;
- social indicator systems based on a set of policy concerns and other systems including Social Accounting Matrices and Satellite Systems.

Whichever approach was used, there appeared to be 'areas of concern' which are more or less common across all these lists (see, for example, the comparison in Carr-Hill *et al.*, 1995). Hence the relative ease with which the Organization for Economic Co-operation and Development (OECD, 1970) were able to agree on a List of Social Concerns. Not surprisingly this List was grouped in a way that closely corresponded to the cabinet portfolios of the typical (OECD) government (health, education, employment, and so on). But at the same time the programme emphasised the measurement of well-being, so that it tried to proceed by breaking well-being down into various components and sub-components, until a precise concept resulted which was capable of measurement.

Once inter-ministerial consensus had been reached on what were the most important aspects of the quality of life (that is, social concerns), the OECD Secretariat took a systematic approach to the elaboration of social indicators: first examining existing literature so as to identify the kinds of data series which would most validly measure the core components of the social concern; second, proposing technical procedures for best measuring those data elements; and then assessing what changes have to be made to current statistical procedures or series so as to best approximate the ideal measure.

In fact, although there was high-level commitment during the completion of the first stage – leading to the publication of Measuring Social Well Being (OECD, 1976) – the programme fizzled out during the 1980s. This was partly because governments became more concerned with the consequences of the hike in oil prices; and, more importantly, partly because it became obvious that very substantial statistical resources would be required to provide systematic data for many of the indicators proposed. The gap between the proposals and what could be derived from existing statistical series was well illustrated by the limited number of series that were included in the final publication of the programme in 1986. As Seers said:

> there are virtually no statistics anywhere on most of the aspects of life that really matter – the average distance people have to carry water and food; the number without shoes; the extent of overcrowding; the prevalence of violence; how many are unable to multiply one number by another, or summarize their own country's history. (Seers, 1983, pp. 5–6)

At the same time, from the beginning, the OECD programme was rooted in the conflict between a concern for social well-being which, although aggregated, was defined exclusively in individual terms, and a concern to elaborate a statistical framework that could serve as an instrument for social planning and therefore for social control. The conflict results in a curious hybrid of indicators. One spectacular example that concerns us here is the way in which the elaboration of indicators for: 'the availability of gainful employment for those who desire it', which may well be relevant for some people, gets transformed into 'unemployment rates' that can only be useful to a Keynesian manager of the economy.

Although this was, in its original conception, a very top–down approach, because of the generality of the approach, the set of social concerns that were generated is actually quite close to many other proposed sets of indicators.

6.3.4 Our way forward

There are several theories of what constitutes well-being and a variety of approaches to measurement, but they tend to converge on a similar list of its main constituents, while of course varying in the way these are organised, the emphasis, weight or rank given to each, and so on. The Basic Needs approach is also quite consistent with the social concerns found in social reports, although it emphasises the achievement of minimum standards in a way that the reports do not.

In other words, there appears to be a considerable degree of consensus about what the major areas of social concern are, although no doubt any number of different views exist about what exactly to include in each, and about their relative importance.[4] Equally, the government social reports tend to be very similar to each other in including data on employment, education and health, the environment, and other sectors (see Carr-Hill *et al.*, 1995). This is not surprising as the areas broadly follow the administrative division of governments, and thus the way that government statistical systems are organised.

On the whole, therefore, we follow the 'eclectic' approach: but with three rather distinctive characteristics that distinguishes our approach from that of other 'eclectic' lists. First, there is our earlier argument (see Chapter 4), consistent with the basic needs approach that, beyond certain minima, it is not always clear how 'more' consumption adds to welfare (although it clearly adds to profit). Second, we argue that a wide variety of perspectives need to be taken into account in order that, as far as is possible, every group's welfare is considered. Third, we place more emphasis on monitoring collective well-being both in terms of inequality and human rights and in terms of reducing ecological damage.

Moving beyond minima

While we do not believe that it is possible to lay down a universal set of basic needs except at the most abstract or general level, we do believe that the concerns with survival and health, autonomy and self-esteem, and many of the other dimensions cited above, generate a set of minima. Accordingly, we shall, in the elaboration of indicators, include many concerns with the minimum conditions for leading an independent social existence that will be similar to those proposed both by theoreticians and international organisations.

We are apparently calling for big sacrifices. But we think that our specification of minima would not be seen as unusual. This is based on the evidence from the series of Poor Britain surveys, in which a random sample are asked which items in a long list should count as *necessities* – and then they are then asked if their household has those goods or access to those services. In the surveys conducted to date in England (Mack and Lansley, 1985; Halleröd *et al.*, 1997), there has been a broad consensus as to what counts as the reasonable minima, rather similar in fact to what we are proposing. They would not therefore involve big sacrifices after all.

A set of social indicators restricted only to these minima would, however, be very bare. Data can, of course, be compiled on the numbers of people disabled and/or homeless and/or illiterate, and/or poor and such compilations are useful in assessing social need (see, for example, Davies, Bebbington and Charnley, 1990). But these data only tell us about one – admittedly very important – extreme of the distribution of welfare. The purpose here is to develop a set of indicators which will comment on the whole of the distribution.

One possible approach would consider the same dimensions as were included in the minima (disability → illness → health; homeless → housing; illiteracy → knowledge; poor → rich) but there are two objections. First, it falls into the same trap as the discussion and measurement of national income in presupposing that more means better. While we could argue cynically that too much knowledge is a dangerous thing, there are difficulties in talking about 'increasing' levels of individual health (see our discussion below). More seriously, if one person or group has more housing and/or income then within certain limits and within a sensible time span another person or group has less – and, indeed, is more likely to fall below the minima. The second objection is that above quite a low level of satisfaction, it is difficult to develop a general criterion as to what would count as the satisfaction of need in order to specify measurable indicators and the collection of data.

At the same time, we want to avoid a categorisation which is simply *dictated by* the administrative structure of government which reflects more a concern with the preservation of the social fabric (from one particular point of view) and so will emphasise elements which correspond with this point of view rather than with the enhancement of individual well-being.

In one sense, therefore, we would advocate a return to the structure of social concerns which grew out of the social indicator movement. For while no overarching theoretical justification was possible, it is surprising how similar the Social Trends style reports are (see Carr-Hill *et al.*, 1995), and how quickly the OECD governments reached agreement on the basic dimensions of well-being. One might argue that this was because, whatever the political persuasion of the government, they all had the same interest in social control: but the OECD programme was distinctive in emphasising the importance of measuring individual well-being: the contradictions appeared at the subsequent stage of developing indicators (see Radical Statistics, 1979).

A variety of perspectives

Rather than basing our framework upon the structure of OECD governments, we have stepped back to ask what *are* the dimensions of interest in terms of a set of world views about what constitutes the good life. For some, the human condition is defined in terms of a healthy body and mind. Obviously, a Platonic emphasis on the constitution of the Republic so as to reach the higher ends of Truth and Beauty is one source. For others, a (wo)man is defined by what (s)he does. In essence, this was

Aristotle's view and followed through by Aquinas and, latterly, Marx (1973) along with several other early Socialist writers arguing for the ennoblement of creative activity. In particular, maintaining long working hours is completely unnecessary in terms of the utility of what is *produced*. Finally, the growth of capitalism brought another definition to the fore: that a (wo)man was defined by what (s)he had. The clearest early exponent of this view was probably Locke (1694), but it is clearly now essential for the continuation of capitalism that people believe that they are what they own. Yet as we have shown in Chapter 4, the urge to consume more is leading neither to more fulfilment nor to greater economic security. These different perspectives on individual well-being can be summarised in terms of the concepts Being, Doing and Having.

But it is equally important is to locate the individual in a social context. The quality of life in society is defined not only by what you are, what you do, or what you have, but also how we relate to each other in society and the extent to which we are free from arbitrary interference whether by other individuals or groups or, indeed, the state. Moreover, we have shown in Chapter 2 that there have to be drastic changes in environmental policies for us to survive. Without too much artificiality in our system, we can summarise these concerns in terms of 'Relating' and 'Surviving'.

Superficially, these are similar to systems that have been proposed by Allardt (1975) and by Ekins and Max-Neef (1992). The former is based on extensive survey work in Scandinavia asking about the following dimensions of welfare: living standards, loyalties, experiences of self-realisation, alienation, happiness and dissatisfaction. The latter also have a 'being' category that represents the personal or collective attributes which might be required in the satisfaction of a given need; their 'having' category refers to the mechanism or tools (including institutions or norms as well as material things) which might be required; a 'doing' category reflects personal or collective actions necessary for the satisfaction of a need; and they chose the term 'interacting' to reflect exogenous factors relating to milieu and location (Max Neef, 1992, cited in Jackson and Marks, 1999, pp. 427–8).

Our approach is somewhat different. We see 'being', 'doing', 'having', 'relating' and 'surviving' as different *perspectives* on the quality of life. Moreover, unlike Doyal and Gough (1991), we believe there are irreducible minima that can be established (although the precise levels will be contentious) in respect of each dimension. Beyond those minima, more might mean better for some along that dimension; but, from our point of view, the issue is whether or not a higher level on that particular dimension constitutes an *overall* improvement in welfare.

But in addition to these specific perspectives that are primarily focused on the individual's welfare, there are a number of 'cross-cutting' more 'societal' concerns that can be grouped into three general themes; and some social constraints on economic activity implied by our earlier arguments in Chapters 2 to 5.

One general theme is *inequality* between social groups within a country or region, whether defined by gender, generation or geography or various measurements of socio-economic status. We could assess this in terms of the statistical combinations of inequality in respect of each of the specific series being considered but this is likely to be difficult to interpret. One possible approach would be to add up the numbers of people who do not reach a basic minimum in respect of each of the one or more of the series. This, however, requires data linkage between the series for each individual with resultant concerns over individual privacy.

A second general theme is *democracy*, or the extent to which people feel able to influence the decisions that affect them. What is crucial are real opportunities to act and change one's life and conditions both day-to-day and in the political arena. People's perceived lack of control over their everyday lives is evident in anti-globalisation demonstrations around the world. One could also argue that the attacks on America on 11 September 2001 were a nihilistic expression of the same lack of control at a global level. Linked to this is the issue of human or democratic rights which should be ensured for everyone.

But most importantly, our earlier arguments that the current situation is unsustainable and policies should be evaluated on a different basis, imply that in order to ensure that ecological damage is being reduced, we need a separate set of collective or *societal* concerns to monitor what we see as necessary constraints on economic activity in terms of reduced levels of consumption and production and in terms of environmental controls.

6.3.5 A proposed framework for discussion

The resulting set of *individual* social concerns is set out in Table 6.2. It conforms broadly to the theoretical specification of needs, to the concerns raised in social surveys and, incidentally, to what was an intergovernmental consensus at the time (see OECD, 1970). The specification of collective social concerns and of constraints on economic activity are set out in Tables 6.3 and 6.4 respectively.

Together, they represent a first step in moving from the very general notion of a citizen's well-being towards specific, operationally-defined social indicators that could then be used to monitor levels of individual

Table 6.2 A possible framework of individual social concerns

General theme	*Suggested concerns*	*Example specifications*
Being	Health	Length and health-related quality of life
	Knowledge	Potential for children's development Level of knowledge and ignorance Opportunities for lifelong learning
Doing	Use of time Quality of activites	Experience when growing up Choice and control over use of time Quality of activities (shorter working hours)
Having	Needs fulfilment	Fulfilment of basic needs (adequate consumption)
	Basic minima	Levels of long-term security Poverty lines
Relating	Social capital Safety in public	Family and/or household security Interactions with strangers and victimisation
Surviving	Environmental health Safety	Adequate quality of air, land and water Safety of collective transport

Table 6.3 A possible framework of collective societal concerns

Collective concerns	*Example specifications*
Inequalities	Combination of individual indicators
Democracy	Perceived lack of control
Human or Democratic rights	Restrictions on movement Due process and liberty of association

Table 6.4 A possible framework of constraints on economic activity

Constraints on activity	*Example specifications*
Consumption	Progressive reductions in GDP
Production	Reductions in production of goods and services with no utility
Sustainable physical environment	Sustainable energy consumption levels Pollution levels

and societal welfare, but in the context of the reductions in consumption, employment and production that are required in order to ensure that the ecological impact of economic activity is reduced (see below).

Of course, the real test of their utility and comprehensiveness will be whether the indicators that are specified provide signals for policy that move institutions and people to behave in ways that help to resolve some of the problems we pointed to in Chapters 2 to 4. A possible set of indicators is set out in Chapter 8.

6.4 Implications for government policies and expenditures

If such a framework were to be adopted, the political and policy implications are considerable. It is true to say that other people's priorities about the specific social concerns might be different, but essentially, the definition of a series of criteria, which are *independent* of current macroeconomic policies (about employment and growth), brings a whole new perspective. Among other policies, increasing employment and higher growth rates have to be evaluated in terms of their (lack of) welfare gains and not applauded simply because they are increases.

In this section, we make a preliminary assessment of current social trends. We also assess the appropriateness and sanity of current government economic and social policies in the light of this argument about the nature of social welfare, and what we know about the likely effects of different kinds of policies. If one believes, as many claim to,[5] that policies should be based on evidence, then policies should change, regardless of whether or not our framework is adopted in its entirety.

It is important to note, that even though the dimensions of welfare that we have outlined are, to a large extent, similar to the lowest common denominator of the cabinet (that is, OECD government) portfolios of Northern governments (as shown above), we start out the analysis with a 'blank slate'. That is, we do not presume that welfare along a particular dimension is best served by the corresponding government department. Of course, this approach raises the whole issue of how the public sector budget *should* be allocated between different sectors. We would see that kind of transparency as one of the bonuses of a more communitarian approach to democracy (see Chapter 8). In other words, this is a thought exercise in 'evidence-based policy evaluation' of current policies. But rather than being couched in terms of 'what works' – the current political mantra advocated by many writers for existing or possible government policies (for example, Nutley *et al.*, 2000) – we have moved upstream to ask how existing trends and government policies contribute or do not contribute to social welfare as defined above.

We repeat that this is not meant to be a comprehensive review, simply an illustration of the welfare-based argument for some of the main current policies towards health, education, employment, social security, the environment, and law and order. Note that although this was the focus of much of the critique in Chapters 2 to 4, we have not explicitly considered economic policies. This is because, as we have explained in Chapter 1, this is not an economic policy problem in the usual sense, given that we are formally abandoning growth as the overall aim. Indeed, as we shall see, nearly all the changes are in the direction of reducing consumption and economic activity in general.

6.4.1 Health policies

In our paradigm, these need to be assessed in terms of length and health-related quality of life as well as in terms of children's development. We should recall that one of the main stated purposes of health care services is to promote health and prevent illness. This is not to deny the importance of 'repair and maintenance' health care services for those who are ill, or of research to find better therapies, especially for chronic conditions, but to suggest that any proposal for massive increases in health care expenditure has to be assessed in terms of the benefits that such increases are likely to bring. And of course most health care is of the 'repair and maintenance' variety rather than on prevention of disease and injury and the promotion of good health, despite the rhetoric. A shift in emphasis towards the latter would have many positive impacts on health (and therefore on welfare); it would probably not involve additional expenditures, but a commitment to evaluate other policies and sectors in terms of their impact on health.[6] The obvious example is transport which is a major cause of death of young people and which is mainly responsible for bringing forward about 8 100 deaths a year (DH, 1998), but there are many others such as employment and housing.

6.4.2 Education and learning policies

In our paradigm these need to be assessed in terms of experience of school, levels of knowledge and ignorance, and lifelong learning. Similar points can be made here with perhaps even more justification (depending on how learning outcomes are to be measured). Some of what children are taught is of little use; and many children are not interested in learning what they are being taught in formal classrooms, even if they might well be interested if taught in other contexts. Indeed, much of what children currently usefully learn at school about the world around them and the way the world works (geography, history, PSE, for example could be replaced in order to encourage children to learn by doing. In addition, much of current (and indeed historical) education policy is to educate for the job market rather than for knowledge *per se* (see Chapter 3 for a discussion of the questionable value of much of present-day employment).

Most would argue that the irreducible minimum would be learning basic communicative strategies (including reading and writing). But most curricula could be reoriented towards enjoyment rather than examination, together with the institution of permanent and relatively formal learning clinics available for children who have not otherwise learnt how to read and write to go to when the children themselves feel ready for that (Carr-Hill, 1987). The school experience itself would be vastly improved through reducing the formal school day and increasing the level of fun and enjoyment (Reimer, 1974).

As the school system is currently structured this would require the employment of dedicated 'fun monitors/teachers', something which would be expensive. But, within a context of more time becoming available, a little common sense would suggest that such an approach would imply wholesale reductions in formal educational expenditure.

At a higher level, we also have to query the utility of many of the qualifications achieved in tertiary education both for the individual and for society. One can, of course, argue that education at that level serves to 'draw out' the latent potential for learning regardless of qualifications or of their utility in the labour market; and with the kind of approach we advocate, we would hope that would become the dominant rationale for further learning. But with current trends and policies, there are two sets of arguments: one about productivity, and one about the real function of qualifications.

In principle, education should lead to higher productivity because those who are well-trained have more transformable skills. There is (disputed) evidence suggesting that educational qualifications were an independent factor in production and growth during the late nineteenth century (Engerman, 1971; Schultz, 1960). But, while there might well be a *comparative* advantage for countries in the early stages of industrialisation, this does not mean that there is an *overall* contribution to global welfare which can be attributed to increased qualifications (see Hirsch, 1977).

The same arguments apply at an individual level. For the majority of learners in the formal school/college system, the purpose of schooling is to provide the 'qualification passport' to a certain level of job status.

In an economy where more means better, this may well be true. Yet, what the evidence shows (Robinson and Oppenheim, 1997) is that what matters is the *relative* not the absolute position in the educational ladder (Nie *et al.*, 1996). At least in terms of occupational and prestige outcomes, we would all have an equally good quality of life if we all had proportionately fewer qualifications.

Indeed, while the expansion of modern 'Western' schooling in developing countries after independence was seized upon by the emergent middle classes as providing the vehicle for social mobility, there is now a wealth of evidence that it has only served to 'label' the existing elite position of higher social strata (Dore, 1976). In Western countries, the realisation that one can be over qualified for any particular job has taken longer, but it is now recognised that educational qualification serves more as a screening mechanism (Arrow, 1962) than as a marker for mobility through talent.

Finally, the current emphasis on the functionally illiterate only underscores our concern with lifelong learning. This would involve wholesale reorientation of the educational enterprise towards those with minimal skills rather than on the privileged elite.

6.4.3 Employment policies

In our paradigm, this needs to be assessed in terms of employment quality, control over (working) life and utility of activity. The current 'no job, no welfare (benefits)' policies do not work in the United States where they began (Meyer, 2000) and neither do they or will they work in the UK or in Europe. Our focus on individual quality of life and societal welfare would lead us, instead, to advocate assessing each type of production and service in terms of its contribution to welfare, and then to eliminate unnecessary jobs (including much of current paid work) and simply spread the remainder around.

This is, of course, one of central features of our whole argument. In Chapter 3 we laid out the way in which much of current employment makes only a marginal contribution to welfare (see also below). Many of those who are employed are therefore at least partially 'wasting' their time and are partially 'victims' of the current emphasis on full employment. We *do* realise, of course, that there has to be sufficient activity and income generated in order to satisfy the other basic minima in this list (although many of these minima do not require any particular level of income); but even with our restriction to eco-friendly technologies, these only require a limited amount of labour (see section 7.5).

The corollary of such a substantial decrease in employment would be that as they will be spending less time in employment, people will have more time for leisure activities which would therefore be less concentrated into short periods of time, and, therefore much less commercialised. This will, of course, take a lengthy period of adjustment for many, but such dynamic change is possible (see Chapter 9 for more developed 'scenarios').

Instead, we would also be increasingly concerned with the content of the employment. Many current jobs are boring and repetitive, and some are simply dangerous; restructuring the working day would lead to much more concern with making the prevailing working conditions for those jobs which are necessary, less alienating.

6.4.4 Social security

In our paradigm, this needs to be assessed in terms of access to specific marker goods. There is now almost a consensus in the Northern over-serviced countries that there is only a small amount of *absolute* poverty in terms of people not being able to access sufficient calories to survive in principle, or because of the lack of sufficient (reasonably warm) shelter. Nevertheless, because of growing inequality of income distribution, homelessness and insecure housing does seem to be increasing in some countries; and, because many people are constrained by other circumstances (perhaps especially transport) shopping cheaply and healthily is often difficult (see, for example, Bradshaw, 1998).

But, for most countries, the crucial concern is now *relative* poverty (Kalisch, 1998; Wilkinson, 1996). However, one of the major causes of (relative) poverty is *ipso facto* the over-consumption (whether or not conspicuous) of the rich, consumption which is not generating or contributing – except in positional terms – even to their own welfare. There could therefore be considerable gain in welfare if that over-consumption were eliminated, or at least reduced substantially through taxation, with the proceeds channelled to the (relatively) poor. Eventually, of course, the need for social security would be very much reduced to a residual safety net because everyone's basic needs would be satisfied through the kind of arrangements discussed here.

6.4.5 Environment policies

These issues have been discussed in detail in Chapter 5, and will be discussed further in Chapter 9. Virtually all policy impacts on resource use and ecological damage (see Chapter 2) and an approach based on welfare entails a completely different attitude to environmental problems. Some of the consequences are discussed in Chapter 9, below. One policy area in particular may be mentioned here, because there is a widespread consensus that new policies are needed, and that is in the area of transport. Here vast (and ever increasing) resources are expended, with huge ecological impact, resulting in an inadequate (and for many people, declining) level of access. Two of the fundamental problems, when judged by the criteria of contributing to welfare or not, are the pointlessness of many journeys undertaken, and the lack of an effective public transport policy.

6.4.6 Law and order policies

With an emphasis on consumerism and the current distribution of income and wealth – exacerbated by the criminalisation of drug users[7] – there will inevitably be substantial levels of property crimes, and this has been the experience over the last few decades. If US history is a guide, these trends are probably being exacerbated by the current 'no work no welfare' policies, which may if anything be contributing to an ever-expanding prison population. While not satisfying the canons of experimental evidence, the increase in the prison population in the US from 1 million to 2 million in just 10 years, together with their racial/class composition and the fact that the Prison Service is one of the largest employers in the US, is an unhappy illustration of the kind of useless employment that is generated by current economic and social arrangements.

Another worrying trend is the increasing availability to the state of surveillance techniques. However, to be effective, they require substantial manpower (for example, to collate and interpret data) and many would question the ethics as well as the sense of employing ever more people to control – at a distance – what we do. At the same time, community support function of the police is being steadily eroded (if indeed it ever existed). The USSR example, where there were 15 million 'statisticians' out of a population of 200 million, is a cautionary example for ourselves.

In principle, at least in the long term, if the emphasis shifted away from consumerism, while income and wealth were more equally distributed, one would expect that healthy communities could resolve their own problems so that both safety and security would be enhanced. We recognise that certain sorts of problems can arise, for example, in the case of vigilantes when the effectiveness of community policing or adequate welfare policies are perceived as failing, but that may also be more prevalent in a situation where one group has or aspires for power.

6.5 Conclusion

Our earlier arguments showed that current patterns of consumption and employment were not conducive to welfare and that the corresponding levels of economic activity were ecologically unsustainable. While measuring the levels of economic activity is relatively uncontentious, there are several different views over how to measure welfare.

After reviewing theoretically based systems, empirically bases, we argue for a more eclectic approach in which we should assess the impact of administrative, political and social arrangements on the individual quality of life in terms of:

- being (knowledge and health);
- having (basic necessities);
- doing (human activities);
- relating (social environment);
- surviving (environment, safety).

In addition, we argue that, collectively, we are concerned both with inequality and human rights, and that, while again relatively uncontentious in terms of measurement, we should not forget to monitor levels of production, consumption and pollution.

In the latter part of this chapter, we showed how the formulation of concerns in terms of welfare provided a base for a substantial critique of current government policies. Indeed, we have suggested a large number of areas in which welfare could probably be *improved* by reducing consumption and activity. Once again we repeat that we recognise that our definition of welfare, while relatively uncontroversial, will not necessarily be shared by everyone, but we have aimed to illustrate the consequence of following an approach which focuses on (aggregate) human welfare rather than on macro-economic indicators.

The following three chapters discuss more specifically the implications of a welfare and ecologically-oriented society. In the next chapter we ask which, among this large variety of possibilities for increasing welfare through reducing consumption and activity, are most likely to have the most impact on reducing ecological damage? In the following chapter we suggest ways in which we could monitor progress or retrogression towards such a society by showing how sets of indicators based on these concerns could be developed. The final chapter returns to the issue of how (and whether) we might get there.

7
Orders of Magnitude of Change

7.1 Introduction

We have argued in Chapters 2 to 4 that our present social order is wasteful, unsustainable and destructive of human welfare. We have argued that a shift to evaluating policies in terms of human welfare rather than output growth – with welfare understood as a broad set of social concerns, rather than as an automatic consequence of output growth – leads to the conclusion that the major direction of change should be towards reduced economic activity.[1]

At the end of the previous chapter, we suggested that in terms of welfare, far from impoverishment, a strategy of lower consumption could offer multiple benefits. This chapter is an attempt to illustrate and make more concrete the implications of such a strategy. The first part illustrates the implications of reducing output and consumption for environment and employment, using the UK as an example. While we don't know precisely what is necessary to achieve sustainability, we outline potential areas for radical reductions in activity that would drastically reduce ecological damage while maintaining welfare. We then show how the reductions in activity work through the economy to: (a) reduce greenhouse gas emissions (GGEs); and (b) employment. The reductions we suggest may seem extreme. However, much of what might appear strange in our proposals is simply because, as a society, we have moved so far away from a focus on welfare. In fact, seen from the welfare viewpoint, it is the emphasis on consumption and growth, continuing well beyond what is necessary for welfare or sustainable ecologically, which is extreme.

As we emphasised in Chapter 6 (and see also Chapter 8), the process of attempting to identify dimensions of welfare and drawing conclusions about where it would be desirable to cut consumption should be a democratic political process. In addition, as we shall see, the best estimates of the effects of consumption cuts on employment and environment are bound to be fairly approximate. So this first section is intended to be both subjective and illustrative. Nevertheless, it has the advantage of raising, in a concrete way, issues about how far we can and should reduce consumption and what the effects will be, and it adds to the evidence that it is at least possible to make large reductions in consumption.

Of course this approach has a number of limitations, in addition to its subjective nature. In the second part of the chapter, therefore, we look at the experience of other countries, many of which (using well-known non-economic measures) achieve similar levels of basic welfare to our own with a fraction of the per capita GDP and ecological impact.

7.2 Reducing consumption in rich countries: some general principles

In Chapter 5 we argued that orthodox solutions which promote ever-increasing consumption will merely make the problems worse. While, at least in the rich countries, many people's jobs have become less unpleasant, and more people try to improve the environment both for themselves[2] and others, overall, both trends stand to be overwhelmed by the continuous drive for more consumption.

Where should we look for substantial decreases in consumption? Essentially, among the possible reductions in consumption of goods and services. We need to look for those which: (1) make little or no contribution to welfare; and (2) whose production is labour intensive, and/or (3) environmentally damaging. The discussion of earlier chapters suggests some promising targets: areas such as transport which have a large positional element; low skilled and low paid service jobs ('McJobs'); and activities with a particularly serious environmental impact, notably the major energy users.

There are also a number of knock-on effects whereby production and consumption themselves lead to further production and consumption – of what are in effect 'intermediate' goods.[3] Jobs and consumption in one industry necessitate jobs and consumption in other industries. This implies that if a set of goods and jobs can be dispensed with, so can a further set dependent on the first. More difficult to document or quantify, but probably at least as important, is the amount of work that has been created in leisure industries to compensate for the stress and boredom of employment.

Much employment and output, especially in the public sector, can be regarded as a kind of 'repair and maintenance' of the social system.[4] Yet, aside from the general point that an undesirable system should be replaced rather than repaired and maintained, much of the need for maintenance stems from consumerism, unemployment, environmental damage, and related problems, and would thus become largely redundant if these were reduced.

The expansion of employment and consumption has not only led to many new activities, but also to the commercialisation of many activities hitherto outside the formal economy. Some of these, while useful or necessary, are better done for free, and perhaps cannot be done properly except for free, because doing them well requires a high degree of personal involvement. Examples include caring, artistic activities and decision-making activities. The shorter working time that would result from reduced production and consumption would make the de-commercialisation of such activities feasible.

Finally, there are other reasons, which do not fit into the categories discussed above, for abandoning certain jobs and the goods that they produce. Deliberate government policies to create jobs, for example (whether directly, as in various youth employment schemes, or more indirectly, for example, through demand management), no longer make sense if the strategy adopted is to: (a) reduce employment; and (b) share the remaining work more equally. In other cases, as already happens, certain activities may be judged sufficiently harmful – particularly to human health, to the ecosystem, or to animal welfare – that individual consumer sovereignty, as expressed in the market, should be overruled by collective sovereignty expressed through the political system.

7.3 Reductions in consumption not contributing to welfare

We have already mentioned several components of consumption which do not contribute to welfare as defined above. If this were the only criterion then we would be focusing mainly on the major areas of consumption which have a large positional or relational element (see Chapter 4), and which reduce the welfare of those on low incomes while only maintaining and not increasing that of the rich and so do not contribute to aggregate welfare. The principal examples here are the educational system, (package) tourism and transport.

However, given that the original rationales for being concerned about replacing a focus on output-oriented growth with a focus on welfare are the current levels of environmental damage and the obsession with alienating employment, we are also concerned: (a) to reduce drastically ecological damage; and (b) to eliminate pointless jobs. We therefore need to search for those sectors where these impacts can be reduced substantially.

The measure we have used for assessing environmental damage is the volume of greenhouse gas emissions (GGEs); for an explanation of this measure, see page 155. The basic data for this and for employment has been extracted from the UK Environment Input–Output tables (EIO) and from the Annual Employment Survey (AES) respectively. Details about both the data and the calculations are given in the annex to this chapter (pp. 161–7).

For the purposes of the argument in this chapter, we show, in Table 7.1, the industries whose products[5] account for either more than 1 per cent (17 million tonnes) of GGEs or more than 1 per cent (200 000) of jobs (or both); and which are not obviously essential (as are, for example, agriculture, sewage and water supplies). Note that, for the purposes of calculating which sectors are above the criterion, some of the sectors that are distinguished in the UK Environmental Input–Output tables annexed to this chapter have been combined (for example, clothing sectors and electricity generating sectors).

Table 7.1 The most ecologically and/or socially costly industries

	Product sector code number	*Greenhouse gas emissions (000)*	*Employment (000 jobs)*
Food processing	8	34 513	476
Clothing	10–12	7 341	395
Coal, electricity, gas	4, 51–56	93 347	144
Construction	58	27 695	948
Wholesale + retail trade except motor vehicles	60–61	35 810	2 860
Hotels and restaurants	62	14 553	1 134
Air transport	70	20 078	62
Financial services	73–75	11 968	990
Real estate	76	4 361	274
Other business	80	3 191	2 008
Public administration	81	14 398	1 052
Public administration – 'defence'	82	13 146	132
Education	83	9 554	1 497
Health	84	24 706	2 145
Leisure	89	7 199	459

The remainder of this section looks at the main categories of consumption in terms of what could be reduced while probably improving welfare and certainly not decreasing it. As we have made clear, our choices involve a large subjective element, with many unknowns involved and much scope for experimentation. It should be emphasised that we are concerned with the relatively long term. Although some consumption cuts could be made immediately, some could only be introduced over a longer period, a couple of generations. There is no way that humankind can plan this far ahead. Nevertheless, we can only move in the direction of a more sustainable and welfare-oriented pattern of consumption if we have some idea, however tentative, of the desired end result.

The notes that follow outline the thinking behind the cuts we propose in Table 7.2.[6] While many of our proposed cuts are substantial, the justification tends to be brief. This is precisely because of the subjectivity and uncertainties involved; a lengthier argument would have been mostly speculation. We hope that, given this explanation, the reader will excuse our brevity.

Food processing (8)

Eating habits have a large positional element in so far as individuals tend to be influenced by what other people around them eat. This is to say nothing of the increasing number of TV cooking programmes, as well as international travel. There are strong ecological, animal welfare and health arguments for eating less meat, for a move away from processed foods towards fresh food, and towards locally available and seasonal food. While immediate 'local availability' may be a problem in major conurbations, this is not a licence for ignoring foods produced nationally in favour of exotic imported foods. In addition, shorter working hours would allow more time for food preparation and even for gardening.

Health data indicate that many people in developed countries overeat, and we largely over-process our food (and waste a lot of it). On the other hand, if we are to eat better quality and less polluted food, we have to avoid the unnecessary adulteration of our food and this means that we have to change our pattern of consumption and production. Although this is linked to the fact that we import a large proportion of our food, we have not, in this analysis, argued that we should become self-sufficient. Instead, we have argued that we have to devote some paid employment to exports to pay for food imports. In the longer term, however, we might want to argue for self-sufficiency.

Table 7.2 Reductions in consumer and government spending

Consumer and government expenditure (non-travel)	*Percentage reduction*	*Reduction in GGEs (000 tonnes)*	*Reduction in employment (000 jobs)*
4 Coal extraction, etc.	20	471	1
8 Manufacture of food and beverages	50	14 334	335
10 Textiles	50	1 210	49
11 Wearing apparel, dressing and dyeing of fur	50	959	70
12 Leather tanning	50	223	13
51 Electricity production – gas	20	1 501	2
52 Electricity production – coal	20	11 884	11
53 Electricity production – nuclear	20	1 573	6
54 Electricity production – oil	20	1 241	2
55 Electricity production – other	20	106	0
56 Gas distribution	20	2 030	11
58 Construction	65	1 611	78
60 Wholesale trade and commission trade, except motor vehicles	30	3 725	186
61 Retail and repair trade, except motor vehicles	30	3 961	591
62 Hotels and restaurants	50	5 905	542
70 Air transport	90	656	5
73 Financial intermediates, except insurance and pensions	90	1 853	202
74 Insurance and pension funding	90	5 658	404
75 Activities auxiliary to financial intermediation	90	405	39
76 Real estate activities	90	3 791	360
80 Other business activities	20	106	18
81 Public administration – not defence	50	7 199	847
82 Public administration – defence	95	12 489	363
83 Education	50	4 620	584
84 Health and veterinary services, social work	50	12 242	1 217

Table 7.2 (*Contd.*)

Consumer and government expenditure (non-travel)	*Percentage reduction*	*Reduction in GGEs (000 tonnes)*	*Reduction in employment (000 jobs)*
89 Recreational, cultural, sporting activities	30	1924	162
All consumer expenditure (non-travel-related)		101638	6112
Consumer expenditure (travel-related)	90	28406	1065
Fuel use by consumers:			
Domestic fuel use	20	18064	0
Motor vehicle use	90	51939	0
Total reduction:		**200046**	**7165**
Current total:		**691708**	**21172**
Reduction as percentage of current usage:		**29**	**34**

On the basis of agricultural products alone, it is unlikely that there would be any significant decrease of expenditure (although the pattern might shift substantially towards organic products). However, much of the processing of food would become redundant as people would have more time to cook from fresh foods rather than buying pre-packaged meals and of course the same comment is true for hotels and restaurants, especially as we would expect the number of business travellers to decrease. At the same time, a substantial fraction of consumer expenditure on alcohol is Excise Tax in order to raise revenue for government activities; this would no longer be necessary given the substantial cuts in public administration that we are proposing.[7] A substantial drop in activity would therefore be possible.

Table 7.2 makes a 50 per cent cut in (8) manufacture of food products and beverages. Any compensating increase in (1) agriculture is assumed to be offset by, for example, reductions in meat eating and an increase in consuming home-grown vegetables.

Hotels and catering (62)

There is a substantial knock-on effect here from less employment, less commuting and less business travel. Table 7.2 makes a 50 per cent cut in (62) hotels and restaurants.

Clothing (10–12)

Fashion is essentially positional as well as being particularly sensitive to manipulation by commercial interests through advertising. People can own fewer clothes and wear them longer with no adverse effect on their welfare at all. There are also good animal welfare arguments against wearing hides and furs. Jackson and Marks (1999) have demonstrated a tenfold increase in the UK consumption of clothing over the 40 years to 1994. Much of that increase is in terms of 'designer' clothing which does not contribute to either comfort (when hot) or warmth (when cold) let alone welfare. At the same time, there are still large numbers of people without adequate clothing in winter and children without adequate and healthy footwear. Moreover, with increasing leisure time, more people might want to be able to use walking boots! While one might therefore envisage a very substantial cut in 'designer' clothing,[8] there would be a modest increase in terms of serviceable clothes for the older age group and in footwear, especially for children. It is, of course, very difficult to provide a 'golden mean', given projected decreases and increases, so we are simply suggesting that there could be a substantial diminution. Table 7.2 makes a 50 per cent cut in (10) textiles, (11) wearing apparel and dying of fur, (12) leather tanning, luggage and footwear.

Electricity and gas (51–56)

We mean by this electricity and gas bought by consumers rather than industry, transport, and other energy, except obviously that used to generate the electricity and produce the gas. Domestic fuel use (mostly for space heating) has a positional element. People turn up heating rather than wear warmer clothing as well as keeping heating high for guests. Table 7.2 makes a 20 per cent cut in (4) coal, (51)–(55) electricity production, (56) gas distribution, and also in domestic fuel use.[9]

Construction (58)

There is a relatively small but growing number of homeless people or people at risk of being homeless, and a significant lack of personal space. In addition, a small proportion of houses still lack basic amenities. These constitute a loss in welfare which can, at least in principle, be remedied.

In the short term, homelessness could be easily abolished by the renovation and re-use of existing housing stock. In the longer term, population movements (for example, away from the suburbs) may mean new building in the new destination areas, although this would be difficult in our crowded island (and made more difficult with any reduction in the road network). But, as well as general maintenance, both renovation and any new building works are likely to be increasingly on a DIY basis, as people have more time and energy, so that the main consumption required would be tools and materials.[10] The presumption is, however, that some paid employment on actual building for real people rather then speculative development would still be required.

Reduction in road transport implies a large cut in road construction. Cuts in production and consumption imply a corresponding cut in construction of industrial and commercial premises. A slower pace of economic change would encourage a move away from house building towards renovating, and generally reduce the need for new construction.

On the basis, then, of a considerably reduced market for speculative development and the considerably reduced demand for a road network, we would suggest there might be scope for a relatively substantial drop in activity. Table 7.2 makes a 65 per cent cut in (58) construction, to be concentrated in road construction and construction of industrial and commercial buildings (i.e. we are not suggesting cuts in small-scale home building).

Transport (63–71)

In addition to including a number of transport sectors, the EIO tables also account separately for the travel-related emissions of all the sectors. Here we are concerned with *all* reductions in transport. It should be noted that the EIO distinguish between 'travel-related' and 'not-travel-related' GGE emissions. 'Travel-related' emissions are 'the quantities of emissions arising solely from road vehicles owned and operated by industry' (Vaze, 1997).

Business travel will reduce, because electronic communication is cheaper. We would except demand for tourist air and road transport to decline steeply to be replaced with slower substitutes (see below and Chapter 9). However, use of bicycles would probably increase and we would need to make lanes safe by erecting barriers. People would still use the railways although with a much simplified and cheaper fare system. Railways are one of the few sectors where we would expect public expenditure to rise. Some travel by road in rural areas would still be necessary, although there would be less dependence on motorways.

The proposed reductions in Table 7.2 assume that cars are virtually eliminated from cities and for commuting. This would come as a result of more efficient zoning policies, more bicycle use and better collective transport. Longer distance travel would mainly use collective transport; air travel[11] would be largely replaced by sea or land travel; most freight transport would be by rail or boat; tourism would be more leisurely and over shorter distances. There are also knock-on effects from less employment and more time.

We have assumed these reductions to be equivalent to a 90 per cent cut in the travel-related categories of the EIO tables, except for railways, buses and coaches, tubes and trams, and taxis. Any increase in the latter, due to cuts in car and air travel, is assumed to be offset by reduction in travel overall. We also assume a 90 per cent cut in motor vehicle use, without any concomitant loss of welfare.

Distribution (60–61)

Given that the volume of goods to be distributed will be reduced, then we would expect a more or less proportional cut in the level of distribution activity. Table 7.2 makes a 30 per cent cut in (60) wholesale trade and (61) retail trade.

Financial Services (73–75)

The financial sector in the main can be described as unproductive. It fails in its textbook role of oiling the wheels of industry, and the 'financial discipline' it exerts (some of the time) on the rest of the economy serves mainly to keep it on a growth-oriented path. It is also often blamed for discouraging environmental and social protection by ensuring that capital is invested in those countries which have the least, and the least enforced, regulation of pollution, and of working conditions. Allowing for a small number of useful functions, Table 7.2 makes a 90 per cent cut in (73) financial intermediation, (74) insurance, (75) activities auxiliary to financial intermediation, and (76) real estate activities.

Advertising/marketing (80)

Most advertising and marketing is 'persuasive' rather than 'informative': it is designed to persuade consumers to buy things they would not otherwise want. It would be desirable to eliminate not only most advertising, but also any additional consumption which it may stimulate; the latter is however largely a matter for speculation. Table 7.2 makes a 20 per cent cut in (80) other business activities (the category which includes advertising).

Other public administration (81)

Some public administration would have to remain in order to regulate many of the reductions that we are proposing. But public administration jobs that become redundant as a consequence of downsizing the economy could certainly be cut. Table 7.2 makes a 50 per cent cut in (81) (non-defence) public administration.

Defence (82)

No one claims that war is good for welfare. Moreover, what goes by the name of 'defence' is in fact often to do with aggression, or at least to do with aggressively promoting a country's global influence. Thus, during the post-World War 2 years, the UK, through high military spending, has attempted to maintain a role in world affairs out of all proportion with its size. Although spending declined in the 1990s, it is still high (around US$500 per head), compared to most countries not at war. The cuts we propose are based on a radical change in the UK's military role, and in its dealings with other countries generally. We envisage a new relationship with other countries, based on cultural exchange and leisurely travel, thereby providing the opportunity to get to know other people, and only a modest amount of trade and other economic interaction. This will enable military spending to be dedicated entirely to genuine defence, and thus to reduce to a very small proportion of its current level. Like many of the changes we propose, this would take time, but it could certainly be achieved over a generation. Reducing per capita military expenditure to about $15 per capita (that is, by 97 per cent) would bring the UK in line with a country such as Costa Rica, which scores highly on basic welfare indicators, and which has remained at peace over the last few decades while war has raged in neighbouring countries. Table 7.2 makes a 95 per cent cut in (82) defence public administration.

Education (83)

Education has a large positional element, where it neither 'educates for life' nor trains for a specific job, but acts merely as a system of selection for jobs. It also has a large ideological component, including inculcating a work-and-consume ethic, which mainly makes it part of the 'repair and maintenance' of the system. Some early education has a child-minding role, so that less would be required (from the formal economy) if adults – especially men, many of whom have managed to avoid the bulk of child care – had more (non-employed) time. Some other (currently formal) education might be better done informally (Illich, 1973).

There is undoubtedly a steady inflation of qualifications. Current policies and a variety of other pressures, of the positional kind discussed in Chapter 4, encourage that trend and mean that further qualifications – however irrelevant to living a satisfying life – are in ever greater demand.

We do not envisage substantial cuts in primary or basic secondary education (the first few years), because these educational sectors do perform important socialising functions. However, there are many reasons to change what kind of socialisation is done and how. There is a strong case to be made for altering the nature of learning, making it far less focused than it is currently on examinations with far fewer specialised resources required. Less pressurised teaching for examinations would reduce the amount of 'cramming' and allow time and space for more enjoyable learning.

At a tertiary level, however, one would want to move as quickly as possible to learning for its own sake, rather than just for qualifications. Some exceptions for professional and technical skills would have to be made since these may still require some form of examinations. On the whole, however, we believe that much of current resources are dispensable. Table 7.2 makes a 50 per cent cut in (83) education.

Health care (84)

For some time, it has been clear that the health care system has only a marginal effect on longevity and (the reduction of) morbidity (see, for example, McKeown, 1936). Moreover, many existing medical interventions are of little use. According to some estimates, as much as 75 per cent fall into this category and a significant proportion of health care expenditure provides profits for the medical technology and pharmaceutical industries. Unsurprisingly, the latter are, of course, committed to further expansion.

Much treatment for illness and accidents results from (excessive) employment, and would not be required if employment time, and the associated stresses, were reduced. Although there might be more accidents from increased DIY activities, there would be fewer pollution-related health problems. If there is less employment there will be less travel to work and much of that travel would not be constrained by time so that proportionately more people would cycle or walk to work. In general, less employment could be part of an approach emphasising prevention and lifestyle factors since these influence health more than health care and social work. Indeed, a network of primary health promotion workers would be much more effective. Reduced employment would also leave more time for caring for ill and older people to be done outside the formal economy and once again men could take their proper role in this.

Emergency services would, of course, still be required, as well as some facilities for looking after the seriously ill, and we would still need to maintain continuing treatment for chronic conditions such as diabetes and asthma.[12]

On the other hand, the concern with child development suggests that we may want to spend more on public health. Broadly conceived this might well include expenditure on health education and renovating housing rather than in the health sector. Similarly, we might want to spend more on research for new therapies. Table 7.2 makes a 50 per cent cut in (84) health (which in fact includes mainly health care and social work) and veterinary services.

Leisure facilities (89)

Much commercialised leisure activity has a positional element and many other activities can be argued to be largely a compensation for under-stimulating employment, where, for example, exercise compensates for a sedentary job, or outdoor activities for a job spent indoors. Table 7.2 makes a 30 per cent cut in (89) recreational activities.

Other possibilities

Government job creation schemes and the military are not included in the employment data used, and have not therefore been included. So have other possibilities, including cuts in, for example (15) publishing (26) pharmaceuticals (27) soap and detergents, and (31) plastic (the first and last are particularly relevant to packaging). The effects of the media, which may not have serious employment or environmental impacts themselves, but may help promote attitudes and sell goods that do, have also not been included.

7.4 Reducing consumption in the UK: some illustrative figures

The implication of the arguments in the preceding section is that we could plan for a wide range of reductions in consumption which would substantially reduce greenhouse gas emissions (GGEs) and employment. The orders of magnitude of the impact on GGEs and employment of the consumption reductions summarised in Table 7.2, above, and are estimated and discussed there.

Ideally, a policy of consumption cuts would be decided through some suitable democratic political process. In the absence of such a process we can only provide an example based on our own preferences. These are not arbitrary, and Chapter 6 and the first part of this chapter have provided some justification for the general pattern of consumption cuts proposed here, though not for particular percentages. Detailed information about calculation methods has been provided in the annex to this chapter. Readers may wish to make their own estimates using this information and the published sources on the basis of their own preferred consumption cuts (or increases!). In a more general way, the annex to this chapter (see Table 7.5 on p. 163) lists the impacts of different industrial sectors, and thus provides an overview of cuts and where they will really make a difference.

The justification for using GGEs as an indicator of ecological impact or risk is that, apart from the likely seriousness of the threat of climate change, GGEs are highly correlated with fossil fuel use and with other ecological threats and nuisances. Moreover, the measures required to reduce GGEs would also help solve a lot of other problems: reducing car use, for example, would affect quality of life in a wide range of ways, from congestion and mobility to respiratory disease and convivial street life. Calculations of the GGE impact are based on the 'Environmental input–output tables for the United Kingdom' (EIO), published in November 1997.[13] Greenhouse gas emissions only are considered here, although it would be easy to extend the calculations to the other air pollution sources covered by the tables. Standard data sources were used to calculate the employment impact. In addition, calculations were made of the impact of corresponding reductions in investment, and of reductions in exports made possible by the reduced imports required (see the Annex to this chapter for further details). The initial and knock-on impacts are summarised in Table 7.3. The effects of the reductions in consumer and government spending, discussed in the previous section, are detailed in Table 7.2. The effect of reductions in all final demand sectors is summarised in Table 7.3.

The data do not allow one to trace the impact of the innumerable, but individually often small, possible consumption reductions, nor all the possible knock-on effects. To get some sense of the magnitudes involved, one has to compensate by hitting the more obvious targets particularly hard. Reductions of 40–50 per cent in both GGEs and employment are arrived at very largely by almost eliminating activity in three sectors, cars, aeroplanes and financial services. If this is thought to be too

Table 7.3 Reductions in all final demand sectors

Reductions	*GGEs (tonnes 000)*	*%*	*Employment (jobs 000)*	*%*
Initial, non-travel-related expenditure	101 638	15	6 100	29
Initial, travel-related expenditure	28 406	4	1 065	5
Domestic fuel use	18 064	3	0	0
Motor vehicle use	51 939	8	0	0
Investment	17 882	3	859	4
Exports	103 563	15	1 302	6
All reductions	321 492	46	9 326	44
Current level	691 708	100	21 172	100

Note: This table includes only those activity codes with substantial expenditure, GGEs or jobs.

extreme, it would be possible to replace this partly by cuts in a number of areas which have been left untouched here.

Obviously the process of chipping away at areas of consumption, whose costs are large but whose benefits are dubious, could be continued, and other knock-on effects could be identified, resulting perhaps in further cuts of 10–20 per cent in both GGEs and employment. But the intention is to arrive at a rough order of magnitude.

What should be emphasised however is that these cuts are *in addition* to what may be achieved through more efficient production methods and product designs (see note 4). This includes improvements not only in technology, but also in organisation. For example, employees may choose to work faster and better, where this results in shorter hours, rather than to do more work, for the same pay. There are huge opportunities for reducing working hours per person through sharing necessary work more widely, since as working hours fall it becomes possible for increasing numbers of people to combine employment with other activities. Something like a doubling of the workforce, to include current home workers and students, and many older and younger people, is easy to envisage.

7.5 Starting from the present situation and counting down

The estimates of the environmental and employment impact of consumption reduction that are presented here are intended to have a limited, illustrative value. But they do suggest the vital role that reducing consumption has to play in achieving sustainability. If 'Factor Four' improvements are feasible, relying on technological improvements alone, but 'Factor Ten' improvements are required, then a 'Factor Two-point-five' reduction in consumption is required as well as factor four technological improvement to bridge the gap. The scenario we have presented suggests, we think, that such a reduction is both possible and desirable.

The 'counting down' approach has some advantages. Studies sometimes just assume that reductions of, say, 2 per cent a year in consumption can be made without providing concrete examples of the type of changes which will have to underlie such a strategy. Yet over a generation 2 per cent a year implies halving consumption, and the question arises – which half? We have tried to provide a tentative answer. And of course any strategy for change will have to start from the present situation. But there are also disadvantages in 'counting down' from the existing situation. It is difficult to specify the changes involved in general terms without getting bogged down in details. Available data have many limitations, including in particular using very broad product categories. The complex interdependence of consumption patterns makes it virtually impossible to trace all the effects of a particular change. The credibility of the type of scenario presented is limited because it involves moving away from the known, real situation to what is, at least for the time being, an imaginary one.

Counting up

In estimating the minimum consumption necessary for a high level of welfare, we did consider an alternative approach which attempted to count up from zero. The problem was that we tended to arrive at an unrealistically and unconvincingly low amount. This seems to be because of the dependence of any estimate on cultural and other assumptions, and these are bound to be arbitrary when 'starting from zero'. When counting down from the present situation, we can reasonably assume that social norms, including things such as eating habits, standards of comfort, and the extent of the division of labour, will change only gradually. In the area of food, for example, we suggested above that people might eat less meat, and more locally produced and less processed food. What assumptions are we to make when counting up? Whether people eat as they do now, eat as cheaply as possible, eat as ecologically as possible, or grow all their own food, will make all the difference to the result. In the last case of course, consumer expenditure on food would be reduced by 100 per cent, as would employment and, very nearly, depending on methods used, GGEs.

Table 7.4 World consumption classes, 1992

Category of consumption	*Consumers (1.1 billion)*	*Middle (3.3 billion)*	*Poor (1.1 billion)*
Diet	Meat, packaged food, soft drinks	Grain, clean water	Insufficient grain, unsafe water
Transport	Private cars	Bicycles, buses	Walking
Materials	Throwaways	Durables	Local biomass

Source: Worldwatch Institute, 1992 (Durning, 1992, p. 27).

Global inequalities

Of course it is not a matter of glorifying very low consumption levels *per se*; on the contrary, lower consumption by the rich would make it possible to *increase* the very low levels of consumption by the world's poor. Indeed, another approach to estimating the possibilities of reducing ecological damage is based on precisely those principles of equity.

This is the point which Table 7.4 reproduced from Durning (1992, p. 27) makes in a simple but concrete way. If 'consumers' (the world's richest fifth) adopted the simpler, but adequate, consumption pattern of the 'middles' (the middle three-fifths), this would free more than enough resources for the poor to adopt this pattern also. Durning also reports that the shares of world income of these consumption classes are 64 per cent, 33 per cent and 2 per cent (using purchasing power parities, explained below). This enables us to make a rough calculation of the impact that redistribution would have. If the 'consumers' and 'poor' adopted the consumption pattern of the 'middle', they would each consume 11 per cent (based on 1992 world income), and total consumption would be 55 per cent (11 + 33 + 11) of 1992 world income. In round numbers, total income, consumption and ecological impact would decline by 45 per cent, consumption by the poor would increase by a factor of 5.5, and consumption by 'consumers' would decline by a factor of 5.8. This suggests that a reasonable level of consumption for all is possible for about half the current ecological damage – even aside from any improvement in ecological efficiency.

7.6 The experience of other countries

These sorts of consideration raise the question whether the real experience of other, less overdeveloped, countries might provide a more realistic view of the amount of consumption required to achieve a high level of welfare. There is a pleasing irony in seeking development models for the 'rich' countries among those which are 'poor'.

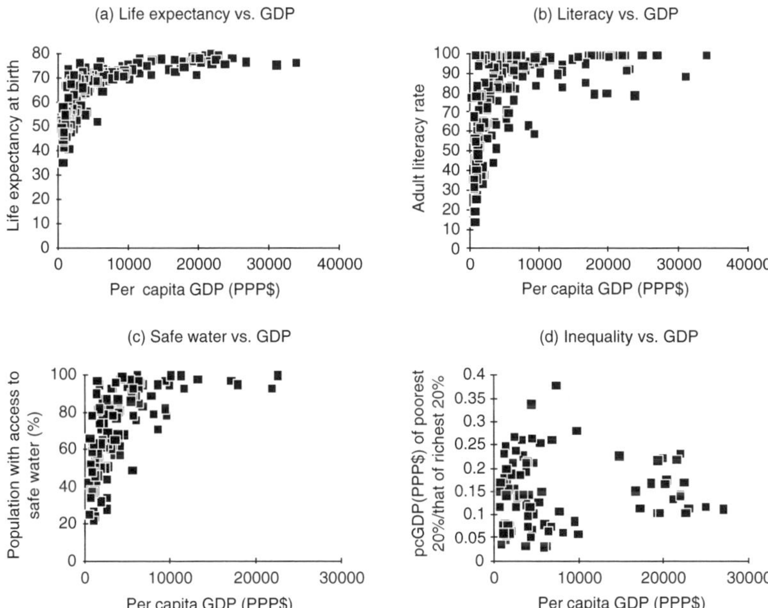

Figure 7.1 Welfare indicators and GDP

Source: UNDP (1998).

Figure 7.1 is intended to shed some light on the relation, or variety of relations, between consumption and some basic aspects of welfare. Based on Human Development Report data (UNDP, 1998), it uses per capita GDP at purchasing power parities as a proxy for consumption. The figure shows data for only a few welfare indicators. These have been chosen because there is a degree of consensus about the indicators' validity as measures of some aspect of welfare; but there are other cases where there is general agreement about the importance of an aspect of welfare (for example, social relations, or risk of physical attack) but no agreed, satisfactory measure seems to exist. The data on which Figure 7.1 is based, including population, age and income, are extremely unreliable for many countries (see Carr-Hill, 1990 regarding the countries of sub-Saharan Africa). Such weaknesses in the data, however, are generalised across countries and so do not detract significantly from the relation (or lack of relation) between consumption and welfare which the figure suggests.

All the same, the figure serves to illustrate a few simple points. A common pattern, illustrated by Figure 7.1 (a) and (b), seems to be that for low levels of per capita GDP/consumption, there is quite a strong relationship between consumption and the kind of basic welfare indicators displayed in the figure; past a certain point, however, there is little or no relation, and there are many examples of low-income countries that nevertheless achieve high welfare levels. On the basis of this data, a per capita GDP of PPP$5 000[14] (the world average is about PPP$6 000) would be more than enough to ensure a similar level of welfare as even the most overdeveloped countries manage. Particular countries or regions of countries (Kerala, India which has a per capita GDP of about PPP$1400 being a well-known example; see UNDP, 1996, p. 81. Other examples are Cuba, Sri Lanka and Taiwan) may provide an illustration of how it is possible to achieve such welfare levels with even lower consumption than that suggested.

A similar pattern exists for other similar indicators not shown here, such as per capita daily calorie intake, and the percentage of the population surviving beyond the age of 40. Figure 7.1(c) may be taken as representative of basic environmental indicators of welfare. It too suggests – as does access to sanitation, for example – that high levels of welfare can be combined with low levels of consumption. Figure 7.1(d), which plots a measure of inequality against GDP, displays a different pattern, where low consumption can be associated with anything from great inequality to relative equality. There is no more a clear relation between consumption levels and welfare than in the other cases, but the data do emphasise another point: just as important as the lack of positive GDP-welfare correlation, is the large range of GDP-welfare combinations which are possible. It certainly seems possible to increase consumption, and the associated ecological impacts and risks, indefinitely without significant improvement in welfare.

7.7 Conclusion

We have not attempted a comprehensive assessment of the impact of lower consumption. Nevertheless, the crude estimates presented suggest that large improvements in both ecological and employment terms are possible through consumption reduction alone – with a concomitant gain in welfare. Some of this potential has been illustrated in the case of one rich country, the UK. Perhaps more revealing is the experience of other countries. This experience gives little support to the idea that consumption beyond a modest threshold amount brings benefits, let alone benefits that offset the undoubted costs.

This is the case without considering the considerable efficiency improvements which are possible through redirecting technological progress and better design, both of which have been the subject of much discussion, but which will be easily offset if tendencies towards consumption growth (particularly by the already relatively rich) are not reversed.

7.8 Annex: calculation details

All calculations were based on environmental input–output tables and official employment figures. These are blunt instruments, in as much as the categories they use, often very broad in any case, are not the most appropriate ones for our purposes. Calculations are therefore in places approximate, but aim to avoid systematic bias. The term 'intensity' is used to refer to the level per £ million of the activity, and the term 'impact' to refer to the absolute level given the volume of activity.

7.8.1 The UK environmental input–output tables (EIO)

In recent years, the UK government has published a set of environmental input–output tables, which are used here. They are based on data for 1993. Standard input–output matrices, such as a use matrix and Leontief inverse, are included. Intensity of emissions of various air pollutants are also included, in two versions: as 'direct emission intensities', which measure the emissions resulting directly from the activity of each industry; and as 'direct and indirect emission intensities' resulting from making all the products used by the industry as well. The latter allow reductions in emissions resulting from cuts in final demand to be easily calculated, and these are the ones used here.

Emissions have also been grouped into a figure for 'greenhouse gas emissions' (GGE), which is what is used here. These 'are calculated by summing emissions of CO_2, CH_4, and N_2O weighted by their Global Warming Potentials at 100 years' (Vaze, 1997, p. 42).

The usual final demand categories have been used, but in addition consumer expenditure is divided into travel and non-travel related. Industrial classification is based on SIC (Standard Industrial Classification) 92, but with a few categories further disaggregated, notably electricity generation (by different fuels) and sewage.

7.8.2 Employment intensities

Analogous direct plus indirect employment intensities were estimated for the EIO product groups. Direct employment intensities were derived from published data, then multiplied by the EIO Leontief inverse. The best source of disaggregated employment figures is the Annual Employment Survey (AES), published in *Employment Gazette* (for a description and assessment, see Pease, 1997). Data for 1995 were used since previous years' data were based on SIC 80. Allocation of employment data to EIO categories was generally unproblematic, but in cases like electricity

Table 7.5 Industrial sectors, intensities and impacts

Product classification	*Intensities*		*Impacts*	
	Greenhouse gas emissions (tonnes/£m)	*Employment (jobs/£m)*	*Greenhouse gas emissions (000 tonnes)*	*Employment (000 jobs)*
1 Agriculture	2633	18	16352	340
2 Forestry	376	45	9	12
3 Fishing	1243	11	293	6
4 Coal extraction, etc.	9514	6	1668	12
5 Extraction of crude oil and natural gas	1625	2	6611	29
6 Extraction – metal ores	11597	4	65	0
7 Minerals and quarrying	1667	12	2568	33
8 Manufacture of food and beverages	1157	10	34513	476
9 Tobacco products	1040	4	2045	8
10 Textiles	899	23	3910	194
11 Wearing apparel, dressing and dyeing of fur	645	33	2730	159
12 Leather tanning	602	21	701	42
13 Timber, wood products	704	23	341	86
14 Pulp, paper and paperboard	2707	45	1420	133
15 Articles of paper, printing and publishing	582	16	4680	370
16 Coke oven products	34655	7	562	1
17 Refined petroleum products	3346	2	12003	19
18 Processing of nuclear fuel	997	10	323	13
19 Industrial gases, dyes, pigments	1952	11	1165	18
20 Inorganic chemicals	2197	8	920	11
21 Organic chemicals	7861	7	16939	28
22 Fertilisers	1925	5	155	3

Table 7.5 (Contd.)

Product classification	Intensities		Impacts	
	Greenhouse gas emissions (tonnes/£m)	*Employment (jobs/£m)*	*Greenhouse gas emissions (000 tonnes)*	*Employment (000 jobs)*
23 Plastics, synthetic rubber, primary form	1 893	7	1 801	25
24 Pesticides, agro-chemicals	1 515	3	775	4
25 Paints, dyes, printing ink, etc.	1 181	11	742	24
26 Pharmaceuticals	875	9	3 053	69
27 Soap and toilet preparations	1 001	10	3 413	45
28 Chemical products not elsewhere specified	1 328	12	2 732	46
29 Man-made fibres	2 884	9	921	6
30 Rubber products	1 095	19	1 033	53
31 Plastic products	1 083	19	2 213	192
32 Glass and glass products	1 663	21	828	42
33 Ceramic goods	994	30	768	49
34 Structural clay products	3 467	26	499	13
35 Cement, lime and plaster	17 071	7	2 469	6
36 Articles of concrete, etc.	1 692	16	946	50
37 Iron and steel	4 651	9	11 968	74
38 Non-ferrous metals	1 537	7	1 296	18
39 Non-ferrous, aluminium	1 844	10	635	14
40 Casting of metals	1 461	27	61	40
41 Fabricated metal products; except machinery	936	28	6 597	462
42 Machinery and equipment	829	19	12 256	438
43 Office machinery and computers	413	7	2 486	57
44 Electrical machinery and apparatus	688	19	3 272	186
45 Radio, television and communications	569	17	2 727	135

Table 7.5 (Contd.)

Product classification	Intensities		Impacts	
	Greenhouse gas emissions (tonnes/£m)	Employment (jobs/£m)	Greenhouse gas emissions (000 tonnes)	Employment (000 jobs)
46 Medical, precision and optical instruments, watches and clocks	508	22	2392	160
47 Motor vehicles, trailers and semi-trailers	718	10	11871	225
48 Other transport equipment	532	15	2862	167
49 Manufacture of furniture, toys, sports equipment and other	772	22	3813	154
50 Recycling	880	31	893	52
51 Electricity production – gas	10452	3	7531	6
52 Electricity production – coal	14636	3	59419	48
53 Electricity production – nuclear	3582	3	7889	24
54 Electricity production – oil	10511	4	6226	8
55 Electricity production – other	3779	5	532	2
56 Gas distribution	1789	5	10109	44
57 Water supply	958	17	1725	51
58 Construction	602	13	27695	948
59 Garages, car showrooms	602	21	8675	454
60 Wholesale trade and commission trade, except motor vehicles	535	15	20320	857
61 Retail and repair trade, except motor vehicles	385	50	15490	2003
62 Hotels and restaurants	474	34	14553	1134
63 Railways	1569	33	3022	112
64 Buses and coaches	1998	38	5393	124

Table 7.5 (Contd.)

Product classification	Intensities		Impacts	
	Greenhouse gas emissions (tonnes/£m)	Employment (jobs/£m)	Greenhouse gas emissions (000 tonnes)	Employment (000 jobs)
65 Tubes and trams	2 620	51	1 630	35
66 Taxi operation	639	7	742	17
67 Freight transport by road	1 430	15	2 155	235
68 Transport via pipeline	331	34	0	1
69 Water transport	3 178	7	10 235	31
70 Air transport	2 924	7	20 078	62
71 Transport services	298	19	685	360
72 Communications	293	20	2 303	486
73 Financial intermediates, except insurance and pensions	247	15	3 296	596
74 Insurance and pension funding	410	7	7 193	213
75 Activities auxiliary to financial intermediation	416	24	1 479	181
76 Real estate activities	84	4	4 361	274
77 Renting of machinery	540	10	3 417	117
78 Computer and related activities	460	18	758	216
79 Research and development	388	20	243	84
80 Other business activities	260	30	3 191	2 008
81 Public administration – not defence	301	22	14 398	1 052
82 Public administration – defence	536	5	13 146	132
83 Education	345	39	9 554	1 497
84 Health and veterinary services, social work	463	29	24 706	2 145
85 Sewage	734	14	1 709	38
86 Solid waste	14 167	7	23 884	20

Table 7.5 (*Contd.*)

Product classification	*Intensities*		*Impacts*	
	Greenhouse gas emissions (tonnes/£m)	*Employment (jobs/£m)*	*Greenhouse gas emissions (000 tonnes)*	*Employment (000 jobs)*
87 Other sanitary services	610	4	280	2
88 Activities of membership organisations	284	37	695	149
89 Recreational, cultural, sporting activities	476	21	7 199	459
90 Other service activities	534	27	2 467	144
Consumer sectors				
Domestic fuel use			90 318	
Motor vehicle use			57 718	
Total:			**691 717**	**21 172**

generation and sewage they had to be allocated proportionately to output. But these are minor employers anyway, so the effect on overall results is certainly negligible.

While the EIO are based on product groups, the employment figures are based on industry groups. However, differences between the two are mostly small (less than 10 per cent); they are only larger for a few small industries. The overall impact of mixing the two classifications is therefore likely to be small. Some adjustment was made for working hours, which vary widely among industries, especially because of differing proportions of part-timers and overtime working. The adjustment was fairly crude, however, using figures for hours worked in broad sectors (manufacturing, distribution, services, and so on). An 'employee' in the calculations is a notional employee working a national average of 34.3 hours weekly.

Unfortunately the AES, though the best source otherwise, excludes the self-employed, work trainees on government schemes and the armed forces. The latter two are relatively small categories.

Table 7.5 gives the EIO product classification, the GGE intensities, the estimated employment intensities, and the current GGE and employment impacts, direct and indirect, of each product group. Note that the impacts listed are those resulting from *all* categories of final demand (consumer expenditure, travel- and non-travel-related, government expenditure, investment, stockbuilding and exports). This is in contrast to Tables 7.2 and 7.3, above, which consider the effects of reductions in each of these categories separately.

7.8.3 Calculation method

The calculations were done as follows. The impact of initial reductions in non-travel-related and travel-related consumer and government expenditure was calculated; and the effects of cutting GGEs due to consumer use (that is, domestic fuel use and motor vehicle use) were added (see Table 7.2, above).

To take investment in GDFCF (Gross Domestic Fixed Capital Formation) and in stocks: the data tell us which products were bought as part of investment, not which product groups did the buying. It is not possible therefore to reduce investment by each product group in proportion to reduction in consumption of its product. All that could be done was to reduce investment of all product groups in proportion to the decline in consumption in general. It was assumed that, after a period of adjustment, investment would settle down at a lower level, in proportion to the lower consumption level. This is conservative, in as much as a steady state economy might be expected to have a still lower level of net investment.

In terms of trade, the data do not allow one to estimate GGE and employment reductions induced abroad as a result of lower consumption at home, nor the domestic/foreign split of lower consumption in each sector. What was done was to estimate the lower level of imports associated with lower consumption, reduce exports by the same amount, and calculate the effects of that. Specifically, it was assumed that, for each category of final demand, there was a decline in imported goods proportional to the decline in domestically produced goods. The EIO use matrix was used to calculate import intensities and thus the reduction in imported inputs resulting from the decline in final demand. Exports were cut by the same amount as the total reduction in all imports. Those exports were chosen which were most GGE-intensive.

8
A First Selected Set of Social Performance/Progress Indicators

> The series a statistical office chooses to prepare and publish exercise a subtle and pervasive influence on political, social and economic development. This is why *the apparently dull and minor subject of statistical policy is of crucial importance.*
>
> (Seers, 1979, p. 3, emphasis added)

In Chapter 6 we set out a framework of social concerns. Later in the chapter, we showed how such a framework would imply very different directions for many government policies, from those currently followed. In Chapter 7 we introduced some concrete estimates of the effects on work and the environment of the kinds of shifts that we think would be required to approach a resolution of some of the problems identified in Chapters 2 to 4, while achieving the same and possibly improved levels of welfare or quality of life for the population.

Clearly, the next step is to suggest how we might get from here to there. This requires the implementation of a whole new political programme and a substantial change in attitudes and values (particularly on consumerism). We do not pretend to set out a whole political programme, although we have suggested possible changes to government policies (at the end of Chapter 6; see also Chapter 9) that would move in the direction of reducing economic activity and therefore reduced ecological damage. In terms of changes in attitudes and values, overall, we think that the necessity of many of the changes we are talking about will become more and more apparent to large fractions of the population; although we do suggest, in the next and final chapter, that there are some indications that values are already changing in some quarters.

In assessing those and other changes, however, there are two crucial tests for us. First, whether or not they actually do reduce ecological damage and second what happens to levels of welfare (in terms of a multi-dimensional approach to defining welfare of the kind that we have outlined). The issue here is how to measure progress in respect of these two crucial tests and then, of course, to design and implement the corresponding systems of measurement. The focus in this chapter therefore is on a possible measurement infrastructure for monitoring change in the desired direction; and on a possible approach to implementing such a measurement framework democratically.

The former test should be relatively easy to verify. It is generally accepted that the level of Greenhouse Gas Emissions is a good measure of the level of ecological damage. The previous chapter has shown how the level could be dramatically reduced through targeted cuts in consumption and employment. But, as we have emphasised several times, although we are convinced of the needed direction and orders of magnitude of change, we cannot be any more precise.

The focus here, therefore, is on how we monitor what is happening to welfare. It should be emphasised that the indicators suggested in the first half of this chapter are only suggestions; just as we would have preferred the estimates in the previous chapter to have been based on a democratic agreement about the priorities for cuts in consumption, we would expect a community to develop its own set of indicators that are most relevant to its own situation. Similarly, the suggested approach to democratic implementation considered in sections 8.4 and 8.5 is only a suggestion, we would expect communities to develop their own approach.

8.1 Monitoring welfare

The essential prerequisite for monitoring levels of welfare are a set of indicators that are practicable to use and procedures for ensuring that they are democratically acceptable. We focus on the first issue in this and the following two sections and on the latter in sections 8.4 and 8.5.

As the quote from Seers at the beginning of this chapter suggests, the measures of performance or progress that a society uses will largely determine the direction of its development. Within the overall constraint of reducing economic activity, we have suggested a set of welfare criteria for judging economic and social policies at all levels (community, regional and national) within that overall constraint. In order for this to be a transparent process, there has to be a set of indicators for assessing any given situation relative to those welfare criteria. Given the variety of contexts and situations, it should be emphasised that these are suggestions for the short to medium term and are only meant to be applicable for rich countries.

For a set of indicators to be useful, they have to be embedded in an institutional process of decision making. In contrast to the current top-down use of performance indicators for management control[1] we argue for democratic, community-based debate and adoption of a set of indicators that best suits their situation, within the overall constraints of reducing economic activity and of bringing no adverse effects to other communities or other countries.

The purpose of this chapter, based on our illustrative specification of the social concerns, is to set out the kind of indicators for which we think data could be collected, and to discuss ways of concretising them in a more democratic fashion.

8.1.1 From concerns to indicators

For the purpose of this book, the crucial difference between systems of social (and economic) statistics and a set of social indicators is that social indicators attempt to measure outcomes for individuals. Thus, in converting the social concerns specified in Chapter 6 into indicators, we need to focus on length and healthfulness of life rather than access to health care; the potential for children's development and levels of knowledge and ignorance rather than schooling; on choice and control over use of time and the quality of activities rather than labour force participation rates themselves; and on fulfilling basic needs and levels of long-term security rather than levels of income. Other foci are enjoyment of, rather than simply accessibility to, a safe and secure physical environment; a caring social environment, whatever the actual 'family' configuration, the risks from encounters with others, and a sense of community; and a minimum of interference into personal liberty. However, while there has been considerable attention to 'outcome measurement' in several areas of social policy (see, for example, Smith, 1996), specifying such indicators is not straightforward. This is for several reasons:

- most routine data systems have been oriented towards administrative interests;
- measurement of outcomes for individuals depend upon taking their existing circumstances into account;
- different value systems prescribe different outcomes.

Nevertheless, the growing public concern with accountability and with the quality of services being provided has generated an increasing pressure to develop more outcome-oriented measures.

8.1.2 Formulating indicators

This first step is to establish an 'optimal need satisfaction', beyond which level, more is not necessarily better (food and housing, for example) and more can even mean worse for many basic foods (for example, in terms of obesity; excess vitamins A and D) and also in terms of excessive security and overweening relationships. This means that in many cases neither a set of 'positive' indicators ('the proportion who are literate') nor a set of purely 'negative' indicators ('the proportion without adequate housing') will be sufficient: instead, it implies relatively sensitive measurement of the proportions of people who are substantially below and substantially above that *critical optimum*.

It is also important to point out that in many or most cases the main concern is not with averages, but with the proportion of people who achieve an acceptable minimum standard – that is, with avoiding poverty and marginalisation. This concern moreover is not simply with ensuring a basic income for everyone; it applies to all the other concerns and includes for example basic literacy, avoiding early death, and the availability of transport providing access to basic facilities.

There is also a problem when there are too many indicators for it then becomes difficult to assess either progress or retrogression. What normally then happens is that a composite indicator is constructed – something that has its own problems (see section 8.1.4).

8.1.3 Reliance on existing data

The content of most quality of life measures is dictated by data and measures that are readily available rather than the demands of prior theory. Etzioni and Lehman (1967), at the beginning of the 'social indicators movement', pointed to the problems this can cause, for example:

- 'fractional measurement', where there is a lack of correspondence between a concept and its operational definition (as with 'unemployment' and its measurement using social security statistics);
- 'indirect measurement' (e.g. measuring educational attainment by years of school), especially prevalent where data is used which was collected for some other purpose.

Worse still, many measures were in fact established on the basis of a previous administrative or, in some cases, theoretical framework. There are two specific concerns here: the tendency for data series which are related to the national accounts to have been developed more systematically than others; and the pressure to use the existing investments in administrative data systems to derive social indicators.

8.1.4 Difficulties with composite indices

One of the apparently obvious things to do with a set of indicators is to combine them into an index. There are many difficulties with devising an overall quality of life (QoL) indexes. In fact, there are two distinct sets of problems: establishing a coherent set of component indicators; and interpreting combinations.

Choice of components

There is no consensus over what should be the components or the weighting procedures that should be employed in 'composite' QoL indexes:

- while everyone needs/wants a certain minima of several conditions, few can agree on what is the optimum level or what combination is required;
- while nodding in the direction of consumer sovereignty as the mechanism for choosing components and how to combine them, few have actually attempted to take that position seriously.

There is the counter argument that each of the components are the product of a gradual developmental process out of which some degree of consensus has emerged, but the problem is that it is an historical consensus. Whether or not such components or weighting are relevant or 'salient' to different population groups today is important. While there is equally no consensus as to how relevance or salience ought to be measured, nor differences reconciled, if public perceptions are to be an eventual component of their experienced quality of life, then the relative importance of different aspects of their situation must also be essential.

Interpreting component indices

The point is that well-being is multi-dimensional, and the different dimensions are incommensurate because, although they are interrelated, they are not substitutes for each other. For example, a sufficient income to ensure good nutrition increases life expectancy, but you cannot compensate premature deaths with high income. Indeed, although an index can, through continued use, be presented as being simple – as has, one might argue, GNP itself – the presumptions underlying the measurement of each component are often quite complex and obscured.

Thus, a very close correlation exists between life expectancy and per capita income and also between the Physical Quality of life Index (a combination of life expectancy, infant mortality and literacy) and per capita income, but economic growth has been associated with deteriorating quality of life in several aspects: for example, the isolation of the elderly and forms of child abuse are more likely in high-income nations. Moreover, our emphasis here is on individuals, looking at extremes rather than averages, and not lumping them all in together in order to formulate a set of bland results.

8.1.5 Lack of disaggregation

Few Quality of Life Indexes address distributional aspects of the different components of the 'quality of life' or 'well-being' of particular population groups. This is principally because, given the difficulty of collecting sufficient nationally comparable data to yield meaningful estimates at the community level or for small groups, such indexes can usually only be calculated for highly aggregated and often inappropriate geographic units of analysis.

8.2 Monitoring the marginalised and more sensitive social surveys

There are many practical difficulties with assembling data, whether we are talking about administrative systems or social surveys. But there is a general difficulty which should be highlighted, given:

(a) increasing – or increasingly recognised (because of the 'new social movements') – diversity within a population;
(b) the purpose of many of these systems is to monitor the living standards/quality of life of those at the bottom of the heap or who are marginalised; and
(c) our overall concern with empowerment – or providing information important and useful to the concerned citizen.

This general difficulty is that the categories used in administrative systems and in most social surveys are often contested by those being monitored. Problems of measurement then arise since the strongest groups tend to be the most vocal and visible, and they may also manipulate the facts – participation of the subject community under study, however, is always vital. Three examples are considered next: disability; ethnic groupings; and sexuality.

8.2.1 Language and official categorisation

Part of this contestation is the development of vocabularies which confront and challenge stereotypes. For example, the politics of disablement movements (for instance, *Handicappes Méchants* in France) involves a critique of terms which mark out disabled people as different and unequal (like 'the handicapped') and confuse the functional limitations affecting a person's body (impairments) with the socially imposed barriers stemming from the design of the physical environment and the attitudes of other people (disability). Re-naming has played an equally central part in debates/struggles around lesbian and gay rights and anti-racism. Words with previously negative connotations, like 'lesbian' and 'queer', are used to assert a positive collective identity; the word 'Black' with a capital letter has been similarly reclaimed.

This can lead to exclusion from official statistics and national surveys seeking to provide a comprehensive picture of the health and social circumstances of the population: either through the criteria governing entry into the official statistics or social surveys, or from the technical procedures used in sampling or data analysis.

For example, there tends to be lower response rates to surveys in the UK among Blacks than among Whites. This is due in part to a concern that their reported experience will be drained of meaning through analysis by White researchers and that the information collected could be used by state agencies against the interests of minority ethnic groups.

8.2.2 Ignoring dimensions

Many dimensions have in fact gone unrecorded. Sexuality remains an unrecorded dimension of identity. For example, although lesbians and gay men are likely to think twice before making their sexuality and sexual relationships visible, in fact, in most social surveys, invisibility is enforced not chosen. In particular, the organising principle in the collection of most data is that people only live together in heterosexual relationships: cohabiting same-sex relationships are written out of the classification procedure. Two male friends, two sisters or a couple in a lesbian or gay relationship cannot 'cohabit' (nor can they be hassled about income support!). While living outside the institution of marriage, they are still classified by their relationship to it (either as single, separated, widowed or divorced).

In the UK 1991 Census, for example, lesbian and gay couples were apparently given the choice of classifying themselves as 'living together'; but the census report remonstrates:

> in the 1991 Census processing, cohabiting couples of the same sex were not recorded as such; instead, after clerical scrutiny of the forms, either the record of the sex of one of the couple or the relationship was changed. (Population Trends, 1993, p. 5)

The issues are: who is included in official statistics and social surveys; and how their lives and identities are represented. First, disability and class, like other dimensions of inequality, are treated in ways that de-politicise them. Secondly, assumptions about the organisation of domestic life guide the classification process, determining how people are allocated to a class, 'race' and marital status category.

Current procedures, therefore, tend to misrepresent the lives of those most affected by disadvantage and discrimination. This leads to a general doubt as to the appropriateness of social surveys for monitoring social problems.

8.2.3 Starting from the user perspective

The problems of 'monitoring the disadvantaged?' is only an acute form of the general problem of monitoring the quality of life where there is increasing attention being paid to user orientations. One general approach is to base the design of the survey on focused group discussion and to develop from that a more formal but still open-ended questionnaire. A further development is to include the community members in the design of the questionnaire itself (see the annex on page 188 for an early example).

Another general class of approach is that adopted in the survey conducted for the ITV, published as *Poor Britain* (Mack and Lansley, 1985). Respondents were asked to select from among a long list those items they thought were essential/necessary for civilised living in today's Britain. They were then asked whether or not they had or had access to those items. The argument is that this will generate a definition of poverty upon which there can be a broad-based political consensus (Hallerod *et al.*, 1997).

A variant of that approach – which has been tried within the health care context – is to ask people to name which are the most important sub-components of any area of concern; and then to ask them how they rate their own situation in respect of each of these components (Ruta *et al.*, 1994). While there are potential problems of class bias with this approach (see Carr-Hill, 1999), the importance of focusing on user orientations and views about what constitutes quality of life is crucial.

8.3 Developing specific indicators

The purpose of this section is to give examples of the kinds of indicators that could be chosen to monitor individual welfare along the various dimensions, together with a brief discussion of their interpretation in a policy context. It is not intended to be a definitive or permanent set in any way: in particular, we would hope that some of these indicators – which we see as contingently necessary because of the command and control nature of our society now – will become rapidly redundant. Moreover, as living patterns change, we would expect different communities to have different priorities and hence choose relevent indicators through a democratic process.

8.3.1 Health: length and health-related quality of life and children's development

These two 'sub-concerns': (a) length and health-related quality of life; and (b) children's development, are chosen as reflecting the individual adult concerns with the health-related quality of their remaining life expectancy and a societal concern for the future generation.

In respect of the length of life, there are a wide variety of life expectancy and/or mortality rates available; but, given improvements in perinatal care in all the developed countries, these are difficult to interpret as indicators of *current* trends. For example, increases in adult mortality can be masked in life expectancy at birth figures by declines in child mortality; that is, increases in deaths due to one condition masked by falls in another (Davey-Smith and Egger, 1996). Attention has therefore turned to more sensitive mortality indicators and considerable work has been put into the development of indicators of 'avoidable mortality' (those deaths which, given current medical technology, could have been avoided, such as tuberculosis and some deaths related to hypertensive conditions). However, the issue of attribution (whether or not, given socio-economic circumstances, a particular death was actually avoidable through improvements in health services) remains contentious.

In terms of health-related quality of life, there have been two kinds of approach. The first data set is aimed at modifying estimates of life expectancy according to levels of disability. There has been a tremendous literature on the appropriate ways to measure disability, impairments and handicaps, since Philip Wood's exposition in the 1970s (published by the WHO in 1980). While used widely in developing country contexts (for example, DALYs – Disability Adjusted Life Years), their relevance in richer countries is limited as disabilities, impairments and handicaps only capture part of what is understood as ill-health.

The second set aims at developing a more global measure of current health status combining health status with length of life (see, for example, Williams, 1985): this debate has generated considerable heat but not much light (for a review of the problems, see Carr-Hill, 1987). This is partly because nearly all the proposed indices and scales have been with reference to health-related quality of life *as affected by medical interventions*. While other self-reported health status measures are closer to the outcome theme being considered here and can be used unrelated to medical interventions, they are sensitive to shifts in population tolerance of illness and morbidity and so are also not very suitable. More fundamentally, there is a considerable body of opinion which argues that people's views of health vary so widely, it is inappropriate to construct a single scale (Blaxter, 1984).

In terms of children's development, there are a wide range of possible physiological and psychological indices of children's progress but, given the difficulties of interpretation, the preference here is for simple anthropometric measures. In developing countries, the *proportion with low birth weight*, is a good measure of socio-economic development in so far as that affects maternal health (Sterky and Millander, 1978), but given improvements in medical technology, there is now much less rationale for associating low birthweight with life chances for the infant or with poverty or deprivation of the mother.

Instead, a reasonable summary measure of healthy development during early years is *the proportion of damaged teeth at different ages*. *Height, adjusted for age and gender*, is also recognised as a good indicator of future potential health (Tanner, 1982); and *weight, adjusted for height and gender* is an important negative indicator.

8.3.2 Learning: experience of school; levels of knowledge and ignorance; lifelong learning

We must first recognise that people spend a substantial fraction of their lifetime at school. For some, school – like factories for workers – is a painful experience, and we should therefore perhaps think in terms of registering the right to get out of school, or at least opting out of some of the official syllabus; or to be able to get a useful job without submitting to the formal educational process as it currently exists.

In terms of educational attainment, a range of indicators/measures are being produced by the OECD. However, these are nearly all process measures (years of schooling, and so on) and, even within that paradigm, where examination results are recorded, there is considerable argument over whether those results should be used as measures of real outcome. This is both for technical reasons (cf. the literature on estimating the added value of schooling), and because many would argue that examinations do not adequately reflect real learning.

Instead, given the overall emphasis of outcome measurement and the specific focus on excluded and marginalised groups, the suggestion here is that the focus should not be on measures of schooling but on minimum levels of attainment. The realisation that school-based measures are insufficient, has prompted the search for survey-based measures of functional literacy amongst the adult population (CERI, 1992), that have being implemented in several developed countries. These surveys could be used to derive simple summary measures such as the proportion who are able to function in the social environment, although any attempts to set up systematic data collection in that area would have to be sensitive to within-cultural variations in language and preferred activities (and in ways that do not yet seem to have been appreciated by OECD). Measurement of the full utilisation of capacities, something that has been favoured by some as an indicator, would be even more difficult.

Finally, it is important also to have a measure of the extent to which people are able to learn over their lifetime after leaving school. The simplest measures – period participation rates which can be obtained from surveys – are probably not very useful; it might be better to focus on cumulative participation over the lifetime, although that would also be difficult to interpret because people perceive their opportunities to learn differently. A more promising alternative to an indicator on levels of further education might be to monitor people's rights to further learning.

8.3.3 Human activities

For several centuries, people's value and worth have been defined by their occupation. The relative permanence of 'structural' unemployment and now, of marginal, precarious employment, has led to a situation where many do not have a role defined in that direct way. At the same time, the (pre-eminence) of paid work (outside the home) has, once again, been challenged by some ecologists and feminists; and it must be obvious that one of the implications of our argument is that much paid work should be abolished. The main indicator is therefore the average number of hours in employed work (with the aim of reducing it).

Broader indicators about activity have to be derived from a time budget approach. There are many detailed sets of indicators that could be developed but, from the point of view of social and economic convergence, the key indicator is probably the proportion of 'dead' time induced by the work environment. A possible proxy for this 'dead time' would be travel time to work. Similarly, an assessment of the amount of time actually spent on essential reproductive activities such as cooking, housework and R&R could be proxied by the proportion of time spent on work at home.

Finally, indicators that can be used to monitor the quality of activities are crucial if we are going to escape the psychological damage of many recent policy innovations. Thus, even if the working week or working year were to be drastically reduced, the conditions of working life should be monitored. At a minimum, one would want to ensure that the workplace scores highly on the Jahoda dimensions (see Table 3.1, above); more positively, that the workplace is convivial. Outside the job-place, deciding on what counts as a good quality activity is not easy: the development of a synthetic indicator would have to be based on community judgements.

8.3.4 Necessities

The preference here is for indicators of the extent to which people's material necessities are being provided for. There are, of course, a wide range of possible indicators for income. However, given the concern with exclusion or marginalisation and the regular changes in social security or welfare schemes, there is some scope for developing *non-income based poverty indicators* showing the proportion without what are considered as basic necessities, regardless of income. The obvious candidates are food and housing.

While food would seem the most transparent, it is difficult to obtain agreement over what is a minimum diet. Moreover, there are obviously a large range of poor quality diets which are 'better' than any prescribed minimum. One possible avenue would be to search for marker indicators such as the numbers of cases of people with food-related illnesses, but this would be heavily dependent upon symptom identification. Another, possibly more promising, avenue is to identify specific marker foods such as fresh fruit and vegetables and ask what proportion of people do not have regular access to such foods. At poverty or near-poverty levels, 'access' (for example, to safe water) can be a matter of strategic choice, or trade off.

Equally, one would want to monitor the numbers of homeless. As well as being an important direct indicator of exclusion, homelessness encapsulates/reflects a range of government policies (housing policies, social security/welfare regulation, breakdown of traditional community support). While this is not easily measurable, via a social survey, for example, there are possible approaches; these are considered in section 8.4.

8.3.5 Physical environment

We have already discussed and dismissed environmental accounts in monetary terms (see p. 108). Even when not monetarised, most of the proposed indicators measure 'process' or even 'input' (for example, measures of the amount of (de?)forestation) rather than the impact upon welfare. Direct measures of impact upon and risks due to environmental damage for individuals are difficult to develop because of the diffuseness of environmental effects. There are also numerous possible confounders, and in addition, mobility, both of individuals and environmental phenomena, have to be taken into account).

Specifically:

- environmental problems are often international in scope, so that the more often available national data is inadequate;
- but they typically affect individual well-being at a local level so that national averages reveal little. On the other hand, if we select a particular locality we often find that pollution has been cleaned up, only to recur somewhere else;
- the effect of environmental degradation on people, while sometimes immediately disastrous, is more likely to manifest itself in a diffuse way, as a combination of stresses.

Instead, we suggest below some approaches to the problem of collecting real data for indicators about energy use and about transport.

8.3.6 Social environment and relationships

While the concerns with the breakdown of the traditional family and the extent to which people are participating actively in the community are clear enough, appropriate indicators are difficult to design. Perhaps the simplest focus in respect of the family, is the welfare of children and therefore to concentrate on the child's situation. While child abuse and violence has been the focus of policy attention and considerable discussion in the literature, it is very difficult to obtain reliable estimates. A possible measure, taking due account of the variety of possible family forms, might be the proportion of children without regular access to both parents if they are alive.

In terms of living in the community, the current issue of major concern in urban areas is the level of criminal violence. However, in terms of the impact upon the individual, while the fear of harm will vary according to the source of possible harm, the risk of unexpected death is the same. It is therefore important to distinguish between: the actual harm inflicted upon an individual; the risks to which they are exposed; and their fear of harm. The first can probably be proxied by examining the rates of unexpected death and then disaggregating those by cause; second, many of the more important risks will have been covered in the area of the physical environment; but the third crucial concern here is the fear of harm from different sources. In this context, this *latter* can probably be most easily measured in terms of the proportions of people who are afraid to go outside their home at night alone.

In respect of active community participation, there have been a large number of suggestions, but all of them are difficult to generalise beyond the specific situation in which they were developed. It might be easier to break down this concern into a number of more discrete areas. Thus, one could possibly measure the strength of the local community via a surrogate measure such as the relative rate of turnover, indicating the extent to which residents are satisfied with their community. Active political participation is traditionally measured in terms of voting or membership of associations but, given the current public view of politics and politicians, this is a less meaningful measure. Self-help activities would perhaps best be measured via local economic audits but that would be extremely time consuming. While it is important to develop surrogate measures, once again this would have to be based on community judgements.

As in many other areas, there is a problem of statistical marginalisation. Thus, we can, to some extent, document the decline of the conventional family – but not the development of unconventional household types or innovative lifestyles, which could be of equal or greater interest. Similarly, in looking at pressure group politics, it is difficult to avoid a bias towards groups which are relatively well organised and have a membership system. It is much more difficult to gauge the strength of the broader environmental movement, or, for example, of the women's and gay movements, in a direct way. And even in the case of organised groups, available data does not allow us to distinguish between various degrees of active participation and passive membership.

8.3.7 People and the law

Although this may seem very specific to the current UK situation, the concern with exclusion and marginalisation makes this a reasonable high priority. While individuals are exposed to state interference in a number of ways, those which result in physical constraint and interference with personal liberty are the most important. The appropriate indicators can be developed by examining the key encounters between the state and the individual, ranging from being stopped on the street to imprisonment. A community where more people are being stopped and questioned on the street is, *ceteris paribus*, less free than another, just as much as one where many people are being imprisoned. Appropriate indicators might be: (a) the numbers of individuals stopped for questioning by police in each age-sex group broken down by ethnicity; and (b) average daily prison population. Indicators such as these would be of particular concern for marginal groups, whether they are ethnic minorities, the unemployed, and so on.

More legalistic concerns are also important for showing the extent to which personal liberties are being safeguarded. Thus, it is of concern whether or not people who are charged and arrested spend their time awaiting trial in liberty or even temporarily in prison (both because of the restriction of liberty and because of the effect of remand in prison upon the likelihood of their being found guilty). The indicator would simply be the proportion of those arrested who are remanded in prison awaiting trial. Equally, the availability of legal support is important and the suggested indicators here would be the proportion of those on trial who are denied access to legal advice.

A broader view might be to take into account the extent to which citizen's rights are being safeguarded; a particular concern here might be the extent to which people are effectively protected from racial discrimination. But it becomes difficult to develop indicators since:

> many of the more important social factors are inherently unquantifiable: how safe it is to criticise the government publicly, or the chance of an objective trial or how corruption affects policy decisions. (Seers, 1983, p. 6)

8.4 Implementation

Actually implementing such a social indicator system is, of course, more complicated. The material in this section is drawn mostly from developing countries because that is where many of the most innovative attempts at implementing such systems have been made. Doyal and Gough conclude

> that some type of state responsibility, control and pressure is a necessary pre-requisite for the redistribution policies which are in turn preconditions for basic individual needs to be met in practice. ... The question is ... what sort of state it should be, and how it could ever meet the needs and rights of those it should serve rather than dominate. (Doyal and Gough, 1991, p. 78)

8.4.1 Constructing democratic monitoring

The thing to be aware of is that, first, data are *produced*, not *collected*: Data depend on underlying concepts and on a system of processing in which different agents have different interests and tasks. Therefore, measurement work and statistical work are neither socially nor theoretically autonomous activities. Equally, the historical and social context of measurement is important: for example, the ready access of quantitative measures and techniques for analysing aggregates of things has dominated the way in which statistical systems have developed.

Consequently, the activity of measurement itself is a potential agent for change. Indeed, the potential of data measurement to influence policy often leads to its suppression, even when no-one disagrees about the concepts or definitions: information has a political role. For example, Gordon (1979) gives a graphic account of her experiences as Director of the Bawku Applied Nutrition Programme in Ghana over a five-year period. She concludes, ruefully, that 'conventionally trained nutritionists and doctors are not always skilled in presenting their case to the right people' (Gordon, 1979, p. 8).

Second, everyone might agree that a particular phenomenon is worth measuring, but the actual indicator chosen would vary according to the clientele. Consider, for example, schools, which everyone wants to know something about. The government planner, typically, will be interested in enrolment, repeater and drop-out ratios, pupil–teacher ratios, construction costs, and so on; people who are not government planners would be more interested in access to different types of educational facilities, what they can learn in different 'institutional' contexts (this need not, of course, involve a building, or even a formal programme); and concerned pedagogues more interested in the type of resources that are needed to impart the type of knowledge that is socially useful.

Third, the same indicator can be used in various ways. Thus, an indicator of individual well-being may reflect a current *condition*, membership of a *risk group*, or a *trend* in the causative factors. Accordingly:

> a change in the use of an indicator from, for example, the diagnosis and treatment of malnutrition in the individual, to the quantifying of risk for families or communities, or to the analysis of trends and changes, requires a change in definition and significance of that indicator. This dependence raises fundamental questions about the procedure for defining indicators, about who should be involved in the process, and about the role and objectives of research. (Dowler *et al.*, 1982, pp. 101–2)

In general one must be very wary of how an index is used, as opposed to how it was developed.

Finally, since social change can only be carried out by people, measures and statistical activities should be on the human level, and, as far as possible, organised around people's possibilities for change. In a developing country context, Chambers suggests three ways in which, for example, poor rural people can benefit from appraisal and research:

> the direct operational use of data; the changes in outsider's awareness, knowledge and understanding, leading subsequently to changes in their behaviour; and the enhanced awareness and capability of the rural poor themselves. (Chambers, 1983)

In principle, this means that we have to understand how people develop their own goals in their social environment and how they develop their own measurement criteria. In practical terms, many authors have remarked that the validity of data depends upon the extent to which the informant understands and agrees with the motivations and objectives of those collecting the data, and at least consents to the use to which the data will be put. Even this pragmatic approach imposes severe constraints on the viability of those surveys that are centrally designed and executed.

A corollary is that measures and statistical procedures should be transparent. That is, although it would be silly for everyone to become a statistician overnight, however sophisticated the procedures used (and we would usually question their utility), the assumptions, and the results and the consequences of varying the assumptions, should be clear to everyone. The obvious example in this context is the ease with which an economic statistician slips from talking about economic welfare to measuring GNP per capita, without explaining the limitations of using the latter as a proxy for the former.

8.4.2 Developing lay reporting and local-level monitoring

There have also been attempts in developing countries to come up with monitoring methods which are more appropriate on a local level, rather than centralised national systems. In the mid-1950s, the WHO explored ways of making use of data collected by non-medical personnel for studying crude cause of death (Uemura, 1988).

In the 1970s, UNRISD set up Development Monitoring Systems (DMS) at the local level (McGranahan *et al.*, 1972). Scott (1988) draws on the experience in the Indian state of Kerala to illustrate the possibilities and problems (here, three of the initial 12 socio-economic observatories were still functioning ten years later). Local level staff had been paid and trained to collect the data on a regular basis. This was not always easy: 'even one of the trained DMS interviewers read the height on the wrong side of the measuring rod for some time' (Scott, 1988, p. 30).

But these attempts were overtaken by the emphasis on the technical aspects of computerisation. This led to a relative lack of attention to ensuring adequate quality in source data, to the practicalities and difficulties of collecting and preparing data for input, and to the capacity of decision makers to use the output. Moreover, although the data were intended for local use, local participation was virtually nil. It has therefore to be demonstrated that the community will benefit in at least one of these ways.

The development of a comprehensive lay reporting system will not always follow the same structure as a centrally-devised system. The technical criteria of a 'good' surveillance system, such as sensitivity, specificity, representativeness, timeliness, simplicity, flexibility and acceptability, are obviously desirable. But the extent to which they can be met will be limited: increasing the sensitivity of a system to detect a greater proportion of a health event may improve representativeness and usefulness, but it also increases the cost and leads to more reporting of false positives (Thacker *et al.*, 1988); second, it is crucially important to involve local people at all stages of planning and execution in order to obtain good quality data which may mitigate against the fulfilment of technical criteria. For while the perspectives of medical professionals and social scientists.

> may help to structure and therefore 'see' empirical data which is not visible to the worker ... worker subjectivity, although containing false

> impressions, contains the seeds of empirical data and new conceptual starting points ... worker participation enhances the validity of collected data. (Myers, 1985, cited in Thacker *et al.*, 1988)

8.4.3 Community-based participatory approaches

The word 'community' is used in a wide variety of ways. Midgley *et al.* (1986) suggests that community has two main meanings in the development literature. The definition most used by those concerned with the *delivery* of (basic) services is the group of people living in a defined area (assumed to be sharing the same basic values and organisations). As the above example shows, the more realistic definition refers to a group of people sharing the same basic interests or problems.

'Participation', similarly, has been used in a wide variety of ways. There is, however, the same basic contrast between the passive spectator ('weak' participation) and the issues of control and power ('strong' participation).

Rifkin *et al.* (1988) point to three characteristics common to all definitions of strong participation. First, participation must be *active*: the purchase or receipt of services does not constitute participation. Second, participation involves *choice*: the right and responsibility to control, have power over, the decisions which affect their lives. Third, their choice must have the possibility of being *effective*: mechanisms must exist or can be created so that their choice can be implemented – ACE (an active effective choice) rather than PAP (passive acceptance of poverty).

None of this is easy. Here is an example from the African context:

> the social dimension of catalysis is ... elusive. Villagers readily participate in development projects but because administration is unable to respond rapidly and because of the organisational problems in the village that we have described, participation is often frustrating. (Feachem, 1980)

The weakness of village institutions contributes to shortages of publicly-available resources. Villages in Africa do not usually have the power – or sanctions – to raise funds on a regular basis for maintenance. While voluntary contributions in cash or labour may be easy enough to mobilise for a specific occasion, such as the building of a new water supply, to maintain it on a voluntary basis does not usually work. In part this is because what counts as salient will vary over time; basic needs, however, are relatively unchanged, though how to meet them might vary.

On the basis of an analysis of over 100 case studies, Rifkin and colleagues (1988) identify six dimensions along which the strength of participation can vary: needs assessment, leadership, organisation, resource mobilisation, management and focus on the poor. Her argument is convincing but it should be emphasised that, while useful suggestions for monitoring participation – or any other aspect of welfare – can be brought from outside, the extent of participation can only satisfactorily be assessed by those who are meant to be participating! Thus Rifkin and colleagues cite a study in Nepal using their framework of process indicators where, apparently, community involvement varied *considerably* between the villages. It would appear here, however, that a uniform scale has been imposed by the researcher, rather than being agreed between (representatives of) the villagers.

Lourié (1987) claims that cultural, political and social pressures – including the expectations that communities will make a material contribution – are following a demand for increased participation. The first question is whether communities can be fully involved in a monitoring process. Campbell (1988) describes the development of a household baseline survey and of water and sanitation profiles in Belize. He claims that villagers were involved at all stages, including survey design, counting the responses, and the use of the survey results for designing a local water supply and sanitation programme. A systematic procedure for conducting such a survey is described in the context of educational planning in the Annex to this chapter on page 188.

The second crucial question is the extent to which communities have achieved any power. In another context, Piven suggests the following test of the effectiveness of a decentralisation programme

> not merely by observing the shifts in inter-agency chains of command, the formal procedures for 'citizen participation' or feedback, but by evaluating the actual political leverages in matters regarding the allocation of tangible resources, including the hiring and firing of personnel, which accrues to citizen groups, especially those citizen groups which have not previously been regarded as significant constituents of the agency. While such a 'test' of decentralisation may seem crude, in the turgid realms of bureaucratic policy, the simpler tests of power may be the most reliable. (Piven, 1977, p. 289)

This poses a dilemma for those promoting social participation from outside. First, given their emphasis upon emancipation – and upon creating bottom–up policies, programmes or projects with a participatory theme – they tend to concentrate on the educational and health care sector, which are not always seen by the communities concerned as the most urgent priorities. Second, the political goals – the redistribution of power and structural change – are long term and do not usually offer short-term solutions to the immediate problems.

Just as there is no easy way to overcome the obstacles in the way of developing a lay monitoring system, there is no easy solution to the dilemma facing advocates of participatory approaches among poor communities. We have no magic bullets: but that process will be facilitated by some of the possible short-term changes we discuss in the next and final chapter.

8.5 Annex: radicalising survey methodology

Freire argued:

> There is no such thing as a *neutral* educational process. Education either functions as an instrument which is used to facilitate the integration of the younger generation into the logic of the present system and bring about conformity to it, *or* it becomes the 'practice of freedom', the means by which men and women deal critically and creatively with reality and discover how to participate in the transformation of their world. (Freire, 1972, p. 13, italics added)

On this basis, Freire developed his method of authentic-education for the oppressed while working with the peasants in north eastern Brazil. His method consisted first of discovering the basic vocabulary and living conditions of the group to be taught; then, through group dialogue, the fundamental interests of the students. They then realise that they need to know more about the world before they can act consciously to control their own lives.

The problem with Freire's method (or similar prescriptions for radical education) is that they only work *if people come to them*, whereas most people's experience of education (whether or not radical) is that the involvement and motivation by subjects of the learning process, which is crucial, cannot be assumed *ab initio*. In fact, one main reason why such methods work (as indeed they do) is because of the ideals and enthusiasm of the committed, highly skilled and motivated educators who employ them. Indeed, it is arguable that someone like Freire would be a successful educator – in terms of raising consciousness so that people can participate in the 'transformation of their world' – with almost any method.

The problem, therefore, is to develop a low-key method of awakening people's interest in the first place (the subsequent level and nature of their motivation cannot, of course, be determined in advance); a tool which will focus people's attention on the issue, without imposing counter-productive discussion on those who do not see any problem or who have no hope of effecting any change. Any approach to uninterested and unmotivated people must, *inter alia*, examine their educational experiences and the part these institutions have played in producing their immediate situation and particularly their understanding of, and reactions to, that situation. An early attempt was made by one of the authors to use an interview/questionnaire approach since this requires a very low level of involvement on the part of the respondent and yet introduces ideas to him/her.

The difficulty is, that when people are asked their reaction to the education they have received or that they would desire for their offspring, the purpose and content of the education being offered are often indeterminate. Even if made precise, there is little incentive for people to reply because they sense that the final decisions will be made elsewhere.

We can go some way towards compiling data on needs in a non-alienating and non-exploitative fashion by involving a selection of the population at each stage. In a pilot study in Brighton, England, in 1974, the following procedure generated considerable discussion about the purpose and content of educational programmes:

(a) an informal discussion with groups of individuals from the projected population, eliciting the categories in which people perceive the reality of their own lives and possible futures;
(b) a more direct semi-structured interview with the same group of individuals about the relevance of present and possible education careers to their own lives; and
(c) a self-completion questionnaire for the population designed so as to compare the purpose and results of present formal educational systems and other forms of socialisation, with the way in which they live their own life and their hopes for improvement in its quality (taken from Carr-Hill, 1987).

The experience of the questionnaire suggested that it was possible for respondents to be clear and coherent about what are desirable outcomes of all kinds from all forms of education in terms of attitudes, roles and skills – and, moreover, that *everyone is capable* of distinguishing between different educational contexts and their effects on these outcomes for themselves.

Similar procedures are the basis of the Participatory Rural Appraisal Approaches used in many developing countries today. Note that they are very different – at least in principle – from the focus groups beloved of spin doctors, as they are led by the community so that the form and content of the discussions and conclusions are decided by them.

9
The Fourth Way in Practice: What Can be Done?

9.1 What needs to be done?

Our starting point in this book was that, while development based on continuing output growth has been the major target of government policy in all the rich countries, its results have been disappointing, and increasingly so. Even judged by traditional criteria, growth has been less, and less consistent, in the last 25 years than in the 25 years before. Such policies have failed to ensure full employment, and have not reduced – in some cases have increased – poverty. But more important, as we have argued in previous chapters, from the point of view of improving general welfare (supposedly the reason for economic activity) a pattern of development based on growth is completely unsatisfactory for three distinct sets of reasons. First, the resulting ecological impacts and likely future risks are such that there is a need to limit, not further increase, production and consumption. Moreover, this is true at a world level, and if consumption is to rise in poor countries, so as to eliminate absolute poverty and reduce inequality, there is most likely a need for *large* reductions in consumption in rich countries. Second, the paid employment required for increased production is alienating and wasteful in a variety of ways and often harmful, so that there are large gains in welfare to be made from reducing employment time. And third, perhaps even more fundamentally, all the evidence suggests that beyond a minimum level required to meet basic needs, increases in the general level of consumption make no contribution to welfare. In so far as consumption (beyond this minimum) does affect welfare, this is mainly because individuals care about their consumption level *relative to others*. This concern drives a process where people generally try to raise their incomes, but it cannot result in any overall improvement in welfare.

This suggests that a variety of welfare gains would result from following a completely different pattern of development, one based on reducing production and consumption, and thus the employment and ecological damage that they necessarily imply. If combined with redistribution of consumption and work, this can be done in such a way that welfare is enhanced. Used in this way, resources – natural and human – are amply sufficient to provide everyone with the material standard of living required for optimum welfare.[1] In the second part of the book we have attempted to make this general proposal more concrete. In contrast with the orthodox framework, based on economic growth and the assumption that welfare will follow, we argue for a framework which is quite different, where welfare, understood as *a set of social concerns*, is the explicit focus (Chapter 6). We certainly cannot produce any kind of blueprint, nor do we wish to, for reasons we have explained. We have however, presented a worked example (Chapter 7) of where some consumption reductions can be made. We think these reasonable, and provide some *ad hoc* justification, but at the end of the day, our suggestions largely reflect our own preferences. We explain where these reductions would lead us in terms of their ecological and employment effects. In Chapter 8, we presented a system of social indicators for monitoring and giving direction to the kind of welfare-oriented development we are advocating. In this chapter we make a few suggestions about where to start, even in the absence of radical change, and about the kind of values which will have to guide any more radical transformation, in the direction of sustainable welfare.

We hope to have convinced readers that this is at least a reasonable plan, and that if it could be put into practice, it would go a long way towards solving the major problems that afflict us. Unlike some environmentalists, we are not calling for sacrifices to be made in the name of sustainability; on the contrary, we are presenting ecological crisis as an opportunity to rethink what the costs and benefits of consumerism really are. We suggest that the costs far outweigh the benefits. In this chapter, we discuss some of the possibilities and difficulties involved in implementing the type of development we are advocating. We suggest some policies which, while insufficient in themselves, could be implemented relatively easily, and we outline the general values and principles that should guide the type of development we are talking about. We do not, however, have a 'programme' to offer. This is partly because, as we explain below, any programme of overall consumption cuts would come into conflict with the profit motive, and thus have to be a programme for radical institutional change rather than merely more efficient consumption habits. We do not propose such a programme because history, especially recent history, suggests that, whatever the factors are which lead to radical change, they have little to do with deliberately implementing a programme. Programmes, Marxist or neoliberal, for example, are rarely properly implemented, and when they are all sorts of unforeseen developments occur.[2] Rather than a programme prepared in advance, we envisage the development of a variety of communities, experimenting in their relationships, their organisation, and the technology they use.

In Chapter 5 we discussed the general thrust of existing policy towards ecological issues, as well as some of the proposals for a 'greener' approach. These policies mostly involve interpreting sustainable development in such a way as to reconcile continued economic growth with reduced ecological damage. This interpretation rests on the 'weak' view of sustainability (that economic growth, as presently measured, must be sufficient to offset ecological damage – a view as likely to lead to more growth as less damage), and on a view of technology and markets as able to push back ecological limits indefinitely. Policies inspired by this view are likely to aim at getting rid of the worst instances of pollution and the most inefficient forms of resource use, especially the mining of (potentially) renewable resources. But they still promote economic growth.

A somewhat more radical version of this approach is possible, aimed at maintaining not growth – the flow of new goods and services – but the stock of consumer goods. It would be possible, for example, to reduce resource use through improved durability and repairability. However, this would lead to lower output than otherwise, and thus also lower potential profits. It would still leave aside problems of inequality, ignore the costs of employment, and take for granted the benefits of consumption. The policies discussed in this chapter take as their aim reducing consumption while improving (or at the very least maintaining) welfare.

Undoubtedly there are some things that can be done in the short to medium term and within the existing economic and political framework (see section 9.2, below). The problem however is that the existing framework makes it almost inevitable that development will continue to follow a growth-oriented path. In Chapter 4 we discussed some of the reasons for this, in particular positional competition and other mechanisms by which the search for improved relative position by individuals stimulate growth of output (but not welfare) in the economy as a whole. In addition, it is difficult to see how the goal of welfare, if it implies limiting consumption worldwide and reducing it among the rich, can be reconciled with interests and institutions which are motivated by profit (see section 9.3, below). Our proposals imply a revolution in institutions and values, as well as employment and consumer habits.

We don't really know whether such a revolution will happen – whether the pressures for change, which are considerable and which will certainly increase, will be sufficient to overcome powerful interests. Past evidence suggests that energy systems, and the economic interests associated with them, are so entrenched (the former rather more so than the latter), that they do not change, except in the face of unavoidable crisis (Debeir *et al.*, 1991). On the other hand, that may be precisely the situation we are in, or moving close to. What we attempt to set out below and in section 9.4 are some of the general principles and values which a low consumption society will require, as well as make possible by virtue of this low consumption.

9.1.1 Rich and poor countries

As in other chapters, the rich, overdeveloped, countries are our main focus. We are not presuming to lecture 'poorer', less overdeveloped, countries, who are entitled to expect the same standard of living as the rich. Nevertheless, 'development' in one part of the world is not unrelated to 'development' in the other.

Reduced resource use in rich countries would enable low income countries to return to using their own resources and the levels of self-sufficiency they enjoyed until recently. For example, 50 years ago the countries of Latin America, Asia and Africa grew enough food for their own needs, with in many cases a surplus for export. Now a far larger proportion of crops grown (and livestock raised) in these countries are for export to the rich world, while the poor are left with various combinations of deforestation, malnutrition, food imports and food aid. Western economists tend to point the finger at population growth, but most poor countries could feed themselves easily if it was not for the diversion of land to export production.

Nevertheless, some of the 'poor' countries demonstrate quite clearly the possibilities for reconciling low consumption with high welfare in a way that provides lessons (and a rebuke) to rich countries. Several countries have been held up as examples, none more so than Kerala State in India. Kerala has rich country levels of health and literacy, for Indian levels of income and resource use (Parayil, 2000). The strategies credited with this achievement also have lessons for the rich countries.[3] In the area of politics the key principle has been to make democracy more participatory. In turn this requires the acquisition by citizens of the knowledge and capabilities they need if they are to be able to exercise their responsibilities. It also requires decentralisation of decision making wherever feasible, since it is only at the local level that full participation is possible. Localisation is the key principle in the economic sphere also, particularly self-reliance in meeting basic needs and in energy supplies (Parameswaran, 2000). Of course rich countries start from a very different situation and cannot simply adopt a Keralan or similar 'model'; but some of the general principles may be the same.

9.2 Stretching existing institutions: (pale) green capitalism

There are undoubtedly some things that can be done, in the relatively short term, by government and by individuals and small groups, without requiring drastic institutional changes, and without seriously threatening dominant interests. These are concerned with reductions in activities which are, in ecological terms, particularly undesirable, and with modest reductions in working hours, rather than the large, economy-wide cuts in consumption and employment that we advocate for the longer term.

Regarding the aims of possible short- or medium-term changes, the consumption cuts proposed in Chapter 7 may provide a starting point. Of course, as we have emphasised, the calculations shown in Chapter 7 are intended as an example of what we mean rather than a blueprint to be imposed on our fellow consumers. In addition, the size of the cuts we propose, for individual industries and for the economy as a whole, would certainly require radical changes. Nevertheless, we would expect the general direction of the cuts to receive support from those who agree with our overall argument. For example, concern with environmental issues leads rather naturally to a focus on transport, the largest and fastest increasing user of energy. Limiting suburban sprawl and car use is already very much a matter of policy discussion (though not yet implementation). Similarly, a concern with reducing meaningless work (less evident at the moment) is likely nowadays to highlight certain service sectors (the 'McJobs').

There is a very broad range of possible small improvements in the ecological impact of what governments and individuals do, and no question of discussing all of them here. We focus on some of the larger improvements, in order to make the case that, in a number of areas of economic activity, there are significant changes that can be made, and there are policies which can achieve these changes.

9.2.1 Some things that government can do

In spite of prevalent ideas about entrepreneurial capitalists, at the service of consumers, leading the way when it comes to social change, it is government whose decisions are crucial in setting the general pattern of development and determining broad consumer 'choices' in most of the areas we are concerned with. These include detailed control over land use and transport infrastructure, legal power (actual and potential) over product standards and employment conditions, the use of taxes and benefits to redistribute income and wealth, and the size and scope of its own spending (even, in the UK, post-privatisation). Between them, these matters ensure that government has the main responsibility for bringing change about. Neoclassical environmental economists argue for a limited government role, one of instituting and facilitating appropriate market instruments – taxes, subsidies, tradeable permit systems, and so on – which essentially rely on the effectiveness of price 'signals' in affecting consumer and business decisions. But belief in the power of prices to determine major decisions (rather than just influence minor ones) is a matter of dogma rather than evidence. What evidence there is is not promising: large fluctuations in the oil price have had a modest effect on car design rather than achieving radical change in transport patterns. Government planning decisions – and pressure from citizens to make those decisions – about road and house building, and privatising railways and buses, are far more important where radical change is concerned.

We primarily highlight here a few large categories where there is significant scope for action rather than the many smaller or less promising areas. We also focus entirely on reductions in consumption, and ignore the huge improvements in the efficiency of production which many have argued are possible (for example, we talk about replacing car use rather than making cars more resource efficient). However, efficiency improvements in both production and consumption are necessary and should be promoted.

Transport and land use

The largest category of consumption reductions we have suggested involves transport. Transport systems have a particular importance in view of their large and increasing role in energy use and greenhouse gas emissions (Chapter 7).[4] Transport and land use are closely associated with positional goods (Chapter 4). The general principles of a sustainable transport policy are not very controversial, and include some goals which even existing policy supports, in principle.

Perhaps most fundamentally, there is much scope for reducing the need for people to travel at all. Reductions in local travel (to work; to the shops) can be achieved through the planning system, by refusal to allow further suburbanisation or building on 'greenfield' sites, or out-of-town shopping centres, and by meeting the need for new housing (which is modest in rich countries, and arises largely as a result of regional inequalities which our proposals would help reduce) through 'brownfield' development. This is official (but half-hearted) government policy in the UK and many other countries. Likewise, a large reduction in the need for goods transport could be achieved, as a result of a shift towards production for local use, and away from global trading. We recognise, however, that this runs directly counter to government policy in most countries, which favours increased trade.

Where there remains a need for transport there is great scope for reducing its environmental impact. Obvious examples are moving away from car use in cities and for commuting, and towards collective transport and cycling; moving away from car use (and air travel) and towards trains for inter-city travel; and moving away from road (and air) transport of goods, and a return to rail and water transport.

Government policy, in particular road building and privatisation of public transport, in practice runs counter to the goal of switching to more environmentally benign transport. Proposals for taxes, on road use or on commuting, could play a part in implementing this goal (and be politically acceptable), if (and only if) genuine alternatives are provided, through better collective transport and cycling facilities. Certainly the removal of perverse price incentives (although it is unlikely to solve the problems by itself) seems desirable. This applies to cars, where currently vehicle tax and insurance premiums are generally payable per time unit rather than per distance travelled, thus drastically reducing the marginal cost of individual trips to the driver. It applies even more dramatically to air travel, where fuel is currently exempt from taxes.

Shorter working hours

There is of course plenty of historical evidence that reducing working hours is feasible, provided the political circumstances are favourable. There have been reductions in the working week since the nineteenth century, though these have slowed down since the 1960s. There have also been other reductions in lifelong working time (increases in holidays and school leaving age, lowering of retirement age). And in the 1990s there has in some cases been a return to the previous trend of reductions in the working week, starting in France and The Netherlands and spreading to other countries of continental Europe. The reductions have been modest (for example, a working week of 35 hours in France), and have been aimed principally at reducing unemployment. They have been achieved through a combination of legislation and negotiation with businesses and unions, with financial incentives (for example, reductions in payroll taxes for firms which recruit more workers) playing an important part, and largely paying for themselves as a result of reduced expenditure on unemployment benefits. What is encouraging is the development of a certain momentum, as firms learn to cope with the restructuring involved in redistributing work among a larger group of workers, as workers experience the positive opportunities arising from a shorter week and gain in enthusiasm, and as the experience of one country provides an example to workers in other countries, who start to demand a shorter working week also (Hayden, 1999). On the other hand, employers and government will become quite unenthusiastic as unemployment falls to a level which boosts workers' bargaining power in negotiating wages and working conditions.

Redistributing income and wealth

If reductions in working time are to go beyond the modest examples discussed, and especially if we are to move towards limits, and eventually large reductions, in average consumption, redistribution of income and wealth becomes essential. If absolute poverty is not to be abolished through growth, then it can only be abolished through redistribution. Moreover, relative poverty, by definition, can only be reduced though redistribution. This implies a reversal of policy for countries such as the UK which have reduced taxes on the rich in recent decades. That it is quite possible, without leading to financial ruin, is shown by the example of those countries (Scandinavia, The Netherlands) which have maintained a more redistributive tax regime.

Reforming government spending

A number of the cuts we have proposed in Chapter 8 are in activities directly undertaken by the government: the military, police, education, health services. Some of the cuts will no doubt only be feasible in the longer term, but others can begin right away. Prime examples are the military, and the prison service, where the futility of imprisoning ever larger numbers of people is becoming increasingly evident. On the other hand, there are also public services, such as public libraries, meeting halls and parks, which make it easier for people to reduce consumption, and which should be maintained and could be extended (though this is something that does not necessarily have to be done by government).

Advertising

A non-consumerist society would only want (and tolerate) a certain kind of advertising: true information about the existence and content of useful products, made available to (rather than deluging) potential users. This implies both ensuring true and complete information, and removing false or misleading claims (see below). The first is easier: there has been some improvement in recent years: for example, in labelling food with its nutritional content. On the other hand, in many cases, there has been a refusal to specify country of origin or whether a product incorporated genetically modified ingredients. It would be a relatively easy step for governments to make it compulsory for manufacturers to label a wide range of products with information about the known ecological impact (in terms of GGEs, the distance the product has travelled, and so on), as well as the health impact of the product itself.

Limiting the extent of advertising, as well as its misleading qualities, is more difficult, even if the powers of the Advertising Standards Authority were made much more extensive. Possible policies include banning advertising in a range of public places (for example, street hoardings), and making it easier for advertisers to be taken to court over false claims. At the very least government should prevent the extension of business involvement, for marketing purposes, into areas such as education.

9.2.2 Things that individuals and groups can do

In the second half of Chapter 4 we raised the question why, if welfare does not increase with consumption, people apparently demonstrate by their market and voting choices their willingness to work and consume more. The answer seems to lie with a number of mechanisms. These include positional competition, the role of expectations, pressure to conform to community norms, and the expression of status. These ensure that people, in their search for improved *relative* welfare, attempt to consume more, even though aggregate welfare does not and cannot rise.

The implication of these mechanisms is that there is limited scope for individuals to break out of the prevailing consumption pattern, and that collective decisions and action are required.

This does not mean however that there is *no* consumer choice. Clearly there are all sorts of possibilities at the margin for people to consume less. In areas of substantial consumer spending such as transport and travel, food, and housing (including all household energy use), which are important ecologically, there is considerable scope for consumption cuts that are entirely non-masochistic. There are often opportunities for reducing car use in cities, for covering smaller distances on holiday, for eating less meat and more locally produced and more organic food, for wearing a sweater and turning down the heating, and much else.

There have of course been many attempts to create and live in communities which embody similar ideas to our own (one review can be found in Schwarz and Schwarz, 1998); and, leaving aside their approach to child care and gender, one could argue that the Amish in the US embody much of what we are talking about. These attempts tend to show the feasibility of combining welfare and ecological friendliness (as well as other values). But they also show the difficulties of cultivating such experiments within a consumer society; and of course they have attracted only a fairly small number of participants. One attempt to study the possibilities for reducing ecological impact without requiring such radical changes of lifestyle, and while maintaining reasonable standards of comfort, is Harper (n.d.). Adopting a 'cultural rather than technological approach', Harper found that there were considerable opportunities in areas such as waste disposal and energy use (car use, holidays and domestic heating). He concludes that '... substantial reductions in environmental impact are possible – often approaching the broadly-agreed sustainable and globally-equitable levels – and it's not as terrifying or alienating as it's supposed to be. In fact often enough it seems to lead to an improvement in overall well-being and quality of life' (p. 9).

There have also been attempts to turn consumption (and work) reduction into an organised programme, without emphasising the ecological aspect so much, as with the 'voluntary simplicity' movement. One approach, for example (Dominguez and Robin, 1992), initially merely requires participants to monitor each item of their expenditure and income, with the aim of finding ways of reducing debt and increasing savings. Gradually the emphasis shifts to questioning each item of expenditure, finding ways of doing things more cheaply, investing any savings, and – most important – reducing the need for employment, leaving time and energy for more important and fulfilling activities.

This type of approach is quite ingenious and has many attractions: it starts from the existing situation and from what individuals can do on their own, and it does not require them to sacrifice themselves, while at the same time it promotes, through a step-by-step approach, a shift in values away from employment and consumption. It represents the limits of an individualistic response to our argument: what each of those of us who accept the argument can do, acting on our own. In the aggregate, however, as a solution to the *social* problems involved, this approach is quite unsatisfactory: it amounts essentially to transforming as many workers as possible into rentiers (living on investment income), albeit low-income rentiers. But there is a core of essential work to do, and someone has to do it, so not everyone can achieve this kind of voluntary simplicity. In view of this it is far more equitable to redistribute necessary work and income across the whole population.[5]

Individual attempts at cutting consumption and employed work are greatly encouraged if anti-consumerist subcultures develop, as the rise in the 1960s of the beatniks, hippies and punks demonstrated. The pressures to conform to community norms, largely responsible for inflated consumption, can work in reverse to promote reduced consumption, encourage dropping out of full-time employment, and assign status to those who achieve well-being rather than wealth. These movements did develop a degree of momentum, but nevertheless ended up having limited and temporary success. The decline in these movements suggests that there are many opportunities and, as the next section suggests, good reasons for the consumer culture to fight back, in particular by recuperating anti-consumerism and offering it for sale, from (formerly free) music festivals to pre-faded (and torn and safety pinned) jeans. Similar attempts – i.e. to channel ecological concern into buying 'green products' – are much in evidence.

9.3 Welfare against profit

9.3.1 The link between profits and economic activity

In the first part of this book we argued that economic activity in rich countries should be reduced, because of its excessive costs as well as its failure to bring benefits. This argument, discussed in section 5.3, above, can be seen in terms of the links which do or do not exist between economic activity, ecological damage, and welfare. Thus debate about how to respond to the ecological crisis has often been expressed in terms of how far ecological damage and economic activity, as measured by GDP, can be 'delinked'. We have argued that they cannot be delinked, at least not sufficiently, and particularly in view of the magnitude of existing damage and the need for greater equity at a global level. Even if, as has been suggested, quite dramatic improvements in ecological efficiency are possible, these will not allow us to continue on the path of economic growth discussed in Chapter 2. But just as important, as we argued in Chapter 4, the link between GDP and *welfare* is virtually non-existent. Therefore, if we are interested in exploring development based on improving welfare, the real issue is delinking welfare, not GDP, from ecological impact, and that, we have argued, is quite feasible.

Figure 9.1 summarises: (a) the orthodox position; and (b) the view we advocate. According to the orthodox view, there is a close link between economic activity and welfare (hence the over-riding importance of economic growth). Any link between economic activity and its ecological impact, however, is, on this view, quite flexible: economic growth can solve as well as cause ecological problems, and appropriate policies can limit damage without any need to curb growth. The view we have argued for in this book however is in a sense the reverse. There is some flexibility in the link between economic activity and its ecological impact, but this is quite insufficient, and they certainly cannot be delinked (see Chapter 2); the link with welfare on the other hand only exists at very low consumption levels (see Chapter 4).

Figure 9.1 also brings in the link between economic activity and *profits*. This link *is* important if the concern is with profit rather than welfare. In particular, for those, such as 'green' entrepreneurs and shareholders, whose aim is profit maximisation but who acknowledge some need to face ecological problems, the link between GDP and ecological impact is crucial, and perpetuating GDP growth while limiting impact ('sustainable growth') is the aim. But equally, those whose aim is welfare must confront the issue, because if profits are inextricably linked to ecological damage, then there is the problem of overcoming the powerful interests defending the profit motive, if such sustainability is to be achieved.

Can profit be delinked from ecological damage? We have argued that the link between ecological damage and economic activity (GDP) can only be stretched to a limited extent; but does this mean that reducing ecological damage is incompatible with increasing profits? Without GDP growth, profits cannot grow (except to a limited extent at the expense of wages). Those who are concerned to find ways to continue increasing profits, while reducing ecological damage, face increasing obstacles. In essence, a reduction in economic activity is necessary, as we have argued, and this reduces the opportunity for profit.

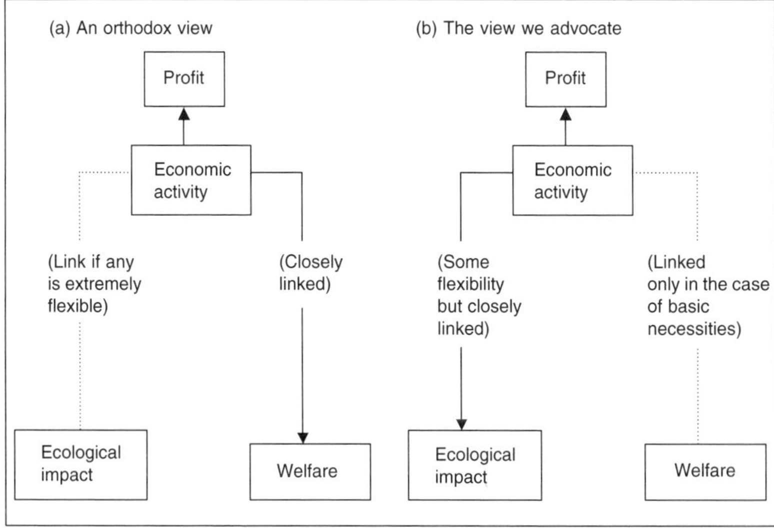

Figure 9.1 Links between economic activity, profit, ecological impact and welfare

The attempt to escape this problem has led to a number of suggestions. We reviewed some of these in Chapter 5 and found them wanting from the point of view of either welfare or profit or both. Some suggestions, such as the idea of renting rather than buying consumer goods, or the 'negawatt' scheme, are essentially devices which are intended to make consumption cuts profitable, and therefore acceptable, to business. Clearly, such schemes appeal to those who see a need for consumption cuts, but who consider any policy which threatens profits to be unrealistic. But they cannot get round the fact that profits have to be paid out of GNP; therefore they can at most be a way of introducing specific consumption cuts, but they cannot be a general scheme for making consumption cuts across the board (of the kind we suggest in Chapter 7) profitable.

Profit seekers face huge difficulties in their search for ecologically harmless products which can nevertheless be sold at a large profit. This is true whether this involves entirely new products, or existing products which are made in a more ecologically friendly way. In the case of more eco-friendly production of existing goods, the most fundamental objection, from the point of view of profit, is that reducing material inputs will reduce costs, and competition will then reduce prices and the opportunity for profit. And this cannot be offset (as generally happens now) by increasing the scale of production, without increasing ecological impact also. Suggestions that are perhaps more promising – since they seem to fit in with existing trends – are those that argue for an economy based more on services and information products than presently. However, as Chapter 5 suggested, there is no trend towards consuming fewer goods, and no indication that consuming more services might lead to such a trend.

Delinking ecological damage and risk from welfare is perfectly feasible (indeed they are not really linked in the first place); delinking them from profit may be impossible. There are thus two very different views of how welfare and profit are related. In the orthodox view, profit is an essential spur to economic activity, which in turn is wholly beneficial for welfare. In our view on the other hand, profit is quite irrelevant for welfare, while the economic activity it spurs has a catastrophic ecological impact.[6]

It is true that capitalism has in the past been flexible in some respects. Defenders of a green capitalism point out how what were perceived to be vicious attacks on the order prevailing at the time such as the 10-hour working day and the abolition of child labour, as well as early air pollution laws, were first resisted and then easily absorbed. No doubt all sorts of ecological improvements could be accommodated in the same way.

However, such improvements were introduced at times of fast expanding output and profit opportunities. It is most unlikely that a system – until now at least – based on the search for output and profit growth could be compatible with the kind of overall, permanent reduction in production and consumption which we are advocating. More sociologically, in the longer term, our proposals involve a radical change in values, presumably affecting capitalists as well as workers; it is difficult to see how a caste of thrusting, profit-driven entrepreneurs could exist in a society where everyone else was aiming to consume less but better. For the profit motive to flourish requires not only the opportunity to continue making profits (something on which we have cast doubt) but also the opportunity to spend them. Yet consumer lifestyles require a huge degree of support from others (see Chapter 4), and it would be even harder to be a 'big spender' in an anti-consumerist society as to be a 'downshifter' in the existing one.[7] In the shorter term, if our proposals are followed, full employment (but with much shorter hours) and the lack of perceived need for more goods would threaten work discipline and thus profits.

9.3.2 Is history on our side?

The implication of our argument is therefore a revolution in institutions and values. How likely is this? Is history on our side? We do not know. Social change seems to be largely chaotic and unpredictable. Certainly all the major social changes within our lifetimes seem to have taken everyone by surprise: the rise of radical politics in the 1960s and 1970s, the neoliberal counter-attack in the 1980s and 1990s, the collapse of 'communism' and the rise of militant Islamic fundamentalism. Neither Marxist accounts in terms of the historical inevitably of a particular direction of change, nor those proclaiming the 'end of history' are particularly convincing (see, for example, Fukuyama, 2000).

At the same time, social change doesn't occur for in isolation. The history of energy systems suggests that they are too fundamental to how the economy and society operate, and become too bound up with dominant economic interests, to change, except under the impact of an unavoidable energy crisis. Such a crisis certainly appears to be unfolding, though it may be some time before it forces fundamental change. An eventual reduction in energy use is inevitable, as well as being linked to other changes. 'This energy revolution is more than ever inseparable from another revolution, a political, social and cultural revolution with no historical precedent' (Debeir *et al.*, 1991, p. 239). We cannot predict how these pressures will generate change, but we can point out the consequences of responding to them – consequences that will be more favourable if we anticipate them – and suggest the values that need to guide this response.

There has been some suggestion of a shift from 'materialist' to 'post-materialist' values across most rich countries (see, for example, Inglehart, 1997, especially Chs 4 and 5). Increasing numbers of people give priority, in response to surveys, to goals such as 'more say on the job' or 'a less impersonal society', over more traditional concerns with the economy. It is unclear however whether this really indicates a decline in consumerism, or merely its channelling into new products (more commercialised leisure, for example).

On the one hand, therefore, it is certainly true that environmental problems will become more urgent, as pressure on resources, including irreplaceable ones, intensifies. Conventional 'solutions', by using the problems as a spur to further growth, will continue to make things worse. Adoption of apparently more ecological policies within a framework which gives priority to profit will at most ensure that the rich continue to enjoy a better environment, rationed out according to 'willingness' to pay. Thus pressure for change will intensify. On the other hand, as we have seen, there seems to be a fundamental problem in reconciling substantial reduction in consumption with the profit motive and thus with prevailing interests.

9.4 Consumers of the world relax!

We will not get very far in the direction of our scenario, or even with the more modest policies proposed in section 9.2, above, without more fundamental changes. Of course we cannot predict what the exact nature and results of these changes will be. If there is one thing that is certain about any more ecological and welfare-oriented society of the future, it is that people will be experimenting – in their relationships, their organisation, the technology they use – and who knows what the result will be? Nevertheless, the discussion of previous chapters suggests some general directions, which are summarised in Table 9.1 and commented on below.

Speed

Increasing ecological impact has largely been associated with increasing speed of travel, of people and of goods. As we have seen, transport in rich countries is the largest and fastest increasing energy user. Ecological crisis can largely be seen as a clash of time scales: the time scales of human resource use and pollution emission, and of natural regeneration and assimilation (Sachs, 1999, Ch. 11).

Living in accordance with ecological limits therefore implies accepting speed limits. The search for improved welfare suggests that we find ways to enjoy the slower speeds; and reducing employed work time makes it much easier to do so. Slower speeds will be easier to achieve where there is less need to cover long distances: less need to transport goods produced for local use (see 'Localisation' below), but also less urge to escape everyday life at every opportunity. But as time is freed up by shorter working hours, it also becomes possible to combine slower speeds with *longer* distances. With less time spent on what they don't really want to do, people may well feel less need to get away, and to get so far away; but when they do get the urge to see the world they will be able to take their time and see more of it. The week in Goa and the weekend in Prague will then give way, for those who want it, to the year-long voyage of discovery[8] (largely overland), as well as the weekend in the countryside an hour or two away by train.

Community

Belonging to a community seems to be essential for individual well-being: because of the identity it provides, the network of support, the

Table 9.1 Development strategies (for rich countries) compared

Development strategy	*Consumption-based*	*Welfare-based*
Economy organised around…	Growth of material production	Meeting basic needs
Impact on human activity	Enough unemployment to ensure social discipline; otherwise, full-time employment and commercialised leisure	Minimise employment but share equally; more time for community participation and for self-fulfilment
Impact on natural environment	Ecological crisis to be a stimulus not a brake on growth; costs and risks shifted onto the poor	Ecological costs kept kept within natural capacity to absorb; natural resources shared more fairly
Rich and poor countries	Globalisation increases and reinforces inequalities	Rich can learn from poor; localisation increases independence
Poverty within countries	Relative poverty inevitable; even absolute poverty quite common	Redistribution eliminates both
Food and agriculture	Productive only if major costs ignored	Local, small scale and organic
Transport and land use	Suburban sprawl; based around the private car	Cycling and collective transport
Trade	Encouraged; used as geopolitical weapon	Limited to luxuries, and what can't be produced locally
Travel	For recuperation; tightly programmed	For discovery; done at a leisurely pace
Community	Non-existent, or based around consumer lifestyles	Combining mutual support and individual freedom

security. The very notion of an individual, considered in isolation from the wider community, and thus of 'individual well-being', may be something that makes little sense where the feeling of community is strong. It seems to be a feature of traditional communities (unlike modern societies, however rich) that members are not allowed to go without the basics, unless the whole community is having to do the same. The loss of community in modern societies is a source of loneliness and misery for many, and may be part of the explanation for the growth of consumerism (see Chapter 4). In the case of 'less developed' countries, it is sometimes argued that community must be protected from 'development', and indeed should spearhead resistance to it (see, for example, Esteva and Prakash, 1998).

In the case of rich countries, where communities are weak or nonexistent, it is not possible to turn the clock back and recreate previously existing traditional forms of community. We have become too individualistic, too used to making our own choices and rejecting authority (usually, but not always, in ways that are trivial in terms of their contribution to social welfare). Once released, the possibility of individual choice cannot simply be abolished. Nor perhaps is it desirable that it should be, since in consumerist societies such communities as exist generally push individuals towards more consumption, and individual choices to reject consumerism are necessary if a more ecologically benign and welfare-oriented development path is to be adopted. More generally, communities can oppress as well as sustain their members. What is required is a search for low consumption, sharing and egalitarian communities which nevertheless provide for greater diversity and choice of beliefs and social roles than most traditional communities do.[9]

Work

After a period of stagnation, and in spite of longer hours in some countries and occupations, the movement towards shorter working hours seems to have taken off again (section 9.2, see above). But this is largely a reaction to unemployment; it could well be reversed, and implies only modest change in terms of hours or overall impact, compared to the work reductions we would like to see.

The scale of consumption cuts discussed in Chapter 7 implies a halving of working hours. In addition, such a reduction makes it possible to envisage spreading employment across a much larger proportion of the population, since the much shorter paid working hours (for both men and women) can be combined with housework, child care, and studying in a way that is not possible with a standard working week of 35–40 hours. An average working week of around 10–12 hours per employed person would result (cf. Andret, 1977).

Of course this would only be an average, and it would be possible for individuals to choose a variety of options: a shorter working week, or working year, earlier retirement, and so on. There is a potential for great flexibility in terms of when we work or don't work, and how paid work fits in with other activities, without the pressure experienced by many individuals faced with existing employment patterns.

Not only time but also effort would be redistributed. When employment, as part of our present system, or employment combined with child care and housework, takes up a large part of people's time and energy, spare time is largely taken up with rest, passive leisure, and compensation for the stresses of work. With a radical shortening of employment time, we would have more time and energy to give to socialising, community participation, and creative activities, with a resulting enrichment of social life.

Equality

According to most economists and politicians, poverty will eventually be abolished as a result of economic growth. This view is not supported by recent evidence, but in any case, if growth is abandoned, the only way to end poverty is through redistribution. Moreover, relative poverty can *only* be reduced by redistribution, and large inequalities, even when they don't result in absolute poverty, are offensive (particularly when, as is not infrequently the case, the wealth results from luck, inheritance, fraud or violence).

The move towards greater equality implies above all a revolution in relations between rich and poor countries, and in the distribution of wealth, in particular natural wealth, among them. That is one reason why we have argued that large consumption reductions are necessary in rich countries. But greater equality within countries is necessary also. Reductions in working hours in poorly paid occupations will only be acceptable to those workers if their hourly rate is increased.

We are thus envisaging a more equal (but lower average) level of consumption, and thus ecological impact, per person. In addition, we are advocating a more equal (but lower average) amount of employment per person. This in turn implies a fairer distribution of 'unpaid work', in particular between men and women.

Localisation

Ecological considerations alone suggest the desirability of a move towards greater (not complete) self-sufficiency, at various geographical levels. Current patterns of production and consumption involve a huge amount of transport. For example, an average plate of food in the US is estimated to have travelled some 1500 miles (Norbert-Hodge *et al.*, 2000); an average supermarket trolley in England has travelled 50 000 miles (Raven and Lang, 1995). The full ecological cost of goods transport is only very partially reflected in the monetary cost.

But in addition, reliance on trade for essentials creates dependence on richer and more powerful countries, and on large multinational companies. It would therefore be desirable to adopt the general principle that necessities should be as locally produced as possible, thus ensuring a community's economic independence, and its ability to survive economic pressure from outside.

The principle of producing as locally as possible and trading only where this is not possible, would require a complete change of direction from the trend of recent years towards (selectively) 'free' trade. It would involve an increase in local control over production and a fairer sharing of the benefits from trade. It would require (but in turn make easier) strict regulation of multinational enterprises. It would involve the return of exchange controls and an emphasis on local rather than global money. Competition would have to be characterised by a 'level but local' playing field, that is, one that does not undermine local environmental and social standards, and lead to a 'race to the bottom', as current 'free' trade threatens. Agriculture would give absolute priority to satisfying local food needs, ahead of any exports (Hines, 2000).

The prospects for a move, if not towards localisation, at least towards slower globalisation, seem brighter than for some years. From the point of view of the globalisers themselves, it is turning out to be impossible to globalise profit opportunities without globalising the problems (financial and agricultural viruses and 'terrorism', for example) as well. Opponents of globalisation meanwhile have become more vocal and organised, and may succeed in at least slowing the pace at which it occurs.

Democratisation

The last 25 years have seen an erosion of democracy, as the economy has become more international, as it has been increasingly driven by global finance, and as government policy has been increasingly constrained by international economic and political factors. In addition, it has been easier for government to blame these factors for unpopular policies even where they were not constraining. The neoliberal paradigm, which views business interests as fundamentally benign and considers that government's role should be exclusively to support them, has become dominant.

The implication of our proposals is that these developments need to be largely reversed. Reducing, then reversing, growth implies contradicting, rather than submitting to, business interests, and requires government intervention aimed at maintaining welfare rather than profits. Reducing energy use, particularly its use in transporting goods, and moving towards production for local use, run directly against the promotion of 'free' trade and a more international economy.

But the extent of democracy which existed before, when national economies were somewhat more self-sufficient, was quite inadequate anyway. There is a large literature concerned with the way that parliamentary democracy is manipulated by dominant interests (see, for example, Carey, 1997). More specifically, much of this book has been concerned with the way that both the market and the ballot box channel behaviour into ever-increasing consumption and continued long employment hours – in spite of the fact that these reduce rather than improve welfare. Clearly, new and better methods of collective decision making are required, which make it possible to overcome positional competition, protect the ecosystem from damage and risk, and ensure that resources are allocated in a way that genuinely contributes to welfare.

Well-being

This brings us back to what is the overarching concern of this book, well-being. Well-being is generally taken to be the ultimate objective of all economic and social activity, and we have no quarrel with that. Indeed it is almost true by definition, if well-being is defined as whatever it is that people seek in their activities. However, as we have argued, the current pattern of development, based on ever-increasing consumption, is harmful to well-being; and the underlying principle of the alternative approach to development we are advocating, involving reduced consumption in rich countries, must be to better ensure that well-being is attained.

We agree with the view of most economists (in principle at least) that what well-being means exactly should be decided by each of us, individually and collectively. However economists generally consider that the best institutions for doing this are the market (for individual decisions) and the ballot box (for collective ones). We have suggested many reasons why this does not work. Better methods of making collective decisions about social goals are required.

Moreover, economists and politicians pay lip service to the goal of well-being, and for purposes of argument in this book we have often taken them at their word. But in practice they equate this very largely with income and consumption levels, hence their emphasis on economic growth. The implication of our argument is that well-being (and thus also 'progress' and 'development') must be redefined, as well as measured and monitored differently. We have developed some of our ideas about this into the framework of social concerns and indicators that we present in Chapters 6 and 8.

In reality of course the present system is run for profit – that is, the income and consumption of a particular group, and not the average consumption level, let alone the general level of welfare. But we take it as obvious that the latter is what should drive the system, hence the need to put welfare before profit, for the rich world to reduce its share of resource use, and for solutions that challenge existing institutions to be discussed rather than discarded as unrealistic.

Notes

1 Introduction: the Purpose and Structure of this Book

1 During the current Labour government, there has been a vogue in UK public sector management-speak for 'joined-up' thinking, referring to the interrelatedness of many government policies and particularly the impact of different government policies.

2 Neoclassical economics is the dominant school of thought within economics, and therefore we have tended to use the various terms – mainstream, orthodox, conventional, neoclassical – interchangeably. It is characterised above all by its belief in markets as the most effective mechanism for allocating resources fairly and efficiently. Other schools of thought have rejected some, but not necessarily all, aspects of neoclassical economics, and some of the criticisms we make apply to some of these schools also.

2 Ecological Impacts and Risks

1 For example, one estimate, based on 'ecological footprints', explained below, is that the world could support 7.9 billion people at the Chinese level of consumption, but only 1.2 billion at the US level (using existing technology) (Chambers *et al.*, 2000, p. 129).

2 The region was originally one of 'mixed evergreen and deciduous forest of oaks, beech, pines and cedars'. Its present state, ranging from scrub to desert, is the result of 'massive environmental degradation', due chiefly to deforestation and overgrazing (Ponting, 1991, p. 75).

3 For example, world coal production increased almost 50-fold during the nineteenth century, while world population roughly doubled. The twentieth century showed a similar trend, but with oil increasingly replacing coal (Ponting, 1991, pp. 241, 289).

4 And two implausible ones, involving, respectively, where physical limits are either very far off, or themselves growing exponentially; and where the limits are 'unerodable' (that is, unaffected by attempts to breach them), or able to recover quickly from erosion.

5 Events since have made it very unlikely that the target will be met: large increases in emissions in many countries for instance, and most recently the rejection of the protocol by the largest emitter, the US.

6 This is the sense in which we use 'poverty' and 'poor' in this section. See section 4.1.2, below, for a discussion of the various meanings attached to these words.

7 For example, Wiezsäcker, one of the *Factor Four* authors, has suggested that 'a factor of four improvement is considered to be readily achievable; a factor of ten is what may actually be necessary to achieve sustainable development' (reported in ENDS Report 272, Sept. 1997). Ekins (2000, Ch. 6) provides some support for the latter figure.

8 That this can lead to a completely unsatisfactory notion of rationality and inefficiency, even aside from ecological considerations, is well illustrated by the 'McDonaldization of Society' (Ritzer, 1993).
9 The fact that 'known deposits' have remained roughly constant, in proportion to annual use, is sometimes taken to indicate that we are not running out of oil, as if they were related to actual deposits. However, this is nonsense: oil companies' exploration strategies are targeted specifically at a particular level of known deposits, and the size of the latter therefore indicates nothing at all about actual deposits.

3 The Employment Problem

1 In France, there has been a legislative move to a 35-hour week, although it has not yet been fully implemented; and there was a similar attempt more than 60 years ago that ended in failure.
2 In the UK, conventionally at the moment, 16–64 for men and 16–59 for women. The latter will be changed to 16–64 in 2020, that is, increasing the size of the labour force.
3 There has always been some ambivalence about the practicability of literally 'full' employment partly because of the belief that the workforce would then be in 'too powerful' a market position leading to wage demands, forcing prices up and thence the 'evil' of inflation (see Chapter 5).
4 For example, the 'hard sell' of cigarettes in developing countries, as markets retract in the North.
5 The pressure to consume – dealt with in the following chapter – is of course the other major determinant.
6 This section and the following one summarise the argument in Anthony (1977).
7 This is not to deny that there had not previously been any concern with economic power. Indeed, the Roman Empire and some medieval courts were monuments to material acquisition and display, but the concept of material value, its production and measurement, were absent.
8 Or, as Perelman (2000) says: '... prisons and factories were created about the same time and their operators consciously borrowed from each other's control techniques'. A worker is a part-time slave.
9 In recent times, self-immolation means suicide: here, the meaning is sacrifice of one's own interest for the sake of others.
10 See Parkinson (1958): 'work expands to fill the time available'.
11 If he 'wins' then, of course, the differentiation may or may not continue; although many would argue (for example, Porter, 1990) that modern corporations – whether or not they are monopolies – have to launch new products continuously (for example, computer software, programes and games).
12 The American Federation of Labour later combined with the Congress of Industrial Organisations to form the AFL-CIO.
13 For a committed argument, diametrically opposed to our own, deploring this process, see Webster, 2001.

14 This, of course, is exactly what has happened through the progressive refinement of the various employment substitutes; but see also the Tract issued by Solidarity (cited in Carr-Hill, 1986), and the extract on pp. 49–50, above.
15 Although this is, in fact, unlikely because the most important of the categories of experience is the structuring of the waking day. That was of course understood very well by the earlier captains of industry.

4 Consumption

1 Given the emphasis on welfare maximisation and preference satisfaction, it is surprising to find that it has been recognised by many economists, going back at least to Adam Smith, that consumption growth leads to dissatisfaction not satisfaction, and that it is this in turn that drives growth (O'Neill, 1998). However, until now this was given a positive gloss: growth was desirable, and dissatisfaction a necessary means to it. The further wants that emerged when one set was satisfied were 'higher' wants. This can no longer be maintained where growth faces ecological limits and where, as we argue below, it is self-defeating, even aside from those limits.
2 Even approaches to economics that are more ecologically oriented tend to be half-hearted in their critique of consumerism (see Lintott, 1998).
3 They are also the 'original information society' since their continued viability depended almost entirely on the accumulation of local information and very little on physical capital. This tends to be ignored by orthodox economists who – whatever their enthusiasm about IT, dematerialisation and so on – are only interested in information that is standardised, generally applicable, tradeable in global markets, and so on.
4 Awareness of the issue goes back much further. Adam Smith, in a famous passage, argued that the need for clothing depended on standards of comfort and decency which varied greatly. For example people could go about without shoes and stockings in Scotland but not in England.
5 Gintis also finds evidence of 'loss aversion' and 'status quo bias', which bears on our argument for a major reduction in consumption habits, though in an ambiguous way: '... individuals often prefer the *status quo* over any of the alternatives, but if one of the alternatives becomes the *status quo*, that too is preferred to any of the alternatives' (Gintis, 2000, p. 315).
6 The label 'the Sixties' has of course been associated with many things and often used misleadingly. Ironically, but not surprisingly, attempts to co-opt radical currents of that time have put a lot of emphasis on consumption habits which became more popular around then (rock, 'drugs', jeans, wholefoods, 'travelling' ...), purposefully ignoring the fact that each of these was originally a rebellion against some aspect of prevailing, mainstream consumer lifestyles (classical music, alcohol, suits, processed food, packaged tourism ...), not least requiring less money and less dehumanising work than them. It is this reaction *against* consumption that Wachtel is referring to.
7 'The prophets of anti-growth depend implicitly on the idea that goods are primarily needed for food and shelter. If that were all, we could cut them down to a healthy level' (1982, p. 31). Douglas has tended to play down

environmental risks, being mainly interested in how perceptions of risk develop (Fardon, 1999, Ch. 7); more generally, she seems concerned with why people consume rather than with the welfare implications of doing so.

5 Orthodox and Green Solutions

1 For an account of how this change in perception was experienced in one intergovernmental organisation, the OECD, see Nectoux *et al.* (1980).
2 The UK government, for example, introduces 'Sustainable Development: the UK strategy' as follows: 'Most societies want to achieve economic development to secure higher standards of living, now and for future generations. They also seek to protect and enhance their environment, now and for their children. "Sustainable development" tries to reconcile these two objectives' (UK, 1994, p. 6).
3 In some countries, notably the US and UK, it has in recent years been possible to lower unemployment somewhat without an increase in inflation or in industrial unrest, since many of the new jobs – especially those for women – are insecure and non-unionised. We are still a long way however from the near-zero unemployment which was a feature of most of the 1950s and 1960s with a full-time, mainly industrial, workforce when most women were still permanent 'housewives'.
4 The renewed move towards a shorter working week in France and elsewhere in Western Europe (see Chapter 9), has been greeted by some as a sign of new thinking by governments, but it remains to be seen whether this trend is maintained if and when unemployment falls substantially.
5 For example, the European Union's rate of growth of real GDP was half (2.4 per cent annually) in the 1980s what it had been in the 1960s (4.8 per cent) and it remained at the lower level in the 1990s (Somers, 1998, p. 367).
6 Whatever the good intentions of both organisers and travellers, ecotourism has all too often had as its main effect to attract more people to ecologically sensitive areas, where they probably do more harm than if they were on an ordinary package holiday (that is, when it is not merely a way of marketing holidays which have some, possibly vague, connection to nature).
7 The 1997 Kyoto Accords illustrate the difficulties of reaching agreement, as well as the power of the richest countries. They also illustrate the role of market instruments: it is the CO_2 reduction targets which are significant for the environment, while emissions trading acts as a way of allowing rich countries to continue emitting more than poor countries, by buying the right to do so. More recently, the US has simply refused to sign up to the agreement.
8 From a paper by Hardin (1968), who showed that 'rational' (in the economic sense) herdsmen would overgraze common land, since each individual herdsman only faces *some* of the cost of grazing an extra animal. In fact, commonly held resources in traditional societies have often been used sustainably for centuries (in contrast to privately owned resources in 'modern' societies).
9 Indeed, they are so systematic and pervasive, in most countries, particularly in areas such as agriculture, mining, energy and transport, that they are better viewed as a normal part of a public–private partnership in favour of

growth at all costs, rather than as an aberration in an otherwise rational system, as the use of the description 'perverse' suggests.

10 This uses a survey approach to estimate individuals' WTP for environmental goods. At its crudest, a sample of respondents are simply asked how much they would pay for good X. More sophisticated versions attempt to introduce a degree of realism, through game playing strategies, for example.

11 Although this terminology may be objectionable: 'In referring to the environment as capital, there is an implicit assumption that it can be substituted by other forms of capital, that it is reproducible and that it is there to be managed in much the same way as manufactured capital' (Victor, 1991, p. 210).

6 Moving from Growth to Welfare – a Conceptual Framework

1 Note that there are situations in which people are paid NOT to work – for example, the EU subsidises farmers to set aside some of their land to avoid over-production.

2 Maslow (1987) later revised the hierarchy to place the different sets of needs on an equal footing.

3 The current version of this approach is the series of EuroBarometer surveys.

4 See, for example, the arguments over the WHO's Index of Health System Performance.

5 For example, the conferences on Evidence-Based Policies and Indicators Systems at Durham have large attendances.

6 We are not claiming that this is a novel idea!

7 'Wars' on drug users have their origin in the USA Hoover administration's campaign in the 1920s. There have been repeated demonstrations that they only serve to make profits for drug barons and that alternative approaches (including treatment as well as legislation) are more cost-effective and provide more security. Following these policies, The Netherlands has managed to avoid the vicious spiral of drug addicts committing crime to fund their habit.

7 Orders of Magnitude of Change

1 Note that this corresponds to the trends observed and projected by several futurologists in the 1960s and 1970s, although it was rarely phrased this way. For example, Gross (1971) said that the post-service society was presumed to have at least the following features

- A sharp reduction in numbers working in large-scale market based service employment that is routine and repetitive and can be replaced by technology;
- Employment will also fall where personalised services can be provided in a centralised fashion;

- Manufacturing will use fewer workers, especially in small firms, because of competition.

2 When people get the chance to express their willingness to pay for a good environment in a real market, they do, as the high prices paid for a house or a holiday in an environmentally clean location demonstrate. The trouble is that the environment is a public good, and treating it like a private good only makes things worse, as we saw in Chapters 2 and 4. But there is little doubt about consumers' *wish* to enjoy a good environment.
3 This is in addition to intermediate goods as usually understood – the outputs of one firm purchased by another – which can be traced using the input–output tables.
4 The phrase was used by Kuznets (1951, p. 184) to describe government activity (in the context of the US), which he argued could not contribute to net welfare, and should therefore be excluded from National Income.
5 In other words, the impacts listed under each industry heading are *not* the ones arising from the operation of that industry, but rather the ones arising from consumers (and governments) buying the products of those industries. For example, there are not 476 000 jobs in food processing; there are 476 000 jobs, in food processing and elsewhere, involved in producing the goods that the food processing industry sells to final consumers.
6 Note that we are not taking into account the potential for efficiency and technical gains (e.g. the Factor Four debate). The focus here is on where we could consume less now.
7 One might, however, in the short term, be concerned about the health impact of lower alcohol prices in a population not yet attuned to living life in a more leisurely fashion.
8 Indeed, there is no real need for designer labels at all; their main function is to project an expensive self image and they encourage notions of elite status.
9 This is an example of an area where there is the potential for much larger cuts with technological improvements – using renewable energy sources, for example – that we are not including in these calculations.
10 The downside in terms of change for its own sake, at the moment, as encouraged by DIY TV programmes, would be avoided by the near-elimination of advertising.
11 The events in America on 11 September 2001 have made many 'look again' at air travel and the increased security measures have slowed down any renewed growth.
12 Although the incidence of some of those conditions would reduce because of lifestyle changes.
13 These are described by Vaze (1997) and can be freely downloaded from the Internet site http://www.statistics.gov.uk.
14 PPP is Purchasing Power Parity. When incomes in low-income countries are expressed in, say, US dollars, using the usual market exchange rates, this generally makes these countries seem even poorer than they really are, because it fails to allow for their (generally) much lower cost of living. PPPs are an attempt to allow for this: an income of 'PPP$5000' is an income that would provide the same purchasing power as US$5000 would in the US.

8 A First Selected Set of Social Performance/ Progress Indicators

1 See Carr-Hill (1999) for a critique in the area of education.

9 The Fourth Way in Practice: What Can be Done?

1 Of course this statement makes no sense from the point of view of orthodox economic theory, where welfare can always be increased through further economic activity and resource use. The idea of welfare developed in Chapter 6 suggests that there are components of welfare, each of which involves aiming to arrive at a sufficient or optimum amount, in contrast to maximising (or minimising) – that is, trying to obtain as much (or as little) as possible.

2 Ashis Nandy, discussing 'evaluating utopias', warns: 'This century has taught us that the search for a non-oppressive society can itself sometimes become a new means of oppression and a technique for expropriating new kinds of surplus – economic, political, cultural and psychological. Our criteria for evaluating utopias must include safeguards against the criteria themselves, Those who advocate a utopia need' … to be accountable for its legitimate and illegitimate brain-children' (Nandy, 1987, p. 6).

3 Unfortunately, far from learning those lessons, rich country governments have so far preferred to promote the 'benefits' of globalisation, which is increasingly undermining experiments in alternative development, in Kerala and elsewhere.

4 Of course other categories of energy use (and thus greenhouse gas emissions) are also important, notably energy use in households, and energy use in production. However both these categories have tended to stabilise or decline in rich countries. Also, and relatedly, efficiency improvements here are less a matter of changing lifestyles and more a matter of improved design (of product and production methods) than in the case of transport.

5 Perhaps the 'rentier' label is unfair in as much as the investment income is derived from saving out of past earnings: the rentiers can be seen as early retirees, who have organised their own pensions. The fact remains that the opportunity to adopt the voluntary simplicity programme is very unequally distributed, especially at a global level, and redistribution of work and income *between* people is required, and not just reduction of the work and income of some people.

6 This activity also leads to much alienating and miserable employed work (Chapter 3). Since the link between economic activity and employment is uncontroversial however, we have omitted it from Figure 9.1 and from the discussion in this section.

7 Where, for example, would a Porsche driver be in a society where he had to make his own car – because others would have more attractive work opportunities than to make it for him – and where speed limits on the remaining roads were set at a prudent 20 miles per hour (not even to mention fuel taxes, road pricing, or emission standards)? He would at worst be indulging in a fairly harmless hobby. To repeat (section 4.1.2), 'Luxury is not possible except when it is paid for by the labour of others' (Smith, 1993, p. 188).

8 With slower speed allowing also an improvement in the quality of the experience: getting to know and learning from a country, its people and culture, and not only enjoying its beaches and museums.
9 More generally, our proposals imply a rejection of many things which seem to be associated with 'modernity', above all the high value attached to novelty for its own sake (and the use of new products as status symbols), but also such things as the lure of ever greater speeds and distances, particular interpretations of 'freedom' and 'happiness', and extreme individualism. But these goals and aspirations are proving to be largely futile or even self-contradictory. The search for the new becomes itself old and boring; the search for speed leads to congestion, and the search for distant and exotic locations leads to the spread of identical modern values and lifestyles everywhere; the pursuit of individualism, taken too far, leads to isolation. In other words, modern values largely fail, even in their own terms. But they do not fail altogether, and in some respects need to be redefined rather than abandoned completely: for example, by searching for, and by exercising individual choice among, new ways of living rather than products, and by adopting a better and broader definition of happiness (see Chapter 6).

References and Select Bibliography

Abramovitz, M., 1979. Economic Growth and its Discontents, in M.J. Boskin (ed.), *Economics and Human Welfare*. New York: Academic Press.

Abrams, M., 1973. Subjective Social Indicators. *Social Trends*, 4, 35–50.

Ahmad, Y.J., El Seraby, S. and Lutz, E. (eds), 1989. *Environmental Accounting for Sustainable Development*. Washington, DC: World Bank.

Allardt, E., 1975. *Dimensions of Welfare in a Comparative Scandinavian Study*, University of Helsinki: Research Group for Comparative Sociology (Research Reports No. 9).

Amez-Droz, Carlos, 1993. 'Indicateurs culturels – cadre général pour les indicateurs de la promotion, de la distribution et de la consommation culturelles', *Schweizerische Zeitschrift für Soziologie*, 19, 153–69.

Adret (Collectif), 1977. 'Travailer Deux Heures par Jour', Paris: Editions de Seuil.

Andrews, F.M. and Withey, S., 1976. *Social Indicators of Well-being*. New York: Plenum.

Anonymous, 1996. 'Recommendations of the Conference "Measuring Social Inequalities in Health", Sponsored by the National Institutes of Health, September 28–30, 1994', *International Journal of Health Services*, 26, 521–7.

Anthony, P.D., 1977. *The Ideology of Work*. London: Tavistock.

Apthorpe, R.J., 1987. 'Two Concepts of Social Development: their Implications for Databases, Indicators and Development Planning', *Regional Development Dialogue*, 8, 2, 43–70.

Aranowitz, S. and DiFazio, W., 1994. *The Jobless Future*. Minneapolis, MN: University of Minnesota Press.

Arber, S., 1991. 'Class, Paid Employment and Family Roles: Making Sense of Structural Disadvantages, Gender and Health Status', *Social Science and Medicine*, 32, 425–36.

Arendt, H., 1958. *The Human Condition*. Chicago, IL: University of Chicago Press.

Argyle, M., 1987. *The Psychology of Happiness*. London: Methuen.

Aristotle, 1912. *Politics*. London: J.M. Dent and Sons.

Armstrong, D., Wing, S. and Tyroler, H.A., 1996. 'Race Differences in Estimates of Sudden Coronary Heart Disease Mortality, 1980–1988: the Impact of Ill-defined Death', *Journal of Clinical Epidemiology*, 49, 1247–51.

Arrow, K.J., 1963. *Social Choice and Individual Values*, 2nd ed. New York and London: Wiley.

Athanasiou, T., 1996. *Slow Reckoning*. London: Secker and Warburg.

Ayres, R.U. and Kneese, A.V., 1969. 'Production, Consumption and Externalities', *American Economic Review*, 69, 282–97.

Bartelmus, P., 1994. *Environment, Growth and Development*. London and New York: Routledge.

Bartelmus, P., Stahmer, C. and van Tongeren, J., 1991. 'Integrated Environmental and Economic Accounting: Framework for a SNA Satellite System', *Review of Income and Wealth*. Series 37, June 1991, 111–48.

Bartley, M. and Plewis, I., 1997. 'Does Health-selective Mobility account for Socioeconomic Differences in Health? Evidence from England and Wales, 1971 to 1991', *Journal of Health and Social Behaviour*, 38, 376–86.

Baudrillard, J., 1998 (orig. 1970). *The Consumer Society*. London: Sage.

Bauer, R.A., 1966. *Social Indicators*. Cambridge, MA: MIT Press.

Bauer, R.A., Rosenbloom, R.S. and Sharp, L., 1969. *Second-Order Consequences*. Cambridge, MA: MIT Press.

Beder, S., 1997. *Global Spin: the Corporate Assault on Environmentalism*. Green Books: Totnes.

Bellamy, E., *Looking Backward, 2000–1887*, 1887 D. Appleton and Company; repr. New York, n.d., pp. 158–60.

Blaxter, M., 1984. 'Equity and Consultation Rates in General Practice', *British Medical Journal*, 288, part 6435, 1963–7.

Block, F. and Burns, Gene A., 1986. 'Productivity as a Social Problem: the Uses and Misuse of Social Indicators', *American Sociological Review*, Vol. 51, 767–80.

Bodley, J.H., 1999. 'Socioeconomic Growth, Culture Scale and Household Well-Being. A Test of the Power-Elite Hypothesis', *Current Anthropology*, 40, 5, 595–620.

Boulding, K.E., 1949. 'Income or Welfare', *Review of Economic Studies*, 17, 77–86.

Bowles S., 1998. 'Endogenous Preferences: the Cultural Consequences of Markets and Other Economic Institutions', *Journal of Economic Literature*, Vol. 36, No. 1 (Mar. 1998), 75–111.

Braverman, H., 1974. *Labor and Monopoly Capital*. New York: Monthly Review Press.

Brown, A., 1983. 'On Socialism', *Solidarity*, 1, 3, 7–11.

Brown, P., 1995. 'Race, Class, and Environmental Health: a Review and Systematisation of the Literature', *Environmental Research*, 69, 15–30.

Brunner, E., 1997. 'Socioeconomic Determinants of Health: Stress and the Biology of Inequality', *British Medical Journal*, 314, 1472–82.

Bryant, C. and Cook, P., 1992. 'Environmental Issues and the National Accounts', *Economic Trends*, November.

Burchell, B.J., 1989. 'The Impact on Individuals or Precariousness in the United Kingdom Labour Market', in G. Rodgers and J. Rodgers (eds), *Precarious Jobs in Labour Market Regulation: the Growth of Atypical Employment in Western Europe*. Geneva: International Institute of Labour Studies.

Campbell, A., 1981. *The Sense of Well-being in America: Relevant Patterns and Trends*. New York: McGraw Hill.

Campbell, D., 1988. Data Collection for the Design of Water and Sanitation Projects in Belize, *Waterlines*, Vol. 6, No. 3, January, pp. 26–8.

Cancian, M. and Meyer, D.R., 2000. 'Work after Welfare: Work, Effort, Occupational and Economic Wellbeing', *Social Work Research*, 24, 69–86.

Carey, A., 1997. *Taking the Risk out of Democracy*. Urbana, IL: University of Illinois Press.

Carr-Hill, R.A., 1978. 'Radicalising Survey Methodology', *Quality and Quantity: the European Journal of Methodology*, Vol. 18, 173–91.

Carr-Hill, R., 1987. 'If I were an Anarchist Dictator', *Libertarian Education*, 2, 6–8.

Carr-Hill, R.A., 1988. 'The Future Demand for Health Care', in A. Harrison and J. Gretton (eds), *Health Care UK 1988: an Economic, Social and Policy Audit*. Hermitage: Policy Journals, 11–20.

Carr-Hill, R., 1990. *Social Conditions of Sub-Saharan Africa*. London: Macmillan – now Palgrave Macmillan.

Carr-Hill, R., 1991. 'Allocating Resources to Health Care: is the QALY (Quality Adjusted Life Year) a Technological Solution to a Political Problem?', *International Journal of Health Services*, Vol. 21, 2, 351–63.

Carr-Hill, R., 1993. 'Social Indicators', in P. Nolan and S. Paine (eds), *Socialist Economies*. Cambridge: Cambridge University Press.

Carr-Hill, R. with Hopkins, M. and Riddell, A., 1999. *Monitoring the Performance of Educational Systems*. London: DFID Educational Research Documents, No. 37.

Carr-Hill, R., Lintott, J., Hopkins, M. and Bowen, J., 1995. Towards Systematic Socio-Economic Reporting of the Quality of Life in Europe, for Eurostat.

CERI (Centre for Educational Research and Innovation), 1992. *Adult Illiteracy and Economic Performance*. Paris: Organisation for Economic Cooperation and Development (OECD).

Ceresto, S. and Waitzkin, H., 1986. 'Capitalism, Socialism and the Physical Quality of Life', *International Journal of Health Services*, 16, 643–58.

Chambers, N., Simmons, C. and Wackernagel, M., 2000. *Sharing Nature's Interest: Ecological Footprints as an Indicator of Sustainability*. London: Earthscan.

Chambers, R., 1983. *Rural Development: Putting the Last First*. London: Institute of Development Studies.

Clarke, R., 1982. *Work in Crisis: the Dilemma of a Nation*. Edinburgh: St Andrew Press.

Clavijo, S., 1992. 'Variations on the Basic Needs Yardstick', *World Development*, 20, 1219–23.

Clemitson, I. and Rodgers, G., 1981. *A Life to Live: Beyond Full Employment*. London: Junction Books.

Clogg, C.C., Sullivan, T.A. and Mutchler, J.A., 1986. 'Measuring Underemployment and Inequality in the Workforce', *Social Indicators Research*, 18, 375–93.

Cobb, J.B., 1990. 'An Index of Sustainable Economic Welfare', *Development*, 3–4, 106–12.

Cobb, C.W. and Cobb, J.B., 1994. *The Green National Product*. Lanham, MD: University Press of America.

Coomes, P.A. and Olson, D.O., 1991. 'An Economic Performance Index for US Cities', *Economic Development Quarterly*, 5, 4, Nov., 335–41.

Costanza, R., 1980. 'Embodied Energy and Economic Valuation', *Science*, 210, 1219–24.

Cross, G., 1994. *Time and Money: the Making of Consumer Culture*. London: Routledge and Kegan Paul.

Cross, J.G. and Guyer, M.J., 1980. *Social Traps*. Ann Arbor, MI: University of Michigan Press.

Csikszentmihalyi, M., 1992. *Flow: the Psychology of Happiness*. London: Rider.

Dahlberg, A.O., 1932. *Jobs, Machines, and Capitalism*. New York: Macmillan – now Palgrave Macmillan, pp. 21, 27, 35.

Daly, H., 1989. 'Toward a Measure of Sustainable Social Net National Product', in Y.J. Ahmad, S. El Serafy and E. Lutz (eds), *Environmental accounting for Sustainable Development*. Washington: The World Bank.

Daly, H. and Cobb, J.B., 1990. *For the Common Good: Redirecting the Economy Towards Community, the Environment and a Sustainable Future*. (Merlin Press, 1990) London: Green Print.

Daly, H.E., 1992. *Steady-State Economics*. London: Earthscan.

Daly, H.E., 1996. *Beyond Growth*. Boston, MA: Beacon Press.

Davey Smith, G. and Egger, M. 1996. 'Unequal in Death. Commentary: Understanding it all – Health, Meta-theories, and Mortality Trends', *British Medical Journal*, 313, 1584–5.

Davies, B.P., Bebbington, A. and Charnley, H., 1990. *Resources, Needs and Outcomes in Community-based Care: a Comparative Study of the Production of Welfare for Elderly People in Ten Local Authorities in England and Wales*. Aldershot: Avebury.

Davies, H.T.O., Nutley, S. and Smith, P.C., 2000. *What Works? Evidence-Based Policy and Practice in Public Services*. Bristol: Policy Press.

Dauncey, G., 1983. *Nice Work if You Can Get It*. Cambridge: National Extension College.

Davey Smith, G., *et al.*, 1998. 'Education and Occupational Social Class: Which is the More Important Indicator of Mortality Risk?' *Journal of Epidemiology and Community Health*, 52, 153–60.

De Angelis, M., 1997. 'The Autonomy of the Economy and Globalisation', *Common Sense*, 21, 41–59.

Debeir, J.-C., Deleage, J.-P. and Hemery, D., 1991 (orig. 1986). *In the Servitude of Power: Energy and Civilisation Through the Ages*. London: Zed Books.

De Haan, M. and Keuning, S.J., 1996. 'Taking the Environment into Account: the NAMEA Approach', *Review of Income and Wealth*, 42, 131–48.

Delande, G. and Négre, M., 1984. 'Travail social et indicateurs sociaux', *Economie Méridionale*, 22, 1/2, 27–36.

Delors, J., 1978. 'The Decline of French Planning', in S. Holland (ed.), *Beyond Capitalist Planning*. Oxford: Blackwell.

Delzell, E., 1996. 'Beyond Social Class', *Epidemiology*, 7, 1–3.

DH (Department of Health), 1998. Department of Health Committee on the Medical Effects of Air Pollutants. *Quantification of the Effects of Air Pollution on Health in the United Kingdom*. London: The Stationery Office.

Diener, E., 1984. 'Subjective Well-being', *Psychological Bulletin*, 95, 542–75.

DiFazio, W., 1985. *Longshoremen*. South Hadley, MA: Bergin and Garvey.

Dominguez, J. and Robin, V., 1992. *Your Money or Your Life*. Harmondsworth: Penguin.

Dore, R., 1976. *The Diploma Disease*. London: Allen and Unwin.

Dorsey, S.D., Hill, J.M. and Woods, M.E., 1989. 'The Human Development Spectrum: Sub-Spectra and Social Indicators for Use in Development Project Planning, Design and Implementation', *Social Indicators Research*, 21, 93–110.

Douglas, M., 1982. *In the Active Voice*. London: Routledge and Kegan Paul.

Douglas, M. and Isherwood, B., 1979. *The World of Goods*. London: Allen Lane.

Dowler, E.A., Payne, P.R., Young, O.S., *et al.*, 1982. 'Nutrition Status Indicators: Interpretation and Policy Making Role', *Food Policy*, May, 99–111.

Doyal, L. and Gough, I., 1991. *A Theory of Human Need*. Basingstoke: Macmillan – now Palgrave Macmillan.

Duchin, F. and Lange, G.-M., 1994. *The Future of the Environment*. New York and Oxford: Oxford University Press.

Duesenberry, J.S., 1949. *Income, Saving, and the Theory of Consumer Behaviour*. Cambridge, MA: Harvard University Press.

Durning, A.T., 1992. *How Much is Enough?* London: Earthscan.

Easterlin, R.A., 1972. 'Does Economic Growth Improve the Human Lot? Some Empirical Evidence', in P.A. David and M.W. Reder (eds), *Nations and Households in Economic Growth*. Stanford, CA: Stanford University Press.

Economic Council of Japan, 1973. *Measuring Net National Welfare of Japan*, Tokyo.

Edwards, S. and Fraser, E., 1970. *Selected Writings of Pierre Joseph Proudhon*. London: Macmillan – now Palgrave Macmillan.

Ekins, P., 2000. *Economic Growth and Environmental Sustainability*. London: Routledge.

Ekins, P., 1990. 'An Indicator Framework for Economic Progress', *Development*, 3–4, 92–8.

Ekins, P., 1992. 'A Four Factor Model of Wealth Creation', in P. Ekin and M. Max Neef *op. cit.*

Ekins, P. and Max Neef, M., 1992. *Real Life Economics*. London: Routledge.

Elliott, R., 1994. 'Addictive Consumption: Function and Fragmentation in Postmodernity', *Journal of Consumer Policy*, 17, 159–79.

Elstad, J.I., 1998. 'The Psycho-social Perspective on Social Inequalities in Health', *Sociology of Health and Illness*, 20, 5, 598–618.

Engels, F., 1958 (orig. 1841). *The Condition of the Working Class in England*; trans. and ed. by W.O. Henderson and W.H. Chaloner. Oxford: Blackwell.

Engerman, S.L., 1971. 'Human Capital, Education, and Economic Growth,' in R.W. Fogel and S.L. Engerman (eds), *The Reinterpretation of American Economic History*. New York: Harper and Row, pp. 241–56.

Escobar, A., 1996. 'Constructing Nature', in R. Peet and M. Watts (eds), *Liberation Ecologies*. London: Routledge.

Esteva, G. and Prakash, M.S., 1998. *Grassroots Post-Modernism: Remaking the Soil of Cultures*. London: Zed Books.

Etzioni, A. and Lehman, E.W., 1967. 'Some Dangers in "Valid" Social Measurement', *Annals of the American Academy of Political and Social Science*, Sept., 1–15.

European Foundation for the Improvement of Living and Working Conditions, 1986. *Living Conditions in Urban Areas*. Dublin: EFILWC.

European Foundation for the Improvement of Living and Working Conditions, 1992. *First European Survey on the Work Environment 1991–92*. Dublin: EFILWC.

Evans, G., 1997. 'Political Ideology and Popular Beliefs about Class and Opportunity: Evidence from Survey Experiment', *British Journal of Sociology*, 48, 450–70.

Eyer, J., 1977. 'Prosperity as a Cause of Death', *International Journal of Health Services*, 7, 125–50.

Fantasia, R., 1995. 'From Class Consciousness to Culture, Action, and Social Organisation', *Annual Review of Sociology*, 21, 269–86.

Fardon, R., 1999. *Mary Douglas: an Intellectual Biography*. London: Routledge.

Feachem, R.G., 1980. 'Community Participation in Appropriate Water Supply and Sanitation Technologies: the Methodology for the Decade', *Proceedings of the Royal Society*, B209, 15–29.

Findlay, A., Morris, A. and Rogerson, R., 1988. 'Where to Live in Britain in 1988', *Cities*, 5, 268–76.

Fine, B. and Leopold, E., 1993. *The World of Consumption*. London: Routledge.

Fisher, I., 1906. *The Nature of Capital and Income*. London: Macmillan – now Palgrave Macmillan.

Foy, G. and Daly, H., 1992. 'Allocation, Distribution and Scale as Determinants of Environmental Degradation: Case Studies of Haiti, El Salvador and Costa Rica', in A. Markandya and J. Richardson (eds), *The Earthscan Reader in Environmental Economics*. London: Earthscan.

Frank, R.H., 1985. *Choosing the Right Pond*. New York and Oxford: Oxford University Press.

Frank, R.H., 1997. 'The Frame of Reference as a Public Good', *Economic Journal*, 107, 1832–47.

Freire, P., 1972. *Pedagogy of the Oppressed*. Harmondsworth: Penguin.

Fryer, D., 1986. 'Employment Deprivation and Personal agency During Unemployment: a Critical Discussion of Jahoda's Explanation of the Psychological Effects of Unemployment', *Social Behaviour*, 1, 3–24.

Fryer, D. and Payne, R.L., 1984. 'Proactivity in Unemployment: Findings and Implications', *Leisure Studies*, 3, 273–95.

Fukuyama, F., 2000. *The Great Disruption: Human Nature and the Reconstitution of Social Order*, London: Profile Books.

Gabor, D., 1964. *Inventing the Future*. Harmondsworth: Penguin.

Gallie, D. and Vogler, C., 1994. 'Unemployment and Attitudes to Work', Chapter 3 in D. Gallie, C. Marsh and C. Vogler (eds), *Social Change and the Experience of Unemployment*. Oxford: Oxford University Press.

Galtung, J., 1977. *A Structural Theory of Imperialism*.

Gardner, G. and Sampat, P., 1999. 'Forging a Sustainable Materials Economy', in L.R. Brown and C. Flavin (eds), *State of the World*. London: Earthscan.

Garraty, J.A., 1978. *Unemployment in History: Economic Thought and Public Policy*. New York: Harper and Row.

Gaskell, P., 1836. *Artisans and Machinery*. London: Frank Cass.

Gee, J., Hill, G. and Lankshear, C., 1996. *The New York Order: Behind the Language of Neocapitalism*. London: Allen and Unwin.

Gershuny, J.I., 1978. *After Industrial Society?: the Emerging Self-Service Economy*. London: Macmillan – now Palgrave Macmillan.

Gershuny, J.I., 1979. 'The Informal Economy: its Role in Post-Industrial Society', *Futures*, Vol. 11, No. 1, February.

Gershuny, J., 1983. *Social Innovation and the Division of Labour* (also trans. into Swedish). Oxford Library of Political Economy, Oxford: Oxford University Press.

Gershuny, J.I., 1994. 'The Psychological Consequences of Unemployment: an Assessment of the Jahoda Thesis', Chapter 7, in D. Gallie, C. Marsh and C. Vogler (eds), *Social Change and the Experience of Unemployment*. Oxford: Oxford University Press.

Gershuny, J.I. and Pahl, R.E., 1980. 'Britain in the Decade of the Three Economies', *New Society*, 3 January, 51, No. 900, 7–9.

Ghai, D., Hopkins, M. and McGranahan, D., 1988. *Some Reflections on Human and Social Indicators for Development*. Geneva: UNRISD.

Giddens, A., 1991. *Modernity and Self-Identity*. Cambridge: Polity Press.

Gide, C. and Rist, C., 1948. *A History of Economic Doctrines*. London: Harrap.

Gintis, H., 2000. 'Beyond *Homo Economicus*: Evidence from Experimental Economics', *Ecological Economics*, 35, 311–22.

Goldberg, D., 1978. *Manual of the General Health Questionnaire*. Windsor: NFER.

Goldthorpe, J.H., 1968–69. *The Affluent Worker: Industrial Attitudes and Behaviour; The Affluent Worker: Political Attitudes and Behaviour; The Affluent Worker in the Class Structure*. Cambridge: Cambridge University Press.

Goodland, R., 1992. 'The Case That the World Has Reached Limits', in R. Goodland, H.E. Daly and S. El Serafy (eds), *Population, Technology and Lifestyle*. Washington, DC: Island Press.

Gordon, G., 1979. 'The Hungry Season in the Savanna of West Africa', presented to the Conference on Rapid Rural Appraisal held at the Institute for Development Studies, University of Sussex, 4–7 December.

Gorz, A., 1983a. *Farewell to the Working Class*. London: Fontana.

Gorz, A., 1983b. *Ecology as Politics*. London: Pluto Press.

Gorz, A., 1989. *Critique of Economic Reason*. London: Verso.

Gorz, A., 1994. *Capitalism, Socialism, Ecology* (trans. Chris Turner). London/New York: Verso.

Gowdy, J., 1994. *Coevolutionary Economics*. Dordrecht: Kluwer.

Green, E. and Woodward, E., 1984. *Gender Relations and Women's Leisure Patterns*, paper presented to Annual Conference of Leisure Studies Association.

Gross, B.M. and Straussman, J., 1974. *The Social Indicators Movement*. Social Policy (Sept.–Oct.), 43–4.

Haber, S.E., 1990. 'Recipient Value and Market Value', *Journal of Economic and Social Measurement*, 16, 41–54.

Habermas, J., 1984. *Theory of Communicative Action*, Vol. 1. Boston, MA: Beacon.

Habermas, J., 1991. *Moral Consciousness and Communicative Action*. Cambridge, MA: MIT Press.

Hakim, C., 1982. 'The Social Consequences of High Unemployment', *Journal of Social Policy*, 2, 4, 433–67.

Halleröd, N., Bradshaw, J. and Holmes, H., 1997. 'Adapting the Consensual Definition of Poverty', in D. Gordon and C. Pantazis (eds), *Breadline Britain in the 1990s*. Aldershot: Ashgate.

Hammond, J., 1933. *The Growth of Common Enjoyment*. London: Oxford University Press.

Handy, C., 1980. 'The Challenge of Industrial Society', in S. Reedy and M. Woodhead (eds), *Family, Work and Education*. London: Hodder & Stoughton/ Open University Press.

Handy, C., 1982. *The Informal Economy*. Wivenhoe, Essex: Association of Researchers in Voluntary Action and Community Involvement.

Hardin, G., 1968. 'The Tragedy of the Commons', *Science*, 162, 13 December.

Harper, P., 1999. *Techno-Anthropology in the Home*, presented at the Joint Radical Statistics and British Society for Social Responsibility in Science Conference, 27 Feb. London: The London School of Economics.

Hawkins, P., Lovins, A. and Lovins, H., 1999. *Natural Capitalism*. London: Earthscan.

Hayden, A., 1999. *Sharing the Work, Sparing the Planet*. London: Zed Books.

Hayward, M.D., Pienta, A.M. and Mclaughlin, D.K., 1997. 'Inequality in Men's Mortality: the Socioeconomic Status Gradient and Geographic Context', *Journal of Health and Social Behaviour*, 38, 313–30.

Henwood, D., 1997. *Wall Street: How it Works and For Whom*. London: Verso.

Hicks, J.R., 1956. *A Revision of Demand Theory*. Oxford: Oxford University Press.

Hildyard, N., 1993. 'Foxes in Charge of the Chickens', in W. Sachs (ed.), *Global Ecology*. London: Zed Books.

Hill, C., 1964. *Society and Puritanism in Pre-Revolutionary England*. London: Secker and Warburg.

Hines, C., 2000. *Localization: a Global Manifesto*. London: Earthscan.

Hirsch, F., 1977. *Social Limits to Growth*. London: Routledge.

Holzner, B., Dunn, W.N. and Muhammad Shahidullah, 1987. 'An Accounting Scheme for Designing Science Impact Indicators', *Knowledge*, 9, 173–204.

Hueting, R., 1991. 'Correcting National Income for Environmental Losses: a Practical Solution for a Theoretical Dilemma', in R. Costanza (ed.), *Ecological Economics*. New York, NY: Columbia University Press.

Illich, I., 1974. *Energy and Equity*. London: Calder and Boyars.

Illich, I., 1973. *Tools for Conviviality*. New York: Harper and Row.

ILO, International Labour Office, 1976. *Employment Growth and Basic Needs: a One World Problem*. Geneva: ILO.

Inglehart, R., 1997. *Modernization and Postmodernization*. Princeton, NJ: Princeton University Press.

Jackson, T., 1996. *Material Concerns*. London and New York: Routledge.

Jackson, T. and Marks, N., 1994. *Measuring Sustainable Economic Welfare – a Pilot Index: 1950–1990*. Stockholm: Stockholm Environment Institute.

Jackson, T. and Marks, N., 1999. 'Consumption, Sustainable Welfare and Human Needs – with Reference to UK Expenditure Patterns between 1954 and 1994', *Ecological Economics*, 28, 421–41.

Jahoda, M., 1979. 'The Impact of Unemployment in the 1930s and 1970s', *Bulletin of the British Psychological Society*, Vol. 32, August.

Jahoda, M., 1982. *Employment and Unemployment: a Social-Psychological Analysis*. Cambridge: Cambridge University Press.

Jahoda, M., and Rush, H., 1980. *Work, Employment and Unemployment*. Falmer: Science Policy Research Unit, University of Sussex (mimeo).

Jahoda, M., Lazarsfeld, P.F. and Zeisel, M., 1972 (first published 1933). *Marienthal: the Sociography of an Unemployed Community*. London: Tavistock.

Jenkins, C. and Sherman, B., 1980. *The Collapse of Work*. London: Eyre Methuen.

Jevons, W.S., 1865. *The Coal Question*. London: Macmillan – now Palgrave Macmillan.

Johannsen, S., 1976. *Towards a Theory of Social Reporting*. Stockholm, Swedish Institute for Social Research.

Johnston, D.F., 1988. 'Towards a Comprehensive "Quality of Life" Index', *Social Indicators Research*, 20, 473–96.

Judge, K., 1995. 'Income Distribution and Life Expectancy: a Critical Appraisal', *British Medical Journal*, 311, 1282–5; discussion 1285–7.

Kåberger, T., 1996. 'On the Combined Use of Economic and Physical Concepts', *Journal of Interdisciplinary Economics*, 7, 191–203.

Kalisch, D.W., Tetsuya, A. and Buchele, L.A., 1998. *Social and Health Policies in OECD Countries: a Survey of Current Programmes and Recent Developments*. Labour Market and Social Policy. Paris: OECD.

Kapp, R.W., 1951. *The Social Costs of Private Enterprise*. New York: Schocken.

Kausman, U. and Löwe, B.P., 1988. 'Zur Methdik der Wertung globaler Modelle', *Deutsche Zeitschrift für Philosophie*, 36, 3.

Kawachi, I. and Kennedy, B.P., 1999. 'Income Inequality and Health: Pathways and Mechanisms', *Health Services Research*, 34, 1, Part II, 215–27.

Keen, S., 2001. *Debunking Economics*. London: Zed Books.

Kelley, A.C., 1991. 'The HDI: Handle with Care', *Population and Development Review*, 17, 315–24.

Keynes, J.M., 1936. *The General Theory of Employment, Interest and Money*. London: Macmillan – now Palgrave Macmillan.

Kruytbosch, C. and Burton, L., 1987. 'The Search for Impact Indicators', *Knowledge*, 9, 168–72.

Kuznets, S., 1951. 'Government Product and National Income', in *International Association for Research in Income and Wealth, Income and Wealth Series I*. London: Bowes and Bowes.

Lafargue, P., 1907. *The Right to be Lazy*. Chicago, IL: Charles Kerr.

Lambert, J.-P., 1998. *Ecologie et distributionisme: la planete des usagers*. Paris: L'Harmattan.

Lancaster, K.J., 1966. 'A New Approach to Consumer Theory', *Journal of Political Economy*, Vol. LXXIV, No. 2.

Lind, N.C., 1992. "Some Thoughts on the HDI', *Social Indicators Research*', 27, 89–101.

Lind, N.C., 1993. 'A Compound Index of National Development', *Social Indicators Research*', 28, 267–84.

Lintott, J., 1996. 'Environmental Accounting: Useful to Whom and for What?', *Ecological Economics*, 16, 179–90.

Lintott, J., 1998. 'Beyond the Economics of More: the Place of Consumption in Ecological Economics', *Ecological Economics*, 25, 239–48.

Lintott, J., 1999. 'Environmental Accounting and Welfare', *Journal of Environmental Assessment Policy and Management*, Vol. 1, No. 2, 177–93.

Locke, J., 1694. *Two treatises of government*. London: Awnsham and John Churchill.

Lodge, D., 1986. *Nice Work*. New York: Macmillan – now Palgrave Macmillan., pp. 85–6.

Lone, O., Nyborg, K. and Aaheim, A., 1993. 'Natural Resource Accounting: the Norwegian Experience', in A. Franz and C. Stahmer (eds), *Approaches to Environmental Accounting*. Heidelberg: Physica-Verlag.

Lourié, S., 1987. 'Are Consequences of Adjustment Policies on Education Measurable?' Paris: International Institute for Educational Planning (UNESCO).

Mack, J. and Lansley, S., 1985. *Poor Britain*. London: Allen & Unwin.

Mandel, E., 1975. *Late Capitalism*. London: New Left Books.

Mander, J., 1978. *Four Arguments for the Elimination of Television*. New York: Quill.

Manuel, F.E., 1956. *The New World of Henri Saint-Simon*. Cambridge, MA: Harvard University Press.

Marglin, S.A. and Schor, J.B. (eds), 1989. *The Golden Age of Capitalism*. Oxford: The Clarendon Press.

Mars, G., 1982. *Cheats at Work: an Anthropology of Workplace Crime*. London: George Allen and Unwin.

Marsden, D., 1975 (2nd edn 1982). *Workless*. London: Croom Helm.

Marshall, P., 1992. *Nature's Web: an Exploration of Ecological Thinking*. London: Simon and Shuster (first published New York, 1988).

Marcuse, H., 1968. *One-Dimensional Man*, repr. 1992. New York: Beacon Press.

Marx, K., 1844. *Economic and Philosophical Manuscripts*, first published 1932, Progress Publishers, Moscow, Marx–Engels Collected Works, Vol. 3.

Marx, K., 1901. *Capital*. London: Swan Sonnenshein.

Marx, K., 1973. *Grundrisse*. New York: Vintage, p. 706.

Marx, K. and Engels, F., 1848 (repr. 1965). *The Communist Manifesto*. London: Penguin.

Masini, E., 1983. *Visions of Desirable Societies*. World Future Studies Federation. Oxford: Pergamon Press.

Maslow, A.H., 1954. *Motivation and Personality*. New York: Harper and Row. (rev. edn 1987 published by Worthington, Brighton).

Massey, D.S., 1996. 'The Age of Extremes: Concentrated Affluence and Poverty in the Twenty-first Century', *Demography*, 33, 395–412; discussion 413–16.

Max-Neef, M., 1992. 'Development and Human Needs', in Ekin and Max-Neef, op. cit.

McGillivray, M., 1991. 'The HDI: Yet Another Redundant Composite Development Indicator', *World Development*, 19/10, 1461–8.

McGranahan, D.V., Richard-Proust, C., Sovani, N.V. and Subramanian, M., 1972. *Contents and Measurement of Socio-Economic Development*. New York: Praeger for UNRISD.

McKeown, T., 1979. *The Role of Medicine: Dream, Mirage or Nemesis?* Princeton, NJ: Princeton University Press.

Meadows, D.H., Meadows, D.L., Randers, J. and Behrens, W.W., 1972. *The Limits to Growth*. New York: Universe Books.

Meadows, D.H., Meadows, D.L. and Randers, J., 1992. *Beyond the Limits*. London: Earthscan (first published 1972).

Midgely, J. with A. Hall, M. Hardman and D. Narine (ed.), 1986. *Community: Participation, Social Development and the State*, London: Methuen.

Miles, I., 1985. *Social Indicators for Human Development*. London: Pinter, for United Nations University.

Miles, I. and Irvine, J., 1982. *The Poverty of Progress: Changing Ways of Life in Industrial Societies*. Oxford: Pergamon Press.

Mill, J.S., 1848. *Principles of Political Economy*. London: Routledge and Kegan Paul. (First Published 1848.)

Misch, A., 1994. 'Assessing Environmental Health Risks', in L.R. Brown *et al.* (eds), *State of the World 1994*. London: Earthscan.

Morris, 1979. *Measuring the Living Conditions of the World's Poor: the Physical Quality of Life*. New York: Pergamon Press.

Mossé, C., 1969. *The Ancient World at Work*. London: Chatto and Windus.

Mukherjee, S., 1974. *There's Work to be Done*. London: HMSO.

Mukherjee, S., 1976. *Unemployment Costs*. London: PEP.

Mumford, L., 1944. *Condition of Man*. New York, NY: Harcourt, Brace and Company.

Murray, C.J.L., 1991. *Development Data Constraints and the HDI*. Geneva: UNRISD, May 1991.

Myers, D.G., 1992. *The Pursuit of Happiness*. New York: Avon Books.

Nagel, S.S., 1989. 'Doing Better than the Optimum', *Social Indicators Research*, 21, 193–220.

Nandy, A., 1987. *Traditions, Tyranny and Utopias*. Delhi: Oxford University Press.

Nandy, A., 1995. 'Consumerism: Its Hidden Beauties and Politics', *ISEE (International Society for Ecological Economics) Newsletter*, July.

Nectoux, F., Lintott, J. and Carr-Hill, R.A., 1980. 'Social Indicators. For Individual Well-being or Social Control?', *International Journal of Health Services*, 10, 1, 89–113.

Nie, N.H., Junn, J. and Stehlik-Barry, K., 1996. *Education and Democratic Citizenship in America*. Chicago, IL: University of Chicago Press.

Norbert-Hodge, H., Merrifield, T. and Gorelick, S., 2000. *Bringing the Food Economy Home*. Berkeley, CA: International Society for Ecology and Culture.

Nordhaus, W.D. and Tobin, J., 1973. 'Is Growth Obsolete?', in M. Moss (ed.), *The Measurement of Economic and Social Performance*. New York: National Bureau of Economic Research.

Novak, T., 1996. 'The Class Analysis of Poverty: a Response to Erik Olin Wright', *International Journal of Health Services*, 26, 187–95.

OECD, 1970. *List of Social Concerns*. Paris: OECD.

OECD, 1976. *Measuring Social Well-Being*. Paris: OECD.

OECD (Organisation for Economic Cooperation and Development), 1986. *Living Conditions in OECD Countries: a Compendium of Social Indicators* (Social Policy Studies No. 3) Paris: OECD.

OECD, 1994. *Managing the Environment: the Role of Economic Instruments*. Paris: OECD.

OECD, 1997. *Evaluating Economic Instruments for Environmental Policy*. Paris: OECD.

O'Neill, J., 1998. *The Market: Ethics, Knowledge and Politics*. London: Routledge.

Ostergren, P.O., Lindbladh, E., Isacsson, S.O. *et al.*, 1995. 'Social Network, Social Support and the Concept of Control – a Qualitative Study Concerning the Validity of Certain Stressor Measures used in Qualitative Social Epidemiology', *Scandinavian Journal of Social Medicine*, 23, 95–102.

Oswald, A.J., 1997. 'Happiness and Economic Performance', *Economic Journal*, 107, 1815–31.

O'Toole, J. *et al.*, 1973. *Work in America*. Cambridge, MA: MIT Press.

Oyen, E., 1992. 'Some Basic Issues in Comparative Poverty Research', *International Social Science Journal*, 44, 4(134), 615–26.

Parameswaran, M.P., 2000. 'What does the Kerala Model Signify? Towards a Possible "Fourth World" ', in G. Parayil (ed.), *Kerala: the Development Experience*. London: Zed Books.

Parayil, G. (ed.), 2000. *Kerala: the Development Experience*. London: Zed Books.

Parker, H., 1982. *The Moral Hazards of Social Benefits*. Institute of Economic Affairs Research Monograph 37.

Parker, S., 1982. *Work and Retirement*. London: Allen and Unwin.

Parkinson, C.H. Northcote and Lancaster, O., 1958. *Parkinson's Law: the Pursuit of Progress*. London: John Murray.

Pauli, G.A., 1998. *Upsizing: the Road to Zero Emissions*. Sheffield: Greenleaf.

Pearce, D., Markandya, A. and Barbier, E.B., 1989. *Blueprint for a Green Economy*. London: Earthscan.

Pease, P., 1997. 'Comparison of Sources of Employment Data', *Labour Market Trends* (December), 511, 516.

Perelman, M., 2000. *The Invention of Capitalism: Classical Political Economy and the Secret History of Primitive Accumulation*. Durham, NC: Duke University Press.

Pigou, A.C., 1932. *The Economics of Welfare*, 4th edn. London: Macmillan – now Palgrave Macmillan.

Piven, F.F., 1977. 'The Political Uses of Planning and Decentralisation in the United States', *Inter Sectoral Educational Planning,* Paris: OECD, pp. 268–89.
Plato, 1970. *The Republic*. London: Sphere.
Polanyi, K., 1957. *The Great Transformation*. Boston, MA: Beacon, p. 33.
Pollard, D., 1965. *The Genesis of Modern Management.* London: Edward Arnold.
Ponting, C., 1991. *A Green History of the World.* London: Sinclair-Stevenson.
Population Trends, 1993. Editorial. London: HMSO.
Porter, M., 1990. *The Competitive Advantage of Nations.* New York: The Free Press.
Radical Statistics, 1979. *Social Indicators: for Individual Wellbeing or for Social Control*. London: BSSRS.
Rao, V.V. Bhanoji, 1991. 'Human Development Report 1990: Review and Assessment', *World Development,* 19, 10, 1451–60.
Raven, H. and Lang, T., 1995. 'Off our Trolleys?'. London: Institute for Public Policy Research.
Rawls, J., 1971. *A Theory of Justice*. Cambridge, MA: Harvard University Press.
Ray, A.K., 1989. 'On the Measurement of Certain Aspects of Social Development', *Social Indicators Research,* 21, 35–92.
Reeve, C., 1976. 'Refus du travail', *Spartacus*. July/August.
Reimer, E., 1974. *School is Dead.* Harmondsworth: Penguin.
Repetto, R., Magrath, W., Wells, M. *et al.*, 1992. 'Wasting Assets: Natural Resources in the National Income Accounts', in A. Markandya and J. Richardson (eds), *Environmental Economics*. London: Earthscan.
Rifkin, S.B., Muller, F. and Bichmann, W., 1988 'Primary Health Care: On Measuring Participation', *Social Science and Medicine,* 26, 9, 931–40.
Ritzer, G., 1993. *The McDonaldization of Society*. Thousand Oaks, CA: Pine Forge Press.
Robbins, L., 1932. *An Essay on the Nature and Significance of Economic Science.* London: Macmillan – now Palgrave Macmillan.
Roberts, K., 1982. *Automation, Unemployment and the Distribution of Income.* Maastricht: European Centre for Work and Society.
Robinson, P. and Oppenheim, C., 1998. *Social Exclusion Indicators: a Submission to the Social Exclusion Unit.* London: Institute for Public Policy Research.
Roodman, D.M., 1996. *Paying the Piper: Subsidies, Politics and the Environment.* London: Worldwatch Paper 133.
Ruskin, J., 1985. *Unto This Last and Other Writings* ed. Clive Wilmer. Harmondsworth: Penguin.
Russell, B., 1976. *In Praise of Idleness and Other Essays*. London: Allen and Unwin.
Ruta, D.A., Garratt, A.M., Leng, M. *et al.*, 1994. 'A new approach to the measurement of quality of life'. *The Patient-Generated Index, Medical Care,* Nov., 32, 11, 1109–26.
Sabine, G.H., 1951. *A History of Political Theory,* 2nd edn. London: Harrap.
Sachs, W., 1992 (orig. 1984). *For Love of the Automobile*. Berkeley, CA: University of California Press.
Sachs, W. (ed.), 1993. *Global Ecology*. London: Zed Books.
Sachs, W., 1999. *Planet Dialectics*. London: Zed Books.
Sachs, W., Loske, R. and Linz, M., 1998. *Greening the North*. London and New York: Zed Books.
Sahlins, M., 1974. 'The Original Affluent Society', in *Stone Age Economics*. London: Tavistock.

Schatan, J., 1990. 'The Deceitful Nature of Socio-Economic Indicators', *Development*, 3–4, 69–75.

Schmidt-Bleek, F. and Weaver, P. (eds), 1998. *Factor 10: Manifesto for a Sustainable Planet*. Sheffield: Greenleaf Publishing.

Schmookler, A.B., 1993. *The Illusion of Choice: How the Market Economy Shapes Our Destiny*. New York, NY: State University of New York Press.

Schor, J., 1991. *The Overworked American: the Unexpected Decline of Leisure in America*. New York: Basic Books.

Schultz, T.W., 1960. 'Capital Formation by Education', *Journal of Political Economy*, 68, 571–83.

Schumacher, E.F., 1974. *Small is Beautiful*. London: Abacus.

Schwartz, W. and Schwartz, D., 1998. *Living Lightly: Travels in Post-consumer Society*. Charlbury, Oxfordshire: Jon Carpenter.

Scitovsky, T., 1976. *The Joyless Economy*. New York: Oxford University Press.

Scott, W. 1988. 'Community Based Health Reporting', *World Health Statistics Quarterly*, Vol. 41, 26–31.

Scott, W. with Argalis, H. and McGranahan, D.V., 1973. *The Measurement of Real Progress at the Local Level*. Geneva: UNRISD.

Seers, D., 1976. 'The Political Economy of National Accounting', in A. Cairncross and M. Puri (eds), *Employment, Income Distribution and Development Strategy: Problems of the Developing Countries*. London: Macmillan – now Palgrave Macmillan.

Seers, D., 1979. 'The Meaning of Development with a Postscript', in D. Lehmann (ed.), *Development Theory: Four Critical Studies*. Bournemouth: Cass.

Seers, D., 1983. *The Political Economy of Nationalism*. Oxford: Oxford University Press.

Sen, A.K., 1992. *Inequality Reexamined*. Cambridge, MA: Harvard University Press.

Sheehan, G. and Hopkins, M., 1979. *Basic Needs Performance: an Analysis of Some International Data*. Geneva: ILO.

Sheldon, E.B. and Moore, W.E., 1968. *Indicators of Social Change*. New York: Russell Sage Foundation.

Shields, R., 1992. *Lifestyle Shopping*. London: Routledge.

Simon, J. and Kahn, H. (eds), 1984. *The Resourceful Earth*. Oxford: Blackwell.

Sivard, R. 1979. *World Military and Social Priorities*. New York: World Priorities Inc.

Smiles, S., 1996. *Self-help: with Illustrations of Conduct and Perseverance;with a foreword by Lord Harris of High Cross*. London: Institute of Economic Affairs.

Smith, A., 1845. *An Inquiry into the Nature and Causes of the Wealth of Nations* (abridged version: The Wealth of Nations [ed. Andrew Skinner] Harmondsworth: Penguin).

Smith, G.A., 1993. 'The Purpose of Wealth: a Historical Perspective', in H.E. Daly and K.N. Townsend (eds), *Valuing the Earth*. Cambridge, MA: MIT Press.

Smith, P.C. (ed.), 1996. *Measuring Outcome in the Public Sector*. London: Taylor and Francis.

Solidarity, 1993. A publication of the United Auto Workers (AFLO-CIO) (May).

Somers, F., 1998. *European Union Economies* (3rd edn). Harlow: Addison Wesley Longman.

Sterky, G. and Millander, L. (eds), 1978. *Birthweight Distribution – an Indicator of Social Development*. Stockholm: SARE Report No. 2.

Stone, R., 1964. *A System of Social and Demographic Statistics*. New York: United Nations.

Tanner, J.M., 1982. 'The Potential of Auxological Data for Maintaining Economic and Social Well-Being', *Social Science History*, Vol. 6, No. 4.

Tawney, R.H., 1920. *The Acquisitive Society*. London: G. Bell & Sons, pp. 139–40.

Tawney, R.H., 1925. *Thomas Wilson: a Discourse upon Usury*. London: Bell and Sons.

Tawney, R.H., 1948. *Religion and the Rise of Capitalism*. Harmondsworth: Penguin.

Tepperman, L. and Laasen, H., 1990. 'The Future of Happiness', *Futures*, Dec., 1059–70.

Thacker, S.B., Gibson Parrish, R., Trowbridge, F.L. and Surveillance Coordinating Group (1988), 'A Method for Evaluating Systems of Epidemiological Surveillance', *World Health Statistics Quarterly*, Vol. 41, 11–18.

Thompson, E.P., 1968. *The Making of the English Working Class*. Harmondsworth: Penguin.

Tokar, B., 1997. *Earth for Sale*. Boston, MA: South End Press.

Trannoy, A., 1986. 'Théorie Economique de la Mésure de l'Inégalité: un reexamen', *Mathémathiques et sciences humaines*, 23/93, 53–60.

Tugwell, R., 1927. *Industry's Coming of Age*. New York: Harcourt, Brace & Co, pp. 223–4.

Uemura, K., 1988. 'World Health Situation and Trend Assessment from 1948 to 1988', *Bulletin of the World Health Organisation*, Vol. 66, No. 6 697–87.

Ujimoto, K.V., 1985. 'The Allocation of Time to Social and Leisure Activities as Social Indicators for the Integration of Aged Ethnic Minorities', *Social Indicators Research*, 17, 253–66.

UK, 1994. *Sustainable Development: the UK Strategy*. Cm 2426. London: HMSO.

UNDP (United Nations Development Programme), 1998. *Human Development Report 1998*. New York and Oxford: Oxford University Press.

United Nations, 1993. *Integrated Environmental and Economic Accounting*. New York: United Nations.

UNRISD (Ghai, D., Hopkins, M. and McGranahan, D.) 1988. *Some Reflections on Human and Social Indicators for Development*. Geneva: UNRISD.

Ure, A., 1965. *Philosophy of Manufacturers*. New York: Harper and Row.

Valaskakis, K. and Martin, I., 1986. 'Measures of Development and Measurement of Happiness', *Journal of Social Development in Africa*, 1, 89–91.

Vaze, P., 1997. 'Environmental Input-Output Tables for the United Kingdom', *Economic Trends*, No. 527, October.

Vaze, P. (ed.), 1998. *UK Environmental Accounts 1998*. London: The Stationery Office.

Victor, P.A., 1991. 'Indicators of Sustainable Development: some Lessons from Capital Theory', *Ecological Economics*, 4, 191–213.

Vitousek, P.M., Ehrlich, P.R., Ehrlich, A.H. and Matson, P.A., 1986. 'Human Appropriation of the Products of Photosynthesis', *BioScience*, Vol. 34, No. 6, 368–73.

Vitousek, P.M., 1994. 'Beyond Global Warming: Ecology and Global Change', *Ecology* 75, 7, Oct., 1861–76.

Walker, A. Maher, J., Coulthard, M. *et al.*, 2001. *Living in Britain: Results from the 2000 General Household Survey*. London: The Stationery Office.

Wachtel, P.L., 1983. *The Poverty of Affluence*. New York: The Free Press.

Wackernagel, M. and Rees, W.E., 1996. *Our Ecological Footprint.* Gabriola Island, BC: New Society Publishers.

Wagener, D.K., Williams, D.R. and Wilson, P.M. 1993. 'Equity in Environmental Health: Data Collection and Interpretation Issues', *Toxicology and Industrial Health*, 9, 775–95.

Warde, A., 1994. 'Consumption, Identity-formation and Uncertainty', *Sociology*, Vol. 28, No. 4 (November), 877–98.

Warr, P., 1987. *Work, Unemployment and Mental Health.* Oxford: The Clarendon Press.

Watkins, S.J., 1982. 'Recession and Health: the Policy Implications', paper presented at the WHO Workshop on Heath Policy in Relation to Unemployment in the Community, Leeds.

Watts, A.G., 1983. *Education, Unemployment and the Future of Work.* London: Routledge.

Watts, H.W., 1992. 'The future of SIPP for Analysing Extended Measures of Wellbeing', *Journal of Social and Economic Measurement*, 18, 177–91.

WCED (World Commission on Environment and Development), 1987. 'Our Common Future' (The Brundtland Report). Oxford and New York: Oxford University Press.

Webster, D., 2002. 'Unemployment: How Official Statistics Distort Analysis and Policy and Why', Presentations to Radical Statistics Conference, 16 February 2002. University of Northumbria at Newcastle.

Weizsäcker, E., Lovins, A.B. and Lovins, L.H., 1997. *Factor Four.* London: Earthscan.

Wiles, P., 1971. 'Crisis Prediction', *Annals of the American Academy of Political and Social Sciences*, January.

Wilkinson, R.G., 1996. *Unhealthy Societies. The Afflictions of Inequality.* London and New York: Routledge.

Williams, A., 1985. 'The Economics of Coronary Artery By Pass Grafting', *British Medical Journal*, Vol. 291, 326–9.

Wisner, B., 1988. *Power and Need in Africa: Basic Human Needs and Development Policies.* London: Earthscan.

World Health Organisation, 1980. *The International Classification of Impairments, Disabilities, and Handicaps.* Geneva: World Health Organisation.

Zimmern, A.E., 1915. *The Greek Commonwealth: Politics and Economics in Fifth-Century Athens*, 2nd edn rev. Oxford: Oxford University Press.

Zolotas, X., 1981. *Economic Growth and Declining Social Welfare.* Athens: Bank of Greece.

Subject Index

Name Index